SURVIVING OPHELIA

SURVIVING OPHELIA

Mothers Share Their Wisdom
in Navigating the
Tumultuous Teenage Years

CHERYL DELLASEGA

PERSEUS PUBLISHING
Cambridge, Massachusetts

Cataloging-in-Publication Data is available from the Library of Congress
ISBN 0–7382-0508-7

Perseus Publishing is a member of the Perseus Books Group.
Find us on the World Wide Web at http://www.perseuspublishing.com
Perseus Publishing books are available at special discounts for bulk purchases in the U.S. by corporations, institutions, and other organizations. For more information, please contact the Special Markets Department at the Perseus Books Group, 11 Cambridge Center, Cambridge, MA 02142, or call (617)252-5298.

Text design by Jeffrey P. Williams
Set in 10.5-point Berkeley by Perseus Publishing Services

First printing, September 2001

1 2 3 4 5 6 7 8 9 10—03 02 01

CONTENTS

part one
⌘

NOT WANTING TO KNOW:
THE JOURNEY BEGINS

p a r t   t w o

❦

HOPING TO HELP:
CRISES BIG AND LITTLE

p a r t   t h r e e

❦

INTERVENTIONS:
ON OUR OWN AND WITH OTHERS

p a r t   f o u r
ᦇ

WHEN TROUBLES GO ON AND ON

p a r t   f i v e

❧

PART OF THE PICTURE:
SIGNIFICANT OTHERS

p a r t   s i x

❧

INTO THE FUTURE

Don't waste your sorrows—
let God use them for your good and His glory.

—ANNE GRAHAM LOTZ

ACKNOWLEDGMENTS

This is not the book I imagined I would write someday, but the call to create it was unmistakable. Each step of the way, help has come to me through an incredible number of people who offered encouragement, support, prayers, and hugs. Most notably, my husband, Paul, and youngest son, Joe, were intimately involved in the day-to-day cheerleading and hand holding that made it possible for me to persevere. My other son, Matt, knew the exact right time to come home from the Navy after a year away, reminding me to always take time for what really counts.

My incredible agent, Laureen Rowland, has, like many of the women in this book, become a valued friend and supporter. Marnie Cochran, my wonderful editor at Perseus (another mom!) and the entire sales/publicity team she has connected me with have all been phenomenal in their own ways. Two other people who helped make this book happen were Sue Horstick, my typist and source of initial feedback, and Maureen Earl, a mentor/friend/mom who voluntarily edited the manuscript—not once, but twice.

I cannot describe in a few sentences the contribution of four people who helped Ellen and me by always believing in the best of her: Dr. Shawna Brent, caseworker Amy Davis, Dr. Richard Levine, and high-school guidance counselor Frank Basehoar. My own therapist, Dr. Barbara Kuhlengel, who is a psychiatrist, mother, and friend, also kept me going, as did the Friends at Harrisburg Quaker Meeting and the community of sojourners at Oasis Ministries.

Lastly, I thank the incredible women who opened their lives and hearts, sharing stories of deeply personal struggles. Although most of us have never met face-to-face, I feel a bond with them that is both mystical and powerful.

And to Ellen . . . I'm sorry it had to be this way. I know it helps that you, like me, will reach many others through the hard times of your life.

Introduction

There are no pictures of me cuddling Ellen to my heart for the first time in the delivery room, but it doesn't matter. Every detail is clear in my mind: her perfect, round face, the fuzz of soft gold hair crowning the very top of her head, and her dazed dark eyes, squinting against the glare of the bright, sterile lights.

"You are the daughter I have always dreamed of," I whispered, resting my cheek against the smooth skin of her forehead. Lying there with her on my chest, I had a vision of the future and all the things she would accomplish. Like a movie on fast-forward, I saw her doing well in school, having loyal friends, and being a kind person. She would go to a good college and would someday make a positive difference in this world. Mostly, I pictured all the good times we would have together.

The year after her birth, 1984, was probably the happiest one of my life. I had a five-year-old son, Matt, from my first marriage, who readily adapted to his role as "big brother," a great second husband, a job teaching at a small university that I liked, and Ellen. When our youngest son, Joe, was born eighteen months after her, I rejoiced again, thrilled she would have a sibling close to her age.

"What a pleasant baby!" was the most frequent comment I heard during Ellen's early years. It was true—she rarely cried and had an unusual laugh that would start deep in her throat and bubble out, drawing smiles from everyone around her. When I cuddled her, she would often pat my back while I patted hers. The developmental tasks I labored over with Matt and Joe came easily to her: she even decided to stop sucking her thumb on her own, doing so in only a few weeks.

My prediction about her academic abilities proved right. She loved math ("There are always right answers") and brought home A's in that and other major subjects. All the sports her brothers tried, she tried, as well as dance lessons. Swimming was the activity that stuck, partly because it helped her asthma, and partly because she was good at it. When her arm was broken in third grade, she wore a waterproof sleeve, still competed, and even finished near the top.

What touched me most about Ellen was her kindness. She (and her brothers) had a special sensitivity for kids who were handicapped or didn't quite fit in for some reason. When holidays rolled around, she was the child who diligently saved her money and thought carefully about the gifts she would buy.

My husband and I followed all the "rules" for parenting we'd learned, providing lots of love, appropriate discipline, spiritual grounding, and security for all three children. When they were old enough, they were encouraged to be independent through summer camp experiences and flying to Chicago to visit their grandparents. They got allowances for the jobs they did around the house to promote a sense of responsibility, and we all looked forward to our traditions for Christmas and Thanksgiving. We went to church together on Sundays so faithfully our occasional absence was noted by the other members.

I wouldn't say I was smug, but, until adolescence, I thought Ellen was going to turn out exactly as I had imagined she would back when I cradled her on the delivery room table. Unfortunately, most of my dreams got shoved aside when she hit her teens and the first of many crises began. She had barely turned fourteen when an eating disorder put a sudden end to the joyful shopping trips, meals out, and lazy evenings of watching videos at home. As her condition worsened, we stopped going to the pool to swim laps and rarely laughed together. Her grades plummeted. I was in a constant state of panic, desperate for reassurance, and afraid to face the future, searching everywhere for answers to the questions that plagued me. What had gone wrong with Ellen? How had I failed her? Would things ever return to "normal"?

I lived in a daze during the early months of Ellen's anorexia. When my coworkers, friends, and family members asked how my daughter was doing, it was hard to know what to say: "She's only eating about 500 calories a day?" "Her hair is falling out?" or "She lost another four pounds?" Even censored versions of what was going on with her seemed so overwhelming, I stopped telling people when she had been admitted to the hospital again or started on yet another new medication.

As the mother of a toddler, there had been more books available on parenting than I had time to read. There were recommendations for every situation I ever faced with my children—in the battered copy of *Dr. Spock's Baby and Child Care* I kept for a decade, in volumes that filled an entire library shelf, or on TV shows. If I needed a second opinion, other mothers were happy to offer advice, and almost every bookstore had a section crammed with parenting literature.

The mothers I knew when Ellen's problems began all seemed to have wonderful, well-adjusted daughters who were doing just fine. That ruled out turning to them for help. There was no comfort to be found in bookstores, either. Sure, there were dozens of books about adolescents written by professionals or parents of "successful" children, but none addressed mothers like me who were in the midst of turmoil. Ironically, we were surrounded by therapists, but there was no one who could really help. I was nearly paralyzed by shame and guilt.

Somehow, slowly, I began to meet other mothers whose daughters were struggling. Amazingly, most were women who looked and acted just like the ones I saw at the shopping mall or high school every day in my own community. Bit by bit, our stories came tumbling out in doctors' waiting rooms, hospital corridors, grocery stores, and school functions. As if confessing to a crime, we shared our experiences in hushed voices, instantly understanding, if not the particulars of a situation, the emotional crisis it evoked.

I began to talk honestly and openly about what I was going through, and other mothers responded instantly. It would only take one question ("How are you getting through all this?") and their answers flowed, sometimes tearful, sometimes relieved, but always honest. I came to realize that all across the country, other "invisible" families were desperately trying to help their troubled daughters with efforts that were nothing short of heroic.

One day, after being lectured by a social worker about my inadequacy as a parent, I picked up my pen in frustration and began to write. There had to be a way to sort out the complicated details surrounding my daughter's problems, and my role in them. I thought of my volunteer work with incarcerated women, who sometimes shared the details of their broken lives with me: abandonment by one or both parents, fear of being shot while walking down the street, physical or mental abuse, or never having enough food to eat or clothes to wear.

As much as I don't like to hear these stories, they explain why problems occur. Ellen hasn't experienced any of these things, yet at times her future seems as bleak to me as that of some of the inmates I counsel.

As I scribbled out the beginnings of a memoir about Ellen and myself, I realized the answers were not to be found in our story alone. The academic side of me wanted to know the extent to which other teenage girls were going through such troubled times and how both they and their mothers survived.

I began an extensive campaign to solicit stories from mothers of daughters who had struggled "more than most" during adolescence. My appeal was simple: I wanted to know how women responded to their daughters' problems. I hoped to write a book that would someday help others who were where I had once been: lost, afraid, and frantic for help.

"Do you really think mothers will write?" one editor asked me skeptically, after reading my proposal. I wasn't sure, but with the encouragement of a wonderful agent and a belief I was meant to create this book, I persisted in asking mothers to describe their experiences, in their own words.

To reach as diverse an audience as possible, I varied the media and resources I used to solicit submissions: the Internet, print newsletters and newspapers, magazines, and fliers. My focus was groups or organizations that involved parents of troubled children, writers, women, and mothers.

As the submissions poured in (over 200, with more continuing to arrive), I realized I had many companions. The topics mothers wrote about ranged from life-threatening crises to time-limited troubles, from suicide attempts, drug abuse, and unplanned pregnancies to struggles with peer acceptance, trust issues, and difficulty communicating. Despite the diversity of situations, our responses to our daughters' problems were similar: confusion, fear, anger, grief, denial, and sometimes panic. Each new story I read reinforced the feeling that I had found a sisterhood that arose from pain but offered strength through the gathered wisdom of women who traveled a similar road.

In addition to stories or poems, many women wrote poignant letters about the need for this book. One said: "Wow, there's a parent out there just like me." Another captured the feelings of many when she wrote: "This is for all the mothers who sat at coffee break with their peers passing pleasantries while trying to sedate their feelings . . . Anger, rage, disappointment (sadness) . . . while they share information on Ivy League colleges their children will be attending in the fall, I just pray that my daughter stays alive."

E-mails poured in from moms, grandmoms, aunts, teachers, fathers, and clinicians. So many grown women who had been "troubled teens" contacted me that I decided to include a chapter on them. I'm still receiving stories—if you have one to share, please visit my web site (www.cheryldellasega.com), e-mail me at opheliasmother@aol.com, or mail to: Cheryl Dellasega, Box 458, Hershey, PA, 17033.

Fathers contacted me as well, as did mothers of sons who were having difficulty. These communications have convinced me that adolescence is the most challenging stage many parents face in raising their children. The vulnerabilities women share with daughters, as well as my own experiences, made me particularly interested in writing about mothers of teenage girls who struggle with a range of issues.

As I selected the stories I wanted to use and began to work with their authors, it often felt like the beginning of a friendship. Each woman I asked for revisions or changes complied happily, intent on sharing her story in an effort to help others. Many were accomplished writers who had already published their own books, while others were first-timers who nervously informed me they'd never written before. Frequently, the authors remarked on how therapeutic it was to commit to paper things they had never been able to speak about. For obvious reasons, some mothers chose not to use their real names, and unless specifically requested otherwise, identifying information has been changed throughout. (However, all authors can be contacted through me.)

More than once, my vision blurred with tears as I read the pieces. I worried that the book might end up being too sad, because so many of the stories described incredibly difficult situations. In two cases, "surviving" actually meant finding a way to go on after the death of a daughter.

However, the writing of this book has ended up giving me hope, easing the discouragement and disenfranchisement I felt when reading books written by professionals or other moms who'd never been in my situation. Although themes in many of the stories overlap, as a whole the writings describe an incredible process of preserving in an effort to navigate the teenage years. It's been a joy to discover and join a collective of women who accept and understand each other regardless of differences in life situations or problems their daughters have.

My belief in the ability of mother love to overcome incredible obstacles has been renewed again and again. Not one mother who wrote to me labeled her daughter as "bad" or spoke of losing any love for her. Best of all, adolescent girls usually found their way through troubled times and emerged as better and stronger people than they might have otherwise. Some stories, like my own, are still evolving, with the mother-daughter relationship continuing to grow and change and the future unclear.

"Ophelia" symbolizes an adolescent girl in crisis. Ever since psychologist Mary Pipher drew parallels between today's teenagers and *Hamlet*'s doomed heroine, the public has been sensitized to the multiple struggles facing young women. Like me, many of my friends read *Reviving Ophelia* and felt both fear that what Pipher described might happen to our daughters and hope that once forewarned, we could prevent it.

Recently, student Sara Shandler gave voice to the feelings of teenage daughters in another book, *Ophelia Speaks*. The missing piece is Ophelia's mother, who never appeared in Shakespeare's *Hamlet* and is still silent today.

To someone who has never gone through crisis, the term "surviving" may sound harsh, but those of us who have seen our beloved daughters struggle, flounder, and fail understand immediately. Sometimes it's hard to get through a day, a night, an afternoon, or even the next hour, because, in the words of one mother, "I'm afraid of what might come next." Surviving is exactly what we do.

At the same time, mothers of troubled daughters try everything within their power to save their child, as I'm sure the original Ophelia's mother would have, had Shakespeare given her a role in *Hamlet*. Ultimately, before we, too, drown in the sorrow of our daughters' struggles, we must learn to step back, stay strong, and fight to keep our Ophelias alive. Still, we never stop praying that someday, somehow, she will follow our example and choose to save herself.

Not Wanting to Know: The Journey Begins

1

Turning Points for Better and Worse: Facing Anorexia, Dishonesty, and Separation

"Is Ellen losing weight?" my husband asked during her eighth-grade Spring Concert. Hearing this from a man who regularly took our daughter out in public with her clothes either on backward or rescued from the Goodwill bag made me pause. I, too, had thought she looked thinner in recent weeks, but knowing she was growing taller and maturing physically had offset my concern.

That night I searched the crowd of children taking their places on the risers to sing and realized I couldn't find Ellen. There was a girl in the same blue dress I had bought for her, but she was too skinny to be my daughter—wasn't she?

Impressions flashed through my brain: Ellen's recent remarks about the fat content of nearly every food she ate or didn't eat and her newfound fussiness about clothes. Hadn't she been a bit irritable, too?

"I'll take her in for a checkup," I told Paul. "She needs a new asthma inhaler anyway."

A week later, our family doctor confirmed that Ellen had lost twenty pounds since the previous fall.

"Ellen, are you throwing up or not eating?" I asked, when we were alone, my heart pounding with fear. She hesitated before nodding slowly, causing tears to spill out onto her cheeks.

Within days, she stopped eating completely and was then admitted, for the first time, to the eating-disorder program at a medical center in our hometown. We were told her stay would only be five days or so, but after thirty days she was still hospitalized and no better. I began to wonder: Was this just a passing incident, or was it an indicator of more serious trouble?

Ellen ended up in institutions for over half of the next sixth months, losing twenty more pounds and missing both graduation from eighth grade and the beginning of high school. I knew what we faced wasn't a temporary problem—it was a crisis.

There isn't always a specific event we can identify as a turning point, but several mothers clearly recalled a "moment of truth" when reality could no longer be denied. A few said (in retrospect) they had played "ostrich," trying to deal with what might be happening with their daughters by "burying their heads in the sand." The following story illustrates how one mother was forced to acknowledge that her daughter was leading a secret life.

A Moment of Unanticipated Clarity

The realization stung me as if I'd been slapped hard across my face. I understood in a word and a look what I'd avoided for a year: I'd been betrayed. My seventeen-year-old daughter, Sara, had lied to me and, because I wanted to believe her, I lied to myself. The way it happened was inevitable in a year marked by emotional opposites—hope, fear, peace, conflict, promises, disappointments—all melted together. Then, in a moment of perfect stillness, the reality I had been avoiding struck with absolute clarity.

I was lying in our backyard in the hammock. My husband was puttering in the garden. My younger preteen daughter, Katie, was in the house giggling with her girlfriend as they tried on clothes for a pool party they'd be going to later on.

I dozed off, waking to the sound of Sara returning from work with her friend Zoe. What I knew about Zoe bothered me: she had a car, didn't work, and had no rules to live by at home.

Sara looked tired. Stubborn wisps of hair refused to stay in her top-knot, and she had deep circles under her eyes.

Sara had spent the previous night at Zoe's house. Before leaving, she had given me the evening's schedule that included some time, but not much, with her boyfriend, Josh, who supposedly had other plans with his guy friends.

"Aren't you happy, Mom, that I'm going to have a girl sleepover, just like you always hoped I would?" she had asked. "We're going to do each other's makeup and hair and rent some movies. So don't worry, Mom. It'll be fine." She had been uncharacteristically chatty but I missed that part of our relationship so much I didn't question it—in fact, I was grateful.

Now, they were making a quick stop at home before going out again. They came over to the hammock to say "hi" and tell me what was up. I asked what they did during the sleepover the night before.

"How did Sara ever get you up to get her to work by seven this morning, Zoe?" I commented.

Sara blurted out, "Josh took me."

Realizing what she had said, she quickly came up with an implausible story of how a boy who I know can never wake up for anything went to Zoe's house at 6:30 A.M. to get her to work.

I hadn't understood before. It was only then, when she turned on me, adopting the familiar arrogant tone of voice, and gave me a look that said "Don't push this, Mom," that I realized what she was telling me. Her life was not what I thought it was, and she wanted me to stay out of it.

In that moment of pain, the sun could no longer touch me. I lay there thinking back to other conversations but with different interpretations: Sara using a belligerent tone when none was warranted, Sara giving sparse details, Sara impatient that I would even ask what her plans were. I never saw the subtext.

My husband drove Katie to her party. Alone, I rushed to Sara's bedroom, a place I rarely went into anymore. I sat on the edge of her bed, looking at the furniture we'd happily picked out together and remembering how elated she'd been when we'd found a tie-dye border. Now this room was a dumping ground and a place to sleep.

Clothes were piled high on the floor, but I was afraid to touch anything, feeling like a suspicious wife, driven to look for tangible proof of defection but desperately hoping not to find any evidence. All around me, there were undeniable signs of a life I couldn't imagine my daughter living.

I picked up a T-shirt displaying a frightening image of the Cradle of Filth band and clutched it to my chest, inhaling deeply to get beyond the smell of stale cigarette smoke to the scent that belonged to the real Sara. The tacky kind of lingerie you'd expect to find in Frederick's of Hollywood was strewn over the floor. It was the room of a stranger that should have been in another house.

There was nothing new that happened that day. It was just until then, I wasn't ready to absorb the choices she was making, but no matter how long I tried to delude myself, the truth was ultimately inevitable. You're never ready, you never want to acknowledge the unimaginable, but in some way, once you do, it's a relief.

Jan Marin Tramontano, New York

Turning points catch us unaware and pivot us in a direction different than the one we originally planned, changing our relationships with our daughters in an instant. Seeing the scaled-down version of Ellen on stage the night of the Spring Concert transformed her into a stranger. Like Jan, I wondered where the child I loved had gone. In a matter of days, it seemed as if the Ellen I thought I knew had been kidnapped and a gaunt, irritable girl sent to live in her place. I began to guard my words and actions, fearful of upsetting her. Mealtimes, once our main family downtime, became tense and unbearable. Here are some other situations that changed the lives of both mothers and their daughters, for both better and worse.

Starting Over and Over

It was October 7, 1996, and I was ecstatic. Even though we'd just made a permanent move after my divorce and I had a full-time job outside the home for the first time in my life, my daughter, Melody, was being admitted to the Beta Club in middle school. Previously, teachers had told me she didn't read well and was "barely teachable," but my mom, a retired schoolteacher, and I had worked to help my daughter. Now she was getting an award, and I had the pictures to capture the moment forever.

Although my parents helped watch the kids while I worked many long hours, all I wanted was to go back to being a full-time mom and "be there" for both my kids. Before the divorce, I had enjoyed being a homemaker/mom, singing, and attending Bible studies. Through dating and chatting about this, I found a man to love me, the kids, and the cats. He spoke of the same "ideals" I had, but in the first year and a half of our marriage it turned out he had trouble fitting in and conforming to those beliefs.

Melody took advantage of his inner battles and my working too many hours. She ignored our house rule "nobody in/nobody out;" if no parents were home, no company was allowed unless planned and approved, and she was to call before going somewhere and tell details and ask time restraints and so on.

She ended up having to repeat tenth grade after her grades and attendance dropped. She also developed a solid smoking habit, confessed to trying many types of alcohol, a little "pot," and was picked up for shoplifting twice in one year. I got calls from sheriffs about that and late-night loitering. One day I got up to go to work and found my car missing—she'd stolen and wrecked it.

We went through all the teen court classes and youth alternatives' classes and available counseling. Some of these counselors could have helped more or differently. The attendance counselor let it slip that sixteen-year-olds aren't actually required by law to attend school and that was all my daughter needed to fuel her apathy. After that, my groundings, positive reinforcements, scoldings, lectures, and tears had little effect.

Three months ago I caught her skipping school one morning. I knew she was up, getting ready, and thought she had left with a friend to walk to the bus stop. I took my shower and then found myself in Melody's room to put away some laundry.

She was there, squatting on her closet floor, hiding. I wanted to know why, but she kept silent. I was beside myself with anger and mixed emotions but had to go to my low-paying but steady-income job. Didn't she understand I had to work a menial job because I, too, had been overly boy crazy and only went through fifty-eight hours of college? My goal was for her to have a better future than mine.

"Come on, Melody—I'll drive you to school," I said. Still, she was silent. I did some preparations for my day until I heard her crying and sobbing, actually freaking out on the phone.

"Who are you talking to now?" I demanded.

"My father!" she cried.

"Why are you calling him long distance and crying and talking to him when you won't talk to me?" I shrieked.

She eventually relinquished the phone. I wanted her to talk, but that was not going to happen for another three hours.

Finally I announced my allegiance to her and her prominent place in my life and said: "Neither of us are going anywhere till you talk to me."

I called in "sick" for work. We ended up talking and crying—it was a truly quality-filled day. She shared that she was five months pregnant and arranging for an abortion, but her ride had canceled and she'd wanted more money from her father to get a taxi.

We prayed together and agonized over every possibility. She was set on getting an abortion—with or without me. I love her. I offered my support and dutifully drove her and held her hand. That was a weird day emotionally and mentally for both of us, but we ended up bonding.

While we still have to get beyond our emotional scars and rebuild our "trust level," she confides more in me now and says she's sure learned her lesson and doesn't want to repeat any more "stupidity" (her word). She comes home on time and we negotiate better. I take the time to iron out all details with her—you see, I announced to my second husband that he no longer has any excuses for gallivanting and he must be the husband/stepdad we discussed on our dates because I quit my job outside the home and will do whatever necessary to put my kids first, at least for this summer. I may have to resort to a part-time job after school resumes, but Melody and her brother are more worthwhile and important to me than that nice retirement plan I'd accumulated.

Lori Stafford, Florida

And Baby Makes Two

I was not quite twenty years old when I gave birth to Tiffany, terrified of the responsibility of raising her properly. She would stretch me beyond what I thought were my limits—especially during her adolescent years!

When she was twelve, we went to Virginia Beach so I could attend a weeklong conference. I was eagerly looking forward to an oceanside vacation with my daughter, who was enrolled in a program for teens whose parents were attending the conference. Tiffany was not very sure she wanted to be there.

My daughter, an Aquarian who finds it imperative to do everything years before others, had decided twelve was the year of her independence. She had been sulky, belligerent, and noncommunicative for almost a year. There had been a new crowd of friends to hang out with in the neighborhood. She tried, then quit, smoking. She experimented with marijuana, and assumed a defiant attitude about contact with boys. As she became more secretive and withdrawn, our communication suffered.

As the conference began, she and the other young people formed a tightly knit group. Their activities during the day were organized, and in the evening they were left to their own resources. Tiffany chose to spend as much time as possible with her new friends. We didn't see a great deal of one another except at meals, and at night in the motel. I would ask her about her day and she would answer in monosyllables. This was the stuff of sitcoms, so I attempted to deal with it humorously by answering my own questions in great detail in what was ostensibly her voice. Her looks were withering! Composure cracking, I alternated between patience and exasperation. This was, after all, my only vacation for the year, yet here I was with a sour-faced twelve-year-old who didn't wish to be there, and certainly not with her mother.

One evening toward the end of the week, I was sitting alone on the beach thinking about our relationship, feeling frustrated and sad. My daughter was slipping through my fingers while I felt powerless to stop her from doing so. I heard voices and laughter coming toward the beach from behind me. A group of adolescents were walking on the beach, so occupied with themselves they didn't notice me. Especially occupied were Tiffany and Thomas, a sweet and charming boy a few years older. They were walking closely together, with his arm around her. I watched them from the distance, seeing the circle of boisterous energy the little group made.

The others noticed me first. I heard them squeal, "Tiffany, your mother . . ." elbowing her and pointing in my direction. She quickly slid out from under Thomas's easy embrace.

I called her over to me. The group split apart not knowing quite where to go, but certain Tiffany was in big trouble. She stopped a few feet away from me, looking sullen and ashamed at the same time.

I said, "Tiffany, did Thomas have his arm around you just now?"

"Yes," she replied in a challenging, if somewhat shaky, voice.

"Did you want him to put his arm around you?"

Again, "Yes."

"Did you think there was anything wrong with his putting his arm around you until you saw me?"

"No." She wondered what I might be getting at. These questions were not what she expected.

"Then don't ever let me catch you going against what you think is right, no matter who is involved. Not even if it's me."

She stared at me in disbelief, trying to reconcile my stern tone with the grace of my message. Tears filled her eyes as she stared hard, seemingly right through me.

That night the floodgates opened and she began to talk to me. This was definitely a turning point in our relationship. She never treated me like a stranger again. Thereafter, even if she knew I wouldn't like it, she found a way to let me know what was going on in her emotional and social life. Sometimes for really difficult things, she would let me know indirectly, by leaving a letter to a friend open on the table for me to glance at, or speaking loudly enough on the telephone for me to over-hear something important. I understood. I had done the same with my mother.

Cie Simurro, Massachusetts

Journey to a Foreign Land

My daughter was a sophomore in high school when she came home and announced that her French class was planning a trip to France. I was divorced and although Sarah's father didn't want her to go, I was determined she would take advantage of this opportunity.

I had begun working at home as a typesetter before the divorce. It was exhausting, mind-numbing work but it allowed me to take the kids to school and pick them up. I didn't get a vacation or holidays, but there was never enough money to go anywhere, anyway. I didn't date because there simply wasn't time.

When her chance to go to France rolled around in 1994, I simply went ahead making plans with Sarah, which meant devoting most of my weekends to helping her with fund-raising, a long, hard job. At the first parents' meeting, I learned that parents who wished to join the trip were welcome. I was thrilled and signed up immediately. My own high-school class had planned a trip to France back in 1965—but my parents had not allowed me to go, or even to participate in the fund-raising. I had been waiting over twenty years for this opportunity.

My daughter was livid.

"I don't want you to go. You'll be hanging around me and treating me like a kid. This is my trip and I want to be with my friends."

I was stunned and terribly hurt. Obviously, I didn't want *my* trip to spoil *her* trip. The "chaperones" were given room assignments with other chaperones—not with their children—so I couldn't understand what was bothering her. I felt I was doing everything I could to give her a wonderful opportunity.

After a while, she and I settled into a state of polite resignation. I *was* going on the trip and she was *not* going to be nice about it. It wasn't until we were in France that I learned from the other parents that my situation was not unique. All of their kids were being snots, too.

We were in Tours when the blowup came. The teens were scheduled to go to a dance with another tour group. The adults were going to explore the old town with the teachers. We left the kids in the care of the tour leader and set off on our walk. We had a lovely time until we started back and saw a young girl approaching us. She was scantily dressed, heavily made up, and a member of our group who had not been accompanied on the trip by a parent. She announced that the dance had been canceled, and that the tour leader told the kids they could entertain themselves for the evening. She had been "driven" from the hotel by "some immature girls who were running up and down the halls with squirt guns getting everybody wet." One of the girls with the squirt guns was my daughter.

We hurried back to the hotel and checked on the whereabouts of all the kids and the tour leader. Once we were certain all were present and safe, we returned to our rooms. Later, my daughter came knocking on our door. She wanted to exchange rooms with us because she and her friends didn't like the one they had been assigned. In front of her friends (since they appeared to be joined at the hip) I told her exactly (and at the top of my lungs) how I felt about her attitude and her behavior— and her nerve in asking me for a favor after treating me so shabbily about the trip. I yelled. I cried. I swore. I held nothing back. We must have screamed at each other for an hour.

When the dust cleared, we were finally speaking again but our relationship had changed forever. After that night, we were people who could travel in the same group without being afraid to show that we cared about each other. Once that moment occurred, there was no going back to the way things were before.

She is almost twenty now, and will begin her junior year in college this fall. She will be an exchange student in England. I wish I could go with her. I think, deep in her heart, she does too.

Glennis Drew, Vermont

Lydia's Adolescence

Lydia is suddenly fighting back and beating her brother up. She has just gotten her period, and I'm horrified to see that she has breasts. She is twelve.

For her thirteenth birthday, Lydia and her girlfriends all dress as hippies and pass a microphone around. Each girl has to perform a song. All of us are dying of laughter, and I am thinking, "This is the time I never want to end. They are still children."

In three months, my daughter has left me. We have moved 150 miles away, to a nightmare of a tract house in a small town of jacked-up trucks and Tammy Faye women. Lydia's hair sticks straight up in the air about seven inches high, jet black, her eyes black lined, her skin creamy white. Boys want her.

A boy I know nothing about who seems to have the IQ of a slug wants to drive Lydia to school. I don't know how to say "no" to this. Years later, I find out that my daughter desperately needed me to take charge and refuse because she was raped by this boy. All I knew at the time was that something was wrong.

I know I am losing my daughter. We hate where we live. Lydia sits in her box-like little room in our horrid little tract house and hardly ever comes out except for school. She keeps her two cats with her and loves them with all her heart.

She makes a friend, the daughter of another troubled single mother who is my friend. We move in with the other mother. Lydia's room is a tiny laundry room, and I hate it that we are so poor that I cannot give her a nicer house.

Lydia and her friend Mary go to a private school together and get in lots of trouble. They like to fill condoms with water, freeze them, and bring them out at parties to shock other kids.

Finally, my mother helps me buy our own house, an old wreck of a farmhouse, but our home, with Lydia's brother, her and me. We're family again, but everything is wrong. One night, about midnight, I am exhausted, grading papers because I spent most of the day driving Lydia around to do her errands. I move to sit down in our big wicker chair and she grabs it out from under me.

I get mad, and Lydia yells, "You fucking cunt!" I'm out of my mind. I chase her up the stairs and start slapping her. Lydia reports this to her counselor, and I am labeled an abusive parent. A friend says to me, one night, "You need to leave when things get abusive."

This becomes a lifeline for me. If Lydia screams at me, I leave, or I hang up. I drive to the park and, in my car, I scream and tell God how much I hate my children and how He will have to help me love them. I settle down, shocked to have finally admitted this. I think, "They will have burned down the house." Instead, when I return, Lydia will come running out, crying, and apologizing.

I am amazed, and watch this scenario happen a few more times over the years. It's as if once I get out of the way, she can finally begin to deal with her stuff instead of foisting it off on me. Finally, I start developing some backbone.

Lydia makes another best friend and lives at her house most of the time. She is in full war paint and far too thin. Men of all ages are at her feet. I hate this, hate finding lacy lingerie in the dryer.

When she turns eighteen, she moves back into my house. She is going to the community college where I teach. Everything changes as she sees me in action and decides that what I do as an English professor is wonderful. The school is small, and everyone knows and loves her. She gets a job in the Writing Center as a tutor and saves up all the complaints she receives about me from my students. Since we have different last names, students don't realize she is my daughter and are shocked when they find out. She and I become allies against stupidity, but there is a brittle pride in it all as I watch the child I knew come back to me, along with the adolescent brashness that says, "I will not be walked on. I will not be ignored."

Dolly Bell, Washington

Life with Lindsay

Lindsay's father and I divorced when she was five; she has one older brother. The worst memory I have of the day we told them Daddy was leaving was her running into her room, slamming her door and telling me what a bad mommy I was and how she hated me for making Daddy go.

Strong-willed and wise beyond her years is the best way to describe Lindsay. She's very determined, with little patience. She gets this from me, which is why we seem to always be butting heads.

Both sides of our family are fairly slender, so weight has never been an issue for any of us. When Lindsay was about eleven or twelve she began to gain weight until she was up to about 156 lbs. She never looked big because of her height, so I told her it was normal. I didn't realize every other weekend her Dad was commenting on how much weight she had gained since he last saw her. It's a wonder she didn't completely fall apart.

We recently spent about three hours one night just sitting on our patio and talking openly and honestly about everything: her dreams for the future, her relationship with her Dad and brother, college, sex, anything you could imagine. I realized how mature she was at fifteen, and it scared me, especially when she said: "Mom, I feel like an old soul in a young body."

It was on that night that she told me what she'd gone through for all those months during her visits to her Dad. Then she told me that she was sorry about the remark she made so many years ago about me and her Dad and said she realized how much I had done for her and it made me feel very good. When she told me she admired me, and wanted to be like me when she grew up, I really lost it. What a great kid. For the first time, I knew I had done something right.

Debi Dilling, Florida

2

Living with Uncertainty: The Search for Why

After Ellen was diagnosed with anorexia, she stopped eating completely, and I went into action mode, frantically calling doctors, therapists, and nutritionists. With each beat of my heart a question pulsed through my mind: Why, Why, Why? Day after day, in between trying to coax Ellen to eat, I spent hours either on the telephone or sitting by it, waiting for a call back. I made lists of places to turn to for help and searched the Internet for information. Underneath all this activity, the question "Why?" continued to haunt me. I thought if I could discover a reason for Ellen's illness, I could make her better.

When I wasn't busy, details of our lives would scroll through my mind as I looked for answers. I scrutinized my past, then Ellen's, then mine and hers together. My husband, who has a great mind for details, obligingly recounted "times when" as I dredged through memories.

"Remember the time when her teacher called and said . . ." I would ask, trying to see if the event seemed as significant to him as it now did to me.

Bewildered, I asked Ellen why she wouldn't eat, but her only answer was a grimace, as if the food she formerly loved was now her enemy. I turned to other members of my family for their insights, hoping someone could pinpoint for me the one pivotal thing that had led Ellen to shut down.

"You and Paul are such wonderful parents" was all my mother could offer, her voice baffled.

There were no answers, yet the pounds continued to drop off my daughter's skeletal frame like the first leaves drifting from trees in the fall. As we became caught up in the mental-health system, I often felt therapists fueled the fire of my obsession to find the reason for my daughter's eating disorder. In medical terms, it's called identifying the "etiology," but basically, the word means the same thing my inner voice was chanting: *Why, Why, Why?*

Eagerly, I answered the battery of questions about our family posed by doctors, nurses, social workers, psychologists, and case-workers, thinking that information I already knew might hold different meaning for them. In particular, they focused on my relationship with Ellen, which both she and I described as "good."

After baring my soul, I would ask for a professional opinion on my daughter's problem in an attempt to uncover the "why" I so desperately needed. Yet each time I did, the experts would shake their head or shrug their shoulders, saying they really didn't know what was going on. She was so young, and there was nothing in the past that would seem to explain the sudden onset of her anorexia or the severity of her symptoms.

I'm not alone in my need to understand why my daughter has struggled so much. Regardless of the type of problems daughters experience, mothers search to understand why it has happened. Perhaps we want to exonerate ourselves from blame, or perhaps it's just the instinct to identify and protect our daughters from whatever it is that threatens them—even if the threat comes from within.

The mothers who wrote for this chapter were at different points in their journey through troubled times with their daughters. Sometimes, possible causes became clear over the course of this journey, but more often they did not, forcing mothers to continue living with uncertainty.

Choices

The first time I saw the movie *Peggy Sue Got Married*, I cried through the second half. The second, third, and fourth times I watched it, I cried through the entire movie. I don't watch *Peggy Sue Got Married* anymore.

Peggy Sue Got Married is the story of a woman who is given the opportunity to live her life over again by confronting the choices she has made in her life. As the mother of an anorexic, I have spent the past four years reliving the choices I have made in my life, searching the past trying to find the cause of my daughter's life-threatening illness. I began sure I would discover that it was my fault: I was responsible, and if only I had been a better mother, if only I had made better choices, this never would have happened to my daughter.

But my search has yielded few answers. I have literally relived our life together over and over again. I have replayed events, searched for hidden meaning in things my daughter said, tried to uncover whether she was subjected to a trauma I did not know about, looked anywhere and everywhere for clues. I have asked myself hundreds of questions, and scrutinized every aspect of her upbringing. Was I too anxious a mother to my firstborn? Did I nurse her for too long and create some sort of dependency? Did I destroy her life by having a second child? Did I set her up for disappointment by telling her she was beautiful, gifted, and talented? As the first grandchild on both sides of the family, was she too adored? I enjoyed being with her—but did I spend too much time with her? Was I wrong to rescue her from uncomfortable situations—did I step in too often, and not allow her to stumble and fall?

Most of all, I question why I didn't recognize the signs that my beloved child was in distress. Or did I really see the signs and subconsciously ignore them? Should I, could I, have intervened earlier so she would not have become so completely disabled? Unlike many parents I have talked to, I noticed the signs of our daughter's anorexia immediately. It was hard not to. She woke up one day, morbidly depressed, almost catatonic, and unwilling to eat. We only let a week pass before seeking help (we were sure she would "snap" out of it), but by that time, she had dropped enough weight to require hospitalization.

Although the recognition of the disease was almost immediate, the slow steady descent to that level of her depression and anorexia was barely noticeable to me when it was happening.

Our daughter had continued to participate in activities (sports, school musical, chorus, academics), but in retrospect, the joy of participation had begun to wane many months before the definitive onset of her disease. She was tired, sometimes withdrawn, and unenthusiastic.

It was easy to dismiss what she was feeling as adolescence since she was thirteen when this all began, but I feel somehow I should have known. If I had addressed my concerns earlier, would she still have become so sick? Maybe I could have helped her. Maybe the illness would not have so completely enveloped her life. Maybe I could have reached her before anorexia so totally consumed her. Maybe . . . maybe . . . maybe . . .

In addition to the questions I ask myself about why I didn't recognize what was happening to her, I also constantly ask myself if my response to her illness was appropriate. My shock and guilt at the seriousness of what was happening to my daughter caused me to act defensively rather than with intuition or positive thought. But how could I have reacted any other way? This was something totally foreign to me, something with which I had no experience, and despite the fact that both my husband and I are intelligent, educated individuals, we felt totally helpless to deal with our daughter's illness. We wanted help, and we turned to "professionals" in the field for advice and guidance.

Unfortunately, our daughter's first therapist gave us advice that, in retrospect, would only set us all up for failure. The therapist told us our daughter was extremely fragile, and needed to be protected from the outside world at all costs. As her parents, we were to intervene at every juncture to be sure that there were no external conflicts so that our daughter could concentrate all of her energy on her internal conflicts. Additionally, we were to do everything possible to "entertain" her, in an effort to hold her depression at bay. Another therapist told us our daughter was suffering from a "Peter Pan" complex (she did not want to grow up), so we were to allow her to remain a child until she was comfortable making the transition to adulthood. In retrospect, these approaches were counterproductive for our daughter. She loved the attention, loved being dependent, and consequently, had no intention of ever giving up her status.

The therapists were right about what our daughter wanted, but were wrong about what she needed. And so, although we ended up giving our daughter what she wanted, it certainly was not in her best interest to foster her continuing sense of dependency on us. We set up a behavioral response pattern whereby the only way she felt she could be nurtured and loved by us was to remain sick/anorexic. Thus, it has become impossible for her to break that pattern; if she became well, she believed she would lose us forever.

I question why I allowed myself to engage in behaviors that I instinctively knew would be counterproductive to our daughter's recovery. Why did I trust "educated professionals" who barely knew our daughter instead of my own maternal instincts? I've come to realize that it is because anorexia takes more victims than the one suffering intimately with the disease; it also affects all those close to the victim. Anorexia scared me enough to relinquish my parental instincts and rights to total strangers who knew nothing about my child.

Our daughter continues to struggle with her anorexia, and I continue to struggle also. Over the past four years, we have seen the worst the mental health profession has to offer, but have also seen some of the best. Unfortunately, the disease is so precious to our daughter that she continues to be unwilling to give it up, even at the risk of death. She has chosen to protect her illness over everything else, including her family. The ultimate dichotomy for her is that she professes to love her family above all else, but her family has become expendable if it means she has to choose between anorexia and us.

I am now at a point where I am trying to accept that I may lose my daughter. There is nothing I can do to make her want to live, to make her want more from her life than the lie of anorexia. Her life is her disease. She has no life outside of the anorexia; she does not go to school, she does not have friends, she has no interests or hobbies at all. My daughter has successfully erased all aspects of her life so that she can concentrate every waking second on nurturing her disease. Her every thought revolves around protecting her anorexia.

As I look back over the seventeen years of my daughter's life, I am overwhelmed by the path she has taken. She has gone from being a vibrant, talented, brilliant, funny, socially responsible person to a mere shell of an individual who barely exists. I recognize that I have taken a parallel road with my daughter; as she has struggled directly with her illness, so have I. On my journey, I have passed through the same stages as someone struggling with a terminal illness; shock and denial, anger, depression, action, and bargaining. I have passed through each stage, and am now at the final stage of acceptance. It took me a long time to get to this point, because the acknowledgment that I need to prepare myself for the possible death of my child is too frightening and overwhelming to deal with on any conscious level. But, in my heart, I know that I must accept the possibility of death as a reality, given the depth of my daughter's involvement with her disease. I have no choice.

In the end, it really is all about choices. The choices I have made, the choices my daughter felt she didn't have, the choices she is now making, the choices I now don't have. In the movie *Peggy Sue Got Married*, Peggy Sue decides not to change any of the choices she made in her past. She eventually comes to a place where she realizes that her life is her life and that by changing any of the events, it would no longer be her life. Maybe she makes this choice because it is too hard to go back and try to figure out what to do differently so that everything will turn out better. I struggle all of the time with the question of what I would have done differently, and in the end, like Peggy Sue, I don't think I would change anything because I am still mystified. Why has this happened to my daughter?

Robin Daniels, Massachusetts

Family and friends often want to know "why" as well. In a letter to her family, one mother struggles to identify "why," even though her daughter's problems have since been resolved. Mixed in with her search for answers is a plea for understanding I know well. How hard it is to find people who will listen, listen, and listen some more, without jumping in to offer judgment or advice.

Letter to My Family

I am Michele's principal caregiver, the one who refused (and still refuses) to give up on her. It's now been almost three years since this horror began, and while Michele is doing well and is determined to stick to recovery, I still live with the knowledge that each day is a potential day for another relapse. I am no longer fooling myself: Michele's recovery is in her hands. Only she can bring about a recovery, just as only she can bring about a relapse.

Putting Michele aside for a moment, I want to talk about me, the caregiver. I recently read a very illuminating article by a man who is taking care of a wife dying of protracted and implied cancer. He writes about something that hit home profoundly: the syndrome of "nobody wants to talk about chronic problems," and his resulting isolation. This is what I have been encountering. At first, when I first learned that Michele was addicted to cocaine, everyone was there to listen, encourage, and support me. While they were obviously very concerned about Michele and seeking ways to help her, they also made it clear they cared about me. I was and am immensely grateful.

Little by little, as the months went by, this began to change. At first I noticed that some friends, still concerned and wanting to be there for me, were getting frustrated because it had become a "chronic" situation, and one that they could do nothing about. Listening to me, over and over again, and seeing how I was suffering, frustrated them. Some began to turn away, because no one wants to listen to pain without being able to help in some way. In turn, I ceased talking to them about it because I *need* my friends, they are my lifelines to sanity. So, in effect, I put a lid on my feelings. Which is what I have been doing for a long time now: bottling my pains up so that I would not bore or frustrate my remaining close friends.

When I say I have come to rely on my family to be there for me, I must add that I cannot bear criticism from you. None of you are in my shoes. None of you can *begin* to understand what it is like to be in my shoes, just as none of us can possibly begin to understand what it is like to be in Michele's shoes. I don't turn to any of you for advice; what I need is to be heard. To know your ears are open for me to talk my heart out, because the more I bottle up my pain and anxiety, the more I am headed to psychic and maybe physical collapse.

I am not a saint. I go through times of tremendous anger and resentment, and times of utter despair, fear, self-pity and rage. Sometimes I feel so utterly alone in this role of caregiver and am faced with feelings of such complete isolation that I just want to call people in my family and *talk*. Not ask for advice, or suggestions, and most certainly not for criticism, but just to talk. I can't do that. No one in my family wants to just sit and hear me talk. They want, out of love I'm sure, to give me advice and in some cases, to criticize me or the way I am handling the situation.

I am told: Kick her out. Don't kick her out. Put her in rehab. Don't put her in a rehab. Pay for her therapy. Don't pay for her therapy. Stop being so kind to her. Just be kind to her. Don't allow her to interfere with your life. Punish her. Don't punish her.

I don't want to hear that anymore. After more than two years, I have done all I can, all that is possible for me to do. Neither do I want to ever have to be defensive with my own family in my actions as to how I handle this. Since I am the primary caregiver, my choices are mine alone, and they are based on over two years' hard experience as well as counseling from professionals.

I am scared to call anyone in my own family to simply talk. To just sound off, unbottle, cry, yell, or scream if I need to. I can't do that because you all want to give me more advice, sometimes demands, and even criticism. I hear the impatience. So, effectively, I have no one at all to turn to, to just talk. I can't call any of you, or e-mail, or fax, because I know full well it will be received as "Oh God, here we go again . . ." I cannot afford to pay for two therapists—Michele's therapy is hard enough on me, so I certainly cannot pay for a second for myself.

In many ways I understand you all. I understand how frustrating and painful it is to stand by and not be able to do anything. To hear the same things again and again, and to hear my pain. It is now a "chronic" situation for all of us, and my calling you, or contacting you, simply serves to bring it all up again. You don't want to be sponges and soak up more emotional pain. I understand that.

What also happens to the caregiver is that, inevitably, their own health suffers. I tire easily, worry more than is normal, have tremendous problems sleeping, laugh less, get aches and minor illnesses often, and seem to have too many accidents. I withdraw a great deal. None of this is the fault of anyone, it's a normal outcome of stress, and yet, if I mention this to any of you, even in the most elliptical way, I hear reproach in your replies. "Somehow," you are thinking, "she must be doing something wrong."

One day Michele will be ready to lead a normal, healthy, and happy life again. I have every reason to believe she will, even with the inevitable problems she will have to deal with upon reentering the world. I have faith in her, and I have that faith because I am with her and see her every day. I see what is going on. She will always be an addict. That will never change. She will be a nonusing addict. I believe that will happen, but in the meantime, what about me? Yes, that sounds like a whining child, and yes I often feel like a whining, complaining child. A very lonely child with no one to talk to. For all this time my life has been on hold; I have been unable to concentrate on work, even on having any fun. To survive I have had to isolate myself, conserve my energy, and bottle my feelings.

Listen to me: I am not at fault. I am not to blame! Nothing I did or didn't do made this happen. My taking Michele in did not make this worse, my kicking her out for a while did not make it worse, and my allowing her back in did not make it worse. My paying for her therapy is not "enabling" her. My lifestyle does not alter any of this. I am not to blame, and neither is anyone else, not even Michele herself.

Maureen Earl, California

Would my suffering or that of these mothers be any less if we somehow magically discovered an answer to "why"? In the following story, a mother does uncover the reason for her daughter's struggles, which offers some consolation but does not completely ease the entire family's suffering.

See Her Smile

"You f–ing bitch."

The words leapt out of her mouth easily and with such hate. Her dark brown eyes were glazed and burning. I waited for an apology or tears, believing she didn't mean it, but my heart was breaking.

She took a deep breath and growled, "I wish you were dead," then stomped up the stairs to her room and as a finishing touch screamed, "I f–ing hate you."

Her bedroom door slammed shut so hard the whole house seemed to shudder. This was not the first rage visited upon me by my thirteen-year-old daughter, but in spite of everything my husband and I tried to help her, she seemed to be getting worse.

My heart shattered at the bottom of the stairs that night. I knew that something was terribly wrong and felt helpless and afraid. I didn't know that in a few more months our daughter would be diagnosed with bipolar depression. Our family's journey to the diagnosis of this illness would take almost three years. After I wrote this piece I realized I couldn't begin to accurately describe the feelings that have swirled around this household. My husband, Gary, and I have been on an emotional roller coaster trying to parent and help our daughter.

Until age eleven, Natalie was a happy, fun, athletically gifted girl. She had been a bubbly baby with an easy temperament, which complemented her older brother's energetic personality nicely. We have a close extended family that we've always seen regularly. I was a preschool teacher, which I enjoyed, especially because my schedule allowed me to be home for my own children during holidays and after school. My husband was busy running a small business but always had time to help coach teams and go to the kids' events. We had an average but sweet life. So how did the wonderful little girl we loved turn into a person who was so miserable?

At first, we thought she was having a tough time because she matured so early. By sixth grade I dreaded hearing the phone ring because she was getting in trouble at school. She had never caused problems before, but started being constantly tardy for class and was getting disci-

pline referrals from teachers for being defiant. Older girls wanted to beat her up because of her attitude.

Teachers were concerned about her behavior because she had always been a quiet polite student. Of course, we would have consequences at home for her transgressions at school, hoping that if we hit upon the right discipline method she could get back on track. This only fueled her anger.

At first, we were shocked and indignant. How dare she turn our life upside down! I didn't want to let go of the way our life had been. I wanted my daughter back; at the same time I was angry with her for causing so many problems.

She was annoyed and upset because she was always in trouble. The word "no" could bring on a two-year-old tantrum. The funny thing is that she rarely ever had a real temper tantrum as a youngster. When her grades plummeted from A's and B's to D's and F's, I knew I could get help from her school.

Through evaluations and teacher input we all agreed Attention Deficit Disorder (A.D.D.) was a place to start. She was having difficulty concentrating and seemed unable to complete tasks. Her defiance could be due to frustration at being unable to keep up at school. So, armed with all the evaluations, we sought out the help of a psychiatrist (for medication and advice) and a counselor to help Gary, me, and Natalie deal with her behavioral problems.

Our home had become such an unhappy place and Natalie was so miserable I had no problems with the psychiatrist's recommendation for a prescription for an antidepressant and a stimulant for her A.D.D. symptoms. The summer between sixth and seventh grade was filled with tutoring to help her catch up on her grades and counseling appointments.

Seventh grade started out pretty well. The medications seemed to be working, but Natalie was growing tired of her counselor, who thought maybe it would be best to put her in an intense outpatient therapy group. Even though things seemed better at home, the counselor could see that we were all missing something. We knew it too, but we decided to forgo this new therapy for a while because her grades were inching up and she was getting good reports on her behavior at school.

Sometime before winter break I noticed Natalie seemed tired all the time. I thought maybe it was the stress of trying to keep up at school and keep her behavior in check. I called to get her in the outpatient therapy program, but they had their maximum amount of kids. She would be at the top of the list for the New Year. Christmas went well but after we had been home a couple of days Natalie began blanking out for a few seconds, sometimes falling to the ground. After these episodes she would be so tired she would sleep for ten or twelve hours. The obvious reason for this was that her antidepressant wasn't agreeing with her, but our family doctor suggested we do some medical tests to be sure that she didn't have heart problems, epilepsy, or a brain tumor.

Then I began to speculate. What if all of her problems could be explained by a health problem? Perhaps this was what we had overlooked. As much as I didn't want her to be physically ill, I wanted to know if there was something that could help her. When all her tests came back normal, I went to my room and cried because I was desperate for an explanation for her troubles.

Her sleep patterns were very disturbed and she had terrible nightmares, so the psychiatrist put her on a new antidepressant and took her off the stimulants. Now she wasn't combative or angry—she was in a major depression and simply couldn't function, missing school because she just didn't have the energy to go. She wanted us to send her away, thinking that somehow a change in scenery would end the problem, but that was too painful to even think about. She went to the outpatient therapy and seemed to like it.

As part of the group, we had to come to family therapy once a week. This was one of the most helpful and valuable experiences Gary and I had. Not all the kids had the same problems, but we learned so much from each other's successes and failures.

I quit my job to home school Natalie for the last six weeks of the school year and she was amazingly grateful. Even though she graduated from her therapy group before school started, Gary and I could still sense that she just wasn't "normal." I fretted about her sleep problems a lot—Natalie could go twenty-four hours without sleeping or sleep for sixteen to eighteen hours. Finally, I decided to take her to another psychiatrist for a second opinion. She recommended slowly weaning Natalie off the antidepressant she was on and trying another one.

I was pleased with this doctor's ability to relate to her and include her in the decisions. By the time eighth grade started in a new, smaller school, her sleep pattern had almost returned to normal, but we could sense an impending storm. No longer in a major depression, she was going back to being angry. I quickly made an appointment with her new psychiatrist and right there in the office Natalie demonstrated her anger. When gently questioned by the doctor about her outburst she became teary-eyed and sad. It was a telling moment because I could see that my daughter was more depressed.

Her psychiatrist explained to Natalie that she had a brain chemical dysfunction which causes her to cycle through many different emotions in a day, even minutes. Her anger and tears were an example of this.

Bipolar depression. I was relieved in a strange way. Yes, I am relieved to know my daughter has a mental illness caused by a chemical brain disorder, and that she isn't always in control. Her rages and bad feelings are caused by this disorder.

She is still the little girl I used to know, but she is sick. I grieve for that sunny, sweet child. I wonder about her future. Will she be happy? Will she be able to hold down a job? I grieve for a simpler life for her. This wasn't what her Dad and I had planned.

For now, she's being treated with new meds and a terrific private counselor to help her deal with her conflicting emotions and behaviors. We will do everything we can to ensure she has the best outcome possible. She thinks we are a pain, but that's okay, we love her anyway. It's going to be a long, difficult journey but each time I see her smile I see the little girl she used to be and I'm filled with hope for the future.

Nancy E. Gibson, Indiana

Although I no longer believe there is any one single cause for Ellen's eating disorder or other problems, there are still times when I fall into that old trap of obsessively looking for "why." All it takes is one bad day to set me searching for clues that might explain the tragedy of her illness. Even on good days, news of a new medication or research study can send me scrambling to the library or Internet, hoping to find that bit of information that might lead to the cure that has so far eluded us.

3

Finding a Way Around Problems: The Magic of Music, Communication, and Hugs

I knew a lot about eating disorders and depression, even before I had Ellen. Several of my close friends had suffered from varying degrees of anorexia or bulimia, as had my youngest sister. Even I had a time during my first marriage when severe stomach ulcers affected my appetite. After I was treated and it no longer hurt to eat, I continued to consciously restrict my intake and was thrilled when I lost weight. Although I don't think depression was the cause of my eating problems, I later struggled with that problem as well, as did many people I knew.

Having experienced all this, I was determined that my daughter would feel so good about herself she would never be tempted to starve or binge and purge. Both my husband and I made a point of focusing more on Ellen's personality than appearance; her wardrobe was interchangeable with her brothers' (with the exception of a brief spell when she wore dresses every day), and her haircuts were always practical. At the same time, we worked to build up her self-esteem, as we did with both Matt and Joe.

Still, I feel there must have been something I missed.

"What did I do wrong?" I asked repeatedly during the first year of Ellen's illness.

My therapist, the mother of a teenage girl herself, understood what I really needed to hear and told me: "Cheryl, I can honestly say there isn't anything I can see that you've done wrong. In fact, I think you've worked harder to help Ellen than many other parents might."

For a short time, that would stop me from wondering how I could have prevented Ellen's life from falling apart completely, but it wouldn't lessen my effort to try and find ways to make things better. The first Christmas after her anorexia started, I bought her a guitar, and she started weekly music lessons she seemed to enjoy. A short time later, when she and her best friend showed interest in designing their own clothes, I found a sewing class for them. They took it, but didn't follow up with the sewing projects. Next, there were jazz dance lessons and volunteer work at a food bank. In between those attempts to stop her from spiraling deeper and deeper into depression and anorexia, I tried hugs, prayers, and praise. Members of my faith community, who witnessed the change in Ellen, tried to help too, spending extra time with her on Sunday mornings, inviting her to their house for an evening, or sending whimsical presents in the mail.

None of these efforts cured her, but who knows? Maybe they prevented far worse consequences than the ones we did experience.

The stories that follow describe the efforts of other mothers who were able to find a way around, or through, real or potential problems with their daughters.

Negotiating a Settlement

The night has closed around us like a jacket
by the time we head back from another
late afternoon walk, my daughter and I
newly together again. Rules spelled out
between us: don't bad-mouth my father;
don't force his life on me, we didn't have much
to say over cardinals crying in the sycamores,
bleaker, bleaker, bleaker.

After two years, I hardly know her.
The pieces our lives split into
I thought, laughing and kicking
dead apples under my feet, but said
nothing when she asked me
what's funny, just pointed to the birds,
little blood-spots in the trees.
I tried a topic, school, which she hates.
She tried a topic, the old farm, which I loathe.
I finally offered to stop for a coffee;
she offered to stop for a Coke
In the corner McDonald's we watched
our reflections grow into the windows
but couldn't see the resemblance.
We're returning in silence when it happens: a melody,
just three minor notes, repeated and repeated.
On a porch somewhere in front of us,
someone's playing a flute. She begins to sing
"Eleanor Rigby," I sing back, "People Are Strange."
We measure our steps in time, we try to harmonize.
We try them until they're right, and they rise
one after one after one, like the street lamps
in the trees, and we can't help but notice
their beautiful symmetry
as we turn onto the lane where, for now,
at least, we agree to say we live.

Sarah Kennedy, Virginia

Sofie on Her Way

"What's wrong with this family?" It is just 6:30 Monday morning and I am pierced, taken off guard by the vehemence of my fourteen-year-old daughter Sofie's tone. She's ready for school, wearing an expression I've been seeing too much of for my own comfort.

"I don't like your attitude. I find it offensive," I begin, searching Sofie's face for a way in. Her brows begin to furrow and she looks down, thick brown hair falling in front of her cheek. She doesn't reply. Her younger sister, Ariel, appears and stands silently in the doorway.

"You know, we hardly spent any time together this weekend. I mean, I like your friends, and I know you enjoy spending time with them, but if you don't make an effort, before you know it you'll be gone and we won't ever have this time again." I let my words tumble, as if they might line up in the space between us to form a bridge. I know I am failing though; to Sofie they must seem like pellets being thrown harshly in her face. I continue anyway, compelled and desperate even as I know I should stop.

"Why are you so angry with me?" I demand, my voice now rising, a hint of hysteria inching in. "You know, I'm not psycho. I don't know why your friend says I'm psycho. My friends never say anything bad about you—only good things, they tell me. Did you set her straight? I'm not psycho?"

I see myself in a flash: I'm spouting and flailing, and I'm aware it's getting late. I don't stop talking, though, but try a different tack: "It's not you. It's me. I'm sorry, for all that's worth." I feel as if I'm talking to some old boyfriend.

The bus comes and the girls are out the door. Not a good start to the day, I think. I finally sit down, resting my face in the palms of my hands.

Sofie was born six weeks premature but otherwise healthy. "She's the tiniest baby I've ever seen," someone commented, but to me, who had no other basis for comparison, she was perfect. A dusting of brown hair covered her head, and in her sleep she seemed to hold the wisdom of ages. She was, however, required to remain in the ICU for two weeks of antibiotic treatment, during which time I was encouraged to spend as much time holding her as I could, which is exactly what I did. After my own discharge, I treated myself to a daily cab ride back to the hospital, where Sofie and I spent our earliest hours together.

Sofie comes home from school a different person from the one who left that morning cross and half-awake. Now she is chatty, animated, as if nothing untoward happened between us earlier. I bring her a glass of chocolate milk as she tells stories of her day, then bounds up to her room and closes the door.

Later, I am stretched out on our couch nursing a rare stomachache. It is unusual for me to stop like this during the evening, and despite my pain, I'm relishing the stillness. I lie on my back, head propped against the side of the couch, and feet together under our sunflower-covered afghan. The room is dimly lit by ambient light from the other rooms.

Suddenly, Sofie bounds in. She's just hung up the telephone after talking with a friend, and she's coming to announce something, but stops when she sees me lying down.

"My stomach hurts," I tell her. "I'm trying to get rid of it."

She approaches the end of the couch and slowly lowers herself onto me, the full length of her body almost the size of mine. First her feet land on mine, falling in and around them. Then her calves and her thighs melt right onto mine, rolling a little in their roundness. Her arms are taut, supporting her upper body, and she looks at me for a moment like she's the mother. Lowering her chest, she places her cheek under my chin, and there we lie, I like a bumpy mattress she is resting upon, her body perfectly lined up with mine. I feel my stomach being pressed, but I don't want to move. We don't speak, and we only stay that way for a few seconds before she's up and about and on her way.

Susan Hodara, New York

Rocker Mom

My thirteen-year-old daughter and I have developed a new bonding ritual. As soon as we're in the car in the morning, she turns on the radio, tunes in to "Elvis Duran and the Z Morning Zoo." The drive to school takes less than ten minutes. By then, I've been awake nearly two hours, my daughter barely forty minutes. I'm caffeine-buzzed, ready to talk about anything. She's still tossing and turning in last night's dreams. Like the apex of an intergenerational triangle, Z100, the radio station of choice for teens in and around New York City, becomes the place where our rock 'n' roll spirits meet.

The joke, of course, is really on me. I may have thought I was programming her for Chopin in utero, but in between the nocturnes and ballades, I gave her a dose of Clapton, Springsteen, and Dylan.

Back to Elvis and his cohorts. Between commercials and songs, there's a lot of good-spirited banter. One day they're analyzing the ramifications of the strike at the Twinkies factory. Another day they're polling listeners on whether to play "The Schlong Song" again. The lives of entertainers or last night's episode of *Sex and the City* are always juicy material. Horoscopes, rattled off, punctuate the hour. It makes us pay attention.

On any given morning the harmony of the ritual is disrupted if I start singing along when a song I like is played. The ones that get me going usually have a familiar ring. Old rockers, so the saying goes, never die. They just keep getting reborn. The embarrassment to my daughter is obviously too much. She rolls her gorgeous, sleepy blue eyes and switches to another station. If I tell her I can't help myself, rock 'n' roll is in my blood, she smirks. If I try to get her to listen to the Rolling Stones, she tells me she's not interested in archeological digs.

One day she wises up. The idea she has is just so, so good (she thinks); she's bubbling like a pot of overflowing pasta.

"You know how much you love rock concerts," she says, practically cooing. "Well, I have an idea, Mom. Tickets for 'Jingle Ball' go on sale tomorrow. Wouldn't you just love to take me?"

I smile. So what if I don't know half the stars of the teenybopper set and like only a limited number of songs from the half I do know? Don't I want to maintain those open lines of communication during the terrible teens? Isn't she handing me, on a silver platter, a key that will grant me entry into an otherwise restricted world?

I'll think about it, I tell her.

If driving our kids (literally and metaphorically) too hard is part of the "soccer mom" syndrome, is there a new syndrome—let's call it "rocker mom"—that's part contrivance, part accommodation? Rock 'n' roller that I am, do I go with the flow of my daughter's longing, willing to accommodate as long as the apple doesn't stray away from the tree? Has menopause, the hormonal trickster, infused me with the tastes and smells and desires of an adolescent waster of youth seeking fun fun fun, is that what it's all about? Or do I harbor some hope that connecting on the unspoken, primal level of song will give my daughter the grounding she needs to make good choices as she stumbles from one rite of passage to the next?

I go into my daughter's room, brightly lit by late morning sun. At the head of her unmade bed, hovering like guards, are Elmo and Cookie Monster, Pooh Bear and Beanie Babies. On the wall across from her bed is a collage of posters and pictures meticulously cut out from magazines—Buffy (the vampire slayer) and Angel (the vampire with a soul), Blink 182, and the cast of *Dawson's Creek*. I resist the temptation to make the bed and risk accusations of snooping around while she's at school.

She's closing the door more and more these days, occasionally slamming it shut and locking it, music screeching a loud-and-clear do not disturb. Straddling the fence of innocence and desire, she tests the limits of my understanding with these outbursts, challenges me to stay one step ahead in this thorny game of good-enough parenting. How good, really, is good enough? If I'm the reason she slams the door shut, can I also be the reason she opens it?

"Enough, Mom," my daughter would say if she could read my mind. It's just a rock concert.

Which is why I found myself doing the mother-daughter rock concert thing.

"Jingle Ball '99 is going to be so-o-o fun," said my daughter.

Ricky Martin and 98 Degrees. Smash Mouth and Lenny Kravitz. The last Jingle Ball of the millennium. It was an easy ploy to get sucked into. Time, the great revisionist, reminded me that "the times they are a-changing" and didn't I enjoy some of the music at the last concert I'd taken her to? I may cringe at the blatantly sexual images on MTV and make a case against the sensual melding of sight and sound, but some part of me eggs me on, whispers to me that vicarious entry into the mosh pit of adolescence is better than none. The years pass oh-too-swiftly—more swiftly than ever, it seems—and even if my rock 'n' roll heart tells me she should be here sans any parental unit at all, I can take advantage, for once in my life, of becoming a cliché. Which is what I am—a fifty-something yoga-entrenched woman with boxes of old LPs from my youth-wasting days, memories contained like tiny scratches in the vinyl. Memories of a generation that brought about a paradigm shift in consciousness. In music. In the way I try to connect with my daughter.

"If you start going to rock concerts now," I say to her, "what's the thrill going to be when you're eighteen?"

"Going to more rock concerts," she answers.

Without me, I think, smiling.

Until then, I guess, I'll ride the wave. Which is why I find myself a few months later bracing against the late May wind at Jones Beach, listening to the punk-ska repertoire of Blink 182. (For this concert, we dragged along the other half of the parental unit.)

My daughter and her friends, standing on their seats, are among the younger fans, and their faces register pure, innocent joy at hearing the music live, seeing the tattooed twenty-something-year-old trio whose songs vibrate with adolescent angst. The pot smoking is minimal here, and you can't even get a beer, which I could definitely use to get me a little more into the groove of the Travis, Tom, and Mark show. I might say it's almost appealing, something my mother would have never said about the music I listened to (with the exception of a couple of McCartney-Lennon tunes). I might say I'm glad my daughter likes music that's got a little more punch and we can have intelligent conversations about good rock, hack rock, and everything in between. It may take years before she acknowledges that nothing was ever created in a vacuum, and even the punk-ska she listens to owes something to the days of doo-wop.

Time it was and what a time it was, it was . . .

All the tea in China will never make me love music the way my daughter does, but that's not why I'm here at the beach bracing the wind of a late spring evening. Call it mother love or primal bonding, whatever. Call it honoring thy child's sense of taste. Call it the raging hormones of midlife, that sense of straddling the fence of time, looking back, looking ahead. Knowing: *I was so much older then, I'm younger than that now.*

Deborah Batterman, New York

Between Mother and Daughter

The morning I turned thirteen, my mother knocked on my door to wish me a happy birthday.

"Now that you're a teenager," she said, holding up a little pink book, "I want to share this with you. It explains everything that you'll need to know about being a teen. Please read it and ask me if you have any questions."

Like most teens craving time alone, I reluctantly took the book, climbed out of bed, and told her, "All right, Mom, now leave me alone." I slammed the door behind her, and glanced at *Learning About Your Body*. On the book's cover was a picture of a girl looking down at her bare breasts. I remember thinking that giving me this book was a corny thing for my mother to do, but she'd often done corny things before.

A few moments later came another knock at my bedroom door. I scurried to hide the new book under my pillow, as I had once done with *Valley of the Dolls*. I cracked the door open and again there stood my mother.

"There's one more thing I wanted to tell you. You're entering some tough years now and, unfortunately, these are just beginning. There're three difficult times in a woman's life—adolescence, pregnancy, and menopause."

As an only child with working parents, I spent a lot of time alone. This helped me develop my passion for letter writing and journaling. When I got older, my hobby turned into my career. When I became a mother, I also encouraged my kids to write. By the age of six, I had bought each one of my three children their first journal. I continued the tradition every year on their birthday. Sometimes they wrote in their journal and other times they'd shelve them with unread books. But, when times were difficult, such as when my father died, I'd catch them pulling those journals off the shelves to share their thoughts with an anonymous piece of paper.

Now, I'm forty-six, and the mother of three teenagers, two of whom are girls. My mother's words still echo in my head. As I struggle with hot flashes, insomnia, mood swings, and efforts to control my weight, my daughters are battling with PMS and trying to figure out who they are and where in the world they fit in. All three of us are in the midst of major hormonal upheavals, and each of us thinks that her predicament is worse than the other's.

I was delighted when my eldest daughter, now seventeen, actually used writing as a venue for her teenage angst. Below is an excerpt of a piece she shared with me when she was fifteen. She walked into my office as I sat glued to my computer and said, "Mom, I want you to read what I wrote."

I extended my arm to grasp the paper and said, "Sure."

In many ways I felt honored that I was the person who she chose to share her thoughts with, yet after reading it I became both frightened and concerned about what she was feeling. I didn't want to overreact because, knowing her, next time she wouldn't share anything with me.

After reading the piece, I handed it back to her and said that it was beautiful. I did, however, feel compelled to share some of my thoughts with her, and therefore wrote her a letter. As you will see, my response was brief and encouraging, as I believe that it doesn't matter what adolescents write, as long as they write. Any form of writing can be therapeutic for teens as they cope with that powerful demon inside of them.

Her words:

Life is all right, life is good, but life itself could be better. My mind goes around and around nonstop like a rat in a wheel as it tells me: "You can't bear it anymore. I can't go on; it's over and time for a new start, a clean slate," as I lay there on the floor unconscious waiting for a prince to kiss me.

So what's going to happen in the future? Should I even think about that shit, or, can I think about it is the question. Or do I want to think about it? It's as if there is a little elf inside of my brain saying "No, no. You can't think about it."

I tell myself that I don't know what I want in life. Maybe to be happy, be free, going around fucking whoever, whenever and whatever. That's good. It gives you a rush, a feeling that you actually have some sort of control and I manage to do it any way possible.

As I look at life in the city, the people, the enemies and things around me, I think and sometimes I think too hard, and that's my problem. My brain explodes and I watch it as it falls like a watermelon drawn to the ground, splitting into a million pieces.

I walk at night alone, just walking until I get hit. As something would catch my eye and drag me towards it like a baby screaming my name, I watch, I glare, I stare and I see how people look at me and how they react. Some people are idiots and just stare and some try to talk to me, but others laugh. I am too tired to even think, nor even give a shit. I just mind myself and no one else. I just keep on walking like a ball rolling down a never-ending hill. I am extremely tired and not in the mood for anyone's problems. I just want a cigarette, a relaxing stick of tobacco ready to give in to my needs and wake me up again. I am too drunk to drive, or get fucked, or even to tie my own damn shoes. Now that's pathetic.

My response:

Dear Rachel:

I know that you won't believe me when I tell you that I know how you feel. Yes, I was a teenager once, and believe it or not, things were not that different in the sixties. I went through times when I wanted to die. I remember loving my parents one day, and resenting them the next. I lived in New York City and there were many temptations; I had to remain strong and make many decisions to keep me out of trouble. I had to say "no" in situations where everyone else was saying "yes."

I'm sorry that you feel so sad and so angry, yet, I'm happy that you have chosen to write. Writing is good therapy, whether you share it or not. I'm delighted that you chose to share yours with me.

You are a special and sensible young lady and I want to tell you that I will love you forever, no matter what. Your friends will come and go, but I will always be there for you, and please, whatever you do, keep writing, you have a special talent. Love you now and forever, your mom.

Diana Marquise Raab, Florida

The Challenge of Junior High School

At age twelve, my daughter started junior high school and boy did life change for us. Seventh and eighth grade became a parent's worst nightmare. She and I became strangers, fighting about everything. Shoes, clothes, friends, activities, makeup—you name it, it became a battle. I tried to talk to her, continued to do the mom and daughter things like going shopping, including her in on cooking, and taking her to our favorite places. I even invited her friends along. She would come, but she remained distant from me.

I feel the change came because she wanted to fit in, and do what her peers were doing whether it was right or wrong. I would always get "Sue's mom lets her do this" or "Jill's mom lets her have this." My answer would be "I am not their mom and if Sue or Jill would jump from a cliff will you too?"

She began to lie to me about the places she went, and to make me the bad guy. I was the one making her life a living hell. She would turn to her dad who saw the little angel in her and thought I was the bully also.

Through all of this I felt confused and often angry and would lose my temper a lot. I would want to throw the towel in and tell her to go ahead and learn the hard way. There were many nights I cried myself to sleep. I would ask God to guide me and ask for patience and the strength and knowledge to deal with my teenage daughter.

During this time I was told by friends, family members, coworkers and even my mom to ask what she wanted. Boy oh boy. Believe me that was not easy, most of the responses and wants were crazy, but we began to communicate and she began to listen to me. I would grit my teeth, thinking this is not the child I have given birth to.

I told my daughter that God gave her to me to look after and nurture, to show her love and respect, and to teach her responsibility so that someday she would move out of our nest into her own. I also told her that I did not choose her and she did not choose me. I have told her also that there are rules and "no's" that she will not understand now. Someday she will thank me as I did my own mother.

Today we both are talking and listening to each other. We still have our differences but we compromise. It's been one year since we have been doing this and she has become an honor student again and chooses her friends a lot wiser. We do things together, and she even offers to help with chores.

To all the mothers out there with junior high daughters, hang in there and listen, listen, compromise, and don't give up!

Sharen Long, Ohio

Singing a song, physical contact, listening to music, and communication: approaches that sometimes came to mothers spontaneously, like a gift, and, at others, resulted from a great deal of deliberation. All of them worked to strengthen the bonds between mothers and daughters, and sometimes even prevented or solved their overriding problems.

4

Shared Vulnerabilities:
Body Image, Fitting In,
and Ghosts from the Past

From the onset, it seemed as if my experience of Ellen's illness was different than her dad's. As I began to write this book, I wondered if I was unique. Did other mothers feel their daughter's struggles more deeply than fathers?

"I know what it felt like to be picked on in high school," one woman told me when I asked how her feelings compared to her husband's. "In looking back, it seems like I might have been super sensitive, but at the time, it hurt! Then my oldest daughter got designated as a target by senior girls when she was just in ninth grade, and my heart broke all over again."

"I matured early, which meant I got lots of attention from boys," said another. "It also meant girls hated me. I developed a pretty thick skin, but when I see the same thing happening to my daughter, it infuriates me."

"All I wanted in high school was a boyfriend. I thought my life would be perfect if I just had a steady guy to date," an attractive mom confided. "But I was a 'late bloomer' and I'm afraid my daughter is exactly the same. I reassured her when she didn't get asked to the prom, but then went in the bathroom and cried because I felt so bad about it."

I know many moms with sons in crisis and am struck by the similarity of our feelings. We share a sense of confusion over what went wrong, guilt over our failure to produce a "successful" child, grief from the pain their struggles evoke, and exhaustion and frustration when our efforts to save him or her fail.

Still, mothers have been adolescent girls, and we know the territory well. The sense of vulnerability we share with our daughters seems to lead to an important difference between the mother-daughter and mother-son relationship during times of trouble. In many of the stories I received, the empathy mothers felt for their daughters stirred up a special angst because they had once experienced similar issues.

My love for Ellen isn't any greater than her father's love for her or the love I feel for my sons, but the quality of our relationship has always been different. No one can make me laugh in quite the same way Ellen can, and there's no one else who can *say* what I'm *thinking* at the very same moment (a phenomenon we call "thought stealing," since she accuses me of the same thing).

It hasn't been hard to empathize with Ellen's low self-esteem, either. I, too, had been dissatisfied with my face, figure, and social life as a teen. Although I was a married adult when I had eating issues, being so miserable you don't know how to nurture your body was a struggle I understood well, just as dark sadness was once an all-too-familiar feeling for me. Consequently, I have cried more tears over Ellen and lost more sleep worrying about her than I have for my two sons combined so far.

In the stories that follow, mothers see some aspect of themselves in their daughter and react—perhaps to both the memory of their personal struggles and the sorrow of seeing their child suffer. The need to help is doubly significant when the issues you deal with may be partially your own.

Snickerdoodles

"I love having you home."

The words spilled out like the pool of flour on the floor by the counter. A hug spiced the moment while the smell of cinnamon wafted from the oven. My fifteen-year-old daughter and I were spending Sunday afternoon in the same house. To call our camaraderie "togetherness" was a stretch, as she probably felt more connected to the *Seventeen* magazine she hid behind. She was baking snickerdoodles on her own initiative and I was repotting plants. Baking and eating sweets on a whim has been a favorite shared activity of ours for at least a decade.

I have always hoped to be the kind of mom that a teenage daughter could confide in. I was working at the kitchen table to share both space and words, but silence surrounded us. It seems we have come full circle from the pre-vocal infant stage. Back then she would touch my hair, my ears, my chin as she nursed. Now it is my turn to touch her hair, her hand, and steal hugs as she twirls away.

We don't talk about anything as we work. She is engrossed in her magazine and I am thinking about my suspicions, finding it hard to ignore the connection between the pan of snickerdoodles she has devoured and her trips to the upstairs toilet.

Am I being paranoid because I remember the struggle of wanting to be thin and wanting to eat cookies? I feel guilty eavesdropping outside her bathroom door, yet I am afraid to broach the subject without proof. I want to rip the pages of skinny models out of her magazine. If I did, would she wonder about my rage? Would she ask? Would I tell her about my own struggles with bulimia in college? She and I have both read a book on eating disorders, and I think she knows the dangers.

She emerges from the bathroom, looking guilty, and asks, "Can we order pizza for dinner?"

I don't hesitate. "Yes, yes, yes."

I want to give her everything, knowing I can give her nothing but love, and space, and hope she'll be able to stomach them long enough to stay alive.

Ann Kornelius, Iowa

On the Perils of Being Different

Emily was a pretty little girl who had an ordinary childhood. We lived in a nice but not elaborate house and had enough money for her to take gymnastics, dancing and other expensive activities, like children from middle-class, middle-America homes.

By the time Em was nine years old, budding breasts and other signs of early puberty were evident. She started her period the summer after fourth grade. I was appalled that she would have to deal with the messy business of womanhood so many years before her classmates. She still needed prompting to brush her teeth regularly!

I pushed to place Em in a Christian school in fifth grade because I wanted her safe. She was already a head taller than most, with breasts and hips other little girls would wait years to possess. The day we arrived for the admission procedures a casual statement was made that "she doesn't look like our other girls." I should have taken this as a warning and escaped immediately, but the combination of my fear for her future and the illusion that a "Christian" environment would protect her spurred me on.

It didn't turn out that way—both boys and girls were fascinated with her body. Their parents' eyes seemed to signal fear that my daughter's physical maturity would somehow ruin their own sons' and daughters' childish innocence. Of course I was frightened too. My fear stemmed in part from my own suffering as a social outcast during my teenage years. As a result of my own adolescent ignorance and poor choices regarding sexual expression, I carried tremendous anxiety around Emily's budding sexuality. I kept my anxiety at bay by believing we'd sheltered her from the worst.

In sixth grade, Em was caught with several other children writing a "dirty essay" using words I didn't know she'd ever heard. The teachers were under the impression that Emily was the ringleader, and although she told us it was one of the boys, she admitted to being an eager participant. Her teachers took the event as a reason to look at her and her home environment as somehow perverse.

My embarrassment over Emily's "difference" combined with the toxic residual of my own shame became more than I could bear. With some bitterness, we returned her to public school in the middle of sixth grade, keeping our feelings to ourselves. At the time it felt like our failure rather than that of the system. Instead of helping us solve what should have been a minor problem, Emily was made to feel dirty and bad. Girls who'd previously been friends were no longer allowed to play at our home.

Em quickly began to experience the power her body had to provoke male interest. I knew we were in trouble, but I tried to view the danger signs as early adolescent rebellion. She started to run with older kids and I intercepted notes that were sexually explicit. At twelve she started to cut school and sneak out of the house to meet boys. She became sexually active and spoke casually of what she would do if she got pregnant.

Then she ran away. I was panic-stricken and could not work or sleep. I wept uncontrollably in her room, rocking her favorite teddy bear in my arms. We filed a police report, made flyers with her picture and posted them everywhere. We knocked on doors, walked the streets and alleys of our neighborhood, and pleaded for people to give us information. We found her after a week, but she ran away two more times within a short period of time. We had her evaluated at the adolescent psychiatric unit and tried family and individual counseling.

Emily was not "bad enough" for the state to consider stepping in to help. There had been no charges pressed against her. It wasn't illegal to be a runaway and having sex with another teenager is called "consensual sex between minors," but I knew we were in serious trouble and needed help. I searched for answers, made dozens of long-distance phone calls, and reviewed numerous packets of information on residential treatment. They were all extremely expensive and we did not have insurance coverage for such programs. When she ran away a third time, I made contact with a woman who gave me hope. She said that when we found her this time, we should head for a facility in Utah.

We found her in a hotel room with her boyfriend, picked her up, and left immediately for the interstate, driving nonstop from central Iowa to a wilderness program for delinquent youth located in Utah. Unfortunately, after forty days in a program that cost $8,000, we brought her home still in the same mess. She began to skip school and sneak out at night again. She was now thirteen and we were out of money and out of ideas. We knew we couldn't live like this for five more years, but we couldn't turn our heads and let her go as we'd seen other parents do with their wayward children.

We admitted her to a youth emergency shelter, started court proceedings to declare her a CHINA (Child in Need of Assistance), and hired lawyers for both her and ourselves. The judge reviewed our case and then mandated treatment in a girls-only behavioral program just three hours from our home. Her diagnosis was "oppositional defiant disorder," a fancy name for rebellion.

Every weekend I made that three-hour trip to spend Sundays with her. Every other weekend her Dad drove with me so he could also be involved. It was harder for him because he was carrying the financial load. I was unable to work due to the extreme and prolonged stress. After two months in the youth shelter and then three months in a highly confrontational treatment program, she accepted reality. She decided she wasn't as mature as she had tried to convince us, and wasn't ready to be on her own. She wanted to come home, back under our protection and guidance. She decided she loved us after all, and she believed that we loved her. After she graduated from the program and returned home, she continued in a six-month aftercare program.

Taking care of Emily for those two years cost a total of $15,000, but we would spend it again if we thought it would save her from destroying herself. My husband does not bring the money up. He and I worked together to get her through the really bad years, but we will never be in full agreement about how to handle her.

Emily went back to school, though her peers would continue to look at her as a "bad girl." She fought to create a new image, but we eventually had to move to give her a chance to start with a clean slate.

She has had experiences that many adults never undergo and will never be innocent again. If she can survive the rest of her adolescence, I believe we will be on safer ground. She already has wisdom regarding life choices and hard consequences that others her age do not understand. She is still different, but she is learning to accept that, as are we. This is not the life I had dreamed for my only daughter, but I have given up my fantasy and choose to love her for who she is. She is a strong young woman and I trust she will have a remarkable life.

Kathy Shriner, Iowa

Another mother echoes this sense of both her and her daughter not "fitting in," due to a shared family history. A low grade on a school assignment might not trouble other mothers, but for JoAnne, the issue that bothered both her and her daughter was much bigger than academic performance.

Our Less-Than-Perfect Family Tree

After school one day, my fourteen-year-old, the middle child of three daughters, stormed into our house, slammed down her book bag, and stuck a piece of paper in front of my face.

All this before I could even get out the words: "How was your day, sweetheart?"

As I tried to concentrate on reading her work, I could hear my daughter's troubled voice trailing through my thoughts.

"Mom, I told the teacher this paper would be hard for me. He said to just do my best and he wouldn't mark me down, and he didn't keep his word."

My daughter excels in school, but I knew this experience had a much deeper meaning than getting one more shiny polished A. Truthfully speaking, at that moment, I should have been listening more attentively to my daughter's feelings. It wasn't the big letter "D" scrawled in red at the top of her homework assignment that was the problem, but what the teacher had asked her to do: name at least thirty ancestors from both sides of the family. As I looked at her paper, I saw a sturdy, brown tree trunk with a lopsided, fluffy-green cloud of the leaves on my husband's side. Obviously, she had been graded down for the many barren branches on my side of the family.

It was all there on paper: my family history, that resembled a soap opera where the leading performers kept leaving me—and therefore my daughter—behind. My birth parents backed out after I was born, replaced by an adoptive mommy and daddy, with him only making a short-lived appearance. These tragic losses have hurt the most when my daughters' friends reminisce about close relatives and large family gatherings. To help ease the pain, we dream about the time when our immediate family, as a seedling, will begin budding out new branches.

Until that day, I didn't realize how much my feelings of loss and abandonment had trickled down to my daughter. Just as I had struggled to make sense of all the inconsistencies and unknowns in my past, my precious child too was attaching her self-worth to the emptiness of my family tree. By rejecting me, my parents had also rejected her. It hurt me to see this sadness, which came out because of a situation completely beyond our control.

For me to gather up enough courage to discuss this humiliating subject with a stranger (her teacher) was a task I just couldn't bring myself to do—so I never did. I still shake all over when thinking of doing such a thing.

It has been comforting to begin sharing with each other the painful feelings of resentment and shame for a less-than-perfect family tree. Life seemed so much easier when my teenager was a small child and I could hold her in my arms until the tears subsided, but now I must just listen to my daughter's hurts with my whole heart. And every now and then I still fall short.

JoAnne Bennett, Oregon

Sometimes, though, the pain mothers experienced as adolescents can actually be a positive motivator, providing the impetus to take action so daughters won't go through the same experience their mothers did, as the following story demonstrates.

In Her Interests

I cried when the doctor said, "It's a girl."

Not because of the joy on my husband's face. Not for relief because the baby was healthy. Not because after two years of infertility intervention we finally had a second child.

I cried because I didn't want to experience a daughter's teenage years.

My older brother was an Eagle Scout who had dozens of friends. He was adored by his teachers. In the middle of a civics test, a teacher read my essay as I was writing it, patted my shoulder gently, and said: "You're good, but you'll never be as good as your brother."

My younger sister was a blue-eyed wisp who floated across the ballet recital stage. A neighbor once sent me home from a party to get my sister because she wanted her relatives to see the beautiful child who lived across the street.

I was the chunky one who read a lot of books.

The books entertained me on dateless Friday nights, became my devoted friends, and, eventually, taught me that confidence begins with self. When I finally stopped trying to be like my brother and sister, I forged my own path and learned to like myself.

From the moment my daughter's midnight-dark eyes looked into mine, I resolved she'd face her teen years with confidence and joy, not hiding in books as I had. I would encourage her interests and through them help her realize her self-value before she ever reached her teens.

"Why are you asking her which cookies to buy? That baby can't even talk to you yet!" an older woman commented as I shopped with my daughter strapped to my chest.

My answer: "Because she will talk soon enough, and her opinions count."

When she was three, she insisted her daddy stop channel surfing so she could dance with Baryshnikov in *The Nutcracker*. She practically wore out the carpet dancing to the video I bought her for Christmas that year.

When she had the flu and a fever of 102 degrees but still put on her tap shoes to dance with Shirley Temple during grade school, I found a teacher for her who taught the delight of dance, not the achievement of perfection. During mini-performances in a nursing home, my daughter grew in confidence and developed compassion from the joyful smiles of the residents.

Recording her poems and stories even before she learned to write helped her realize school essays were not to be feared. She won't be the valedictorian or even in the top 10 percent, but her teachers celebrate her thirst for knowledge.

There have been some hard lessons she's learned. Pursuing her own path means sometimes people, including herself, get hurt. At twelve, she was snubbed by other girls at school when she qualified for and excelled on the dance squad. She was devastated when we wouldn't let her give her heart away to a fourteen-year-old boy who told her she was his soul mate. When the "soul mate" became jealous of the male friends she made, she decided Mom and Dad were right. She's now fifteen, and the teen years haven't yet been the terror I anticipated: there's been joy and laughter with occasional screaming and tears.

Recently, after two months as a zoo volunteer, she informed me she wanted a python. I glanced at her laughing face and hoped she was joking. I'll always do whatever I can to help her have confidence, but my devotion to her interests stop at the door to the zoo's snake house!

Betty Glasgow Hanawa, Texas

Mothering Ophelia: From Stroller Brigade to Solitary Beat

I was fresh out of college when I read Nancy Friday's book *My Mother, Myself,* laughing in agreement with the first sentence: "I have always lied to my mother." It spoke to me and for me, as someone who had always lied to her mother about the important things: who I was with, what I had really done, and where I had actually been. At the ripe age of twenty-one, it didn't dawn on me that one day I might have a daughter and that she might lie to me.

When I became pregnant with my first child, I was determined to be a far better mother than my own had been. I was raised by a succession of nannies and mother's helpers while my mother "did her thing," whatever that was. In contrast, I was going to be a full-time mother to my child and renounce any outside help in raising her.

When Melanie was born I gladly opted to trade my briefcase for a diaper bag. For the first two years I was happy to be home full-time with my daughter. I loved our play dates: she would share toys with another toddler while the mother and I shared coffee and conversation. I was quite fortunate to live in a neighborhood where there had been abundant fertility and a large "stroller brigade." Every afternoon a group of us would line up our strollers and walk our young offspring while we

compared notes on mothering. It was a good life and when the road became rocky, I knew I was not walking it alone.

By the time Melanie entered kindergarten, I was back at work part
time in a job that permitted me to be off for holidays and the summer.
Still, I had difficulty parting with her. Even though she had been in daycare, sending her off to be cared for by strangers felt different. As she
boarded the school bus for the first time, I felt as if a piece of my self
had been wrenched from my body.

I compensated for our separation by becoming a parent volunteer. I
made sure that I was selected to be a room parent and a chaperone for
every field trip and helped out in the classroom once a week. I knew
Melanie's peers and their parents became part of my new social network.

As the elementary school years progressed, there were fewer opportunities to be present in my daughter's school, but I was involved in all
of her extracurricular activities as either a helper or a spectator. These,
too, provided ways to interact with other parents and to have an im-
promptu forum for sharing some of the challenges of parenting.

Things began to change the year Melanie turned twelve and entered
seventh grade. She went through the classic middle school deterioration
I had read about in the professional and popular literature. Foolishly, I
thought that my years of "preventive parenting" would help us escape
the perils of adolescence. I knew we would encounter bumps in the
road, but thought we would avoid the major potholes.

The year began on a positive note. Melanie had entered a new school
she loved and the phone rang constantly with calls from friends. I was
happy because the school not only welcomed parental involvement, but
actually required us to volunteer on a regular basis. By then, Melanie
was no longer eager for me to be part of her school life, but she tolerated my presence.

I often look back on November as the last calm before the eu-
phemistic storm. On one of those bleak gray days that harbinger the
arrival of winter, I was taking a walk when I encountered a neighbor
whose daughter attended school with Melanie. We chatted and I was
surprised when Margaret abandoned her usual reserve and confided
that she was having a terrible time with her daughter, Rachel. I listened and sympathized as she told me how Rachel was becoming

anorexic, doing poorly in school, and exhibiting alarming signs of psychological distress.

Margaret had consulted the family physician and a psychologist but her daughter refused to talk and refused to eat. My neighbor was beside herself with a combination of worry, anger, and helplessness as she struggled to find a way to help her daughter. The two of us groped for straws together but neither of us could figure out why Rachel was falling apart or what could be done to help her. The issues were much more complex than those we had pondered as members of the stroller brigade.

I had always considered Margaret and her husband the epitome of "perfect parents." Both were human service professionals who made family a top priority, providing their two children with unique educational and extracurricular opportunities and family activities. It was difficult to understand how Rachel could be in so much distress when she had been surrounded with so much love, caring, and good intentions.

Later that day, I told my husband about my conversation with Margaret. We talked about how we might be of help to the family and I remember saying: "I'm so glad we won't ever have to deal with any of those issues with Melanie." After all, she was an active, involved, well-adjusted youngster who seemed to have her act together. We would soon discover otherwise.

In December, Melanie started to become sick, and stayed home from school frequently. I figured the cause was flu season, coupled with an airtight "sick" school building. When a friend suggested my daughter's frequent absences and illnesses might indicate something was bothering her, I sloughed the idea off. Melanie just wasn't the depressed type. If something was bothering her, she would tell us.

We went away over the vacation week and although Melanie did have a respiratory virus, it seemed like she wanted to sleep all the time. I began to get concerned when she was too tired to talk to friends on the phone, since until then she would overcome any malady to take a call. Then one night we went out for Chinese food and she didn't want to come with us, preferring to stay home and sleep. The red flag unfurled completely: she loved to go out for dinner, and Chinese was her favorite.

I took Melanie to the doctor the next day to have her checked for "mono." When the results were negative, I was willing to acknowledge that she might be depressed, but thought it was most likely a seasonal affective disorder or the by-product of hormonal changes, not a "deep-seated" depression. I was in denial and would remain there a while longer. After all, I had done things right, so how could things be going wrong?

The signs of depression persisted. I felt a great sense of loss along with helplessness. It was as if the daughter I had known and raised had disappeared. Her body was with us, but the light had left her eyes, and she carried herself as if there were great weights on her shoulders, the bangs of her hair hanging over her eyes so she could hide behind their dark shield.

It was extremely scary and frustrating to watch the child whom I loved so deeply floundering and to feel like she was rejecting my efforts to help her and shutting me out of her life. Suddenly, my "job" had been restructured. I had spent over thirteen years as a mother and caretaker and now I was being told by my child and "employer" to "get away, I don't need you, want you, or have to listen to you."

It was very difficult for me to entrust my daughter to a therapist. Although I knew that her father and I could not be the only influences in her life and that there were some problems we couldn't fix, on a more emotional level, it felt like a loss of control and a failure on my part. I had not succeeded in keeping her out of trouble and once there, I could not extricate her on my own. It was hard for me to realize as a professional, I could help other people's children, but when it most counted, I couldn't help my own child.

Perhaps some of my ambivalence was obvious, or maybe it was just that Melanie didn't like the process of therapy, for she claimed the therapists I found were too judgmental and just didn't "get" what it was like to be a kid with her problems. She felt that only other kids could understand her and wanted to join a group. Fortunately, we were able to find a group for adolescent girls but she did what I feared and gravitated toward the most disturbed and flamboyant members of the group. At the same time, the group enabled her to see how other kids were handling similar issues and to have a confidential forum for discussing her own concerns.

There were a few sessions for parents offered along with the group for teenagers but only one other mother attended. This was an irony that would pervade my journey through my daughter's adolescence. During the most difficult years of child rearing when the challenges were greatest, the supports were either unavailable or unattended. There were no "stroller brigades" or coffee klatches for parents of teenagers. We were all too busy working or taking care of our other children and the excuses to come together around our children's school and extracurricular activities were reduced as our children shunned these activities or were able to get to them on their own.

Even when we could gather together on the sidelines, certain topics were extremely difficult to broach. It was one thing to talk about our children's struggles with siblings, peers, or school, but it was quite another thing to introduce the subject of experimenting with drugs, alcohol, and sex or to acknowledge a struggle with depression, eating disorders, acting-out, or self-destructive behavior. Occasionally a window would open, as it had on that November day when Margaret had confided in me about her struggles with Rachel, but invariably the window would close again and remain tightly shut. There was too much at risk to let others know what was really happening behind the curtained windows of our homes.

The volume in our house escalated, as there were countless arguments. The mounting anger and frustration on all of our parts sometimes led verbal quarrels to become physical. I am able to laugh about it now, but one day after a particularly heated argument, Melanie didn't come home from school. I tracked her down at a friend's house and she informed me in very catty tones that I would be getting a call from her guidance counselor. The next day my husband and I were called in and questioned about physically abusing our daughter. The counselor was a bit more understanding when he heard both sides of the story. The volatility of her emotions at that time led me to suspect that Melanie might be using drugs, a fact that she hotly denied even in the face of a urine screen that suggested otherwise.

My early laughter at the words "I have always lied to my mother" came back to haunt me: it was my turn to have a daughter who lied to me. Now my job as mother had been restructured as a combination of detective and warden. Over the next two years my daughter would weave a web of lies surrounding her whereabouts and activities; I already knew that many of her companions were not constructive influences. I found myself snooping for evidence and inconsistencies and then, like a cop, going in to make the arrest and enforce the sentence.

Things bottomed out to the point where I threatened to send Melanie to an all girls' parochial school and even took her on an interview to prove my seriousness. This was a radical step for me, since I am an observant Jew, but I was willing to do anything to keep my daughter from further deterioration. Boarding school was another option that we dangled over her head. She didn't want either and was willing to show us that she could turn things around in order to remain in public school.

Melanie met a young man who would become a significant boyfriend. He was nineteen and working at a gas station, but they fabricated a story: he was seventeen and a senior at another high school. Although we disapproved of the relationship for many reasons, we knew the enticement of forbidden fruit and tried to use the relationship as an incentive. A good week earned the privilege of being able to go out with Carl on the weekend and if all homework was done he could come over during the week. We figured that Carl would soon tire of being with a fourteen-year-old, especially when we enforced so many strict rules and curfews. Surprisingly, the relationship ended up lasting for almost two years, during which time Melanie's grades went from C's and D's to honor roll and even high honor roll.

Another incentive that we used to bring Melanie's behavior back in line was the privilege of driving. We made it very clear that she had to maintain honor roll status in order to get her learner's permit and license and that any behavioral infraction would delay the process. Good behavior could be used to earn back time. There was a lot of negotiating and testing but in the end she was able to get her license only a few weeks late.

The next carrot became use of the car. Within weeks of earning her license, Melanie was grounded from the car for a month for breaking a rule and lying. She hated going back to bumming rides and being chauffeured by her mother and hasn't lost the car again—at least, not yet!

Writing about my experience as the parent of a struggling adolescent has been a difficult task. It's been hard to be completely open and honest for fear of violating Melanie's privacy. Going back over the details also stirs up a certain level of guilt, shame, and responsibility on my part. I recall the days in my twenties when I vowed not to repeat the mistakes my mother had made, and how I had deliberately countered my own mother's absence by being a constant presence in my daughter's life.

In spite of all of my efforts and good intentions, my daughter became a modern-day Ophelia and floundered in a river that robbed her of much of the self-esteem and cheerful optimism that had marked the first twelve years of her life. We are no longer caught in the raging current of that river and I would like to think that we have found firm footing along its shores. Neither of us are the same people we used to be, but I like the person she is becoming, and I have learned there are no guarantees in child-rearing.

Melanie has made tremendous progress in school and is very successful in her work with young children. I am gradually rebuilding my trust in her and we are able to talk about many things, to share our thoughts and feelings, and to laugh together again. There are still many days when we storm at each other and exchange harsh words, but now we apologize and forgive. As with any recovery, I take things one day at a time. The river is still beside us; today its waters are cool and calm.

Elizabeth Stein, Massachusetts

PART TWO

Hoping to Help:
Crises Big and Little

5

The Contrary:
On Being Smarter, Prettier,
or More Unique Than Others

Not long ago I was reading about Native American culture and came across an explanation of the "contrary," a person within the community who does things in unusual ways or appears rebellious. However, the contrary is not viewed negatively but rather as a helper because he or she illustrates alternative ways of approaching problems and issues.

In our society, being different is usually a liability rather than an asset, especially for adolescent girls.

"When my son let his hair grow long and refused to wear brand name clothes, he was admired. My daughter tried dressing and acting different, and ended up losing her friends," the mother of a teenage girl told me.

Her comment led me to realize that my sons, too, had faced far less peer pressure when it came to appearances than Ellen or the other young women I knew through my years as a swim coach and teacher of nursing students. Girls face the challenge of trying to conform to an impossible role model: the bright-eyed, clear-skinned, shiny-haired, perpetually smiling young woman with a slender but curvaceous body that greets us from virtually every magazine cover and television show.

In looking back, I can see now that in the year before her eating disorder surfaced, there were signs that Ellen felt different and unusual. She was in an advanced math class and had progressed beyond the other students, but instead of seeing this as a good thing, she was ashamed.

"My teacher made me help other kids," she complained one afternoon when I asked how her day had gone. "What really sucked is one of the guys I had to help was Ben."

I knew she had a crush on the boy, and I could well imagine how miserable she would feel being put in that situation. When I called the teacher to ask if he could provide more challenging activities for Ellen, he told me it was too late for her to be on the Math Scholastic Team (ironically, he'd enrolled a boy in Ellen's class). I wondered why I was the one suggesting more satisfying class work for Ellen, but later met another mom whose daughter had gone through a similar experience the year before.

While I don't think being made to feel uncomfortable in one class led to Ellen's problems, I do think it set her up to view her uniqueness as negative. It wasn't surprising to me later when she became part of a crowd of students who made a point of dressing and acting as differently from everyone else as possible.

I was a "contrary" too, but in a quiet way: a cheerleader who never pursued the popular crowd, spending all my free time in the Special Education classroom as a reading volunteer. When Title IX legislation was passed during my junior year of high school, I was one of two girls who qualified for the boy's swim team. Although I adored the attention of my male teammates, I didn't have a serious boyfriend until months later, and then, we never got beyond an occasional heavy kiss. My memories of high school are ones of being different but obedient: My mother will tell you I was a "good" daughter.

This book is filled with stories of girls who were also unique in some way: They matured earlier, looked different, or had some other characteristic that caused difficulties with their peer group. The mothers who wrote the following pieces describe teenagers who, like Ellen, had to deal with challenges related to being a "contrary."

Second-Born

Rather than share a room with her sister, she has moved to the basement, covering the walls with murals; moon and stars and rainbows partly effaced with murky white. The high basement window is open to damp and creeping creatures. Smoke from burning incense swirls through the room like fog in a cave full of artifacts: drying weeds suspected of herbal value, bird feathers, incense burners, sketches, sewing, a wet bathing suit, dirty jeans with scenes painted on the legs.

When did I lose my second daughter, and why? Her hair is like a lion's mane, tawny and thick, her eyes gold-speckled jade. Her body is thin and strong. She lies on the floor on a moldy mattress and listens to recordings of whining young men with electronically amplified voices. She feels she is herself, whatever that is.

In the morning, instead of going to school, she wanders through town, striking up conversations with homeless people. She knows all the bag women and street people in town by name, as well as their stories. They are more interesting to her than school.

In the counseling office, I try to explain to the Girls' Dean with upswept hair and a phony smile why my daughter does not like school, but fail. When I get home she is in the kitchen baking cookies. The sun catches her hair through the window, surrounding her face with a halo like a Renaissance angel's.

"If you do not get to school tomorrow," I tell her, "they are going to arrest me."

She decides to complete her classes and graduate from high school early. I find myself in the principal's office, asking why, since my daughter is a National Merit Finalist, they have taken her name off the list posted on the wall of the office. It turns out that this is because she is graduating early.

A vagrant dies in Madison, Wisconsin. My daughter's name and address are found in his pocket and someone calls to ask if she knows who he is. She comes home dissolved in grief, as though her best and most promising friend had died broke and alone.

In fall, just when it starts to freeze at night, she disappears. We get a card of a cornfield, postmarked from Iowa. "Hitchhiking West. Don't worry. I am in good hands."

She is eighteen. Even if we found her, we couldn't make her come back, they tell us. I sleep with one of her old socks against my cheek.

Months later, a card comes from California. Then, weeks later, a call. She wants us to wire money so she can take the bus home. They were picking fruit, she says, and a plane came and sprayed all the workers with poison.

She moves from one seedy place to another, tries to stay with her grandmother for a while, then moves into a hippie compound north of town. My mother is horrified—her granddaughter living in a place like that! What will everyone think?

She becomes a devout follower of yoga, then studies with a Catholic priest. Suddenly she joins a fundamentalist sect, moves into a group home with a chaperone, and gets very pious. Somehow I am relieved. She must need something like that, I think. We should have given her something like that.

She is fired from her first and only professional job for a mistake that seems very important to them, but not to her. She goes to work as a cook in a day care center for low-income kids.

She tells me wives should always obey their husbands, and makes her own wedding dress out of white linen. One of the seams is crooked, which upsets her very much. The wedding, outdoors on a cold rainy day, is attended by an uneasy collection of fundamentalists, Midwestern Presbyterian relatives, and academics. Neither the bride nor groom think the rain and cold constitute inclement weather. They are a perfect couple.

Maybe she has recovered from her childhood, but I can't. I know I'll never get another chance to do better, especially since I have no idea what "better" would be. In my heart I'm pretty sure what happened would have happened no matter what I did, given the person I am and the collection of genes she inherited. When I am in an honest mood, I know she is exactly the daughter I really wanted her to be—though I see more clearly now the price the world can exact for this.

Netta Gillespie, Illinois

Early Matriculation

Emily slammed the front door, ripped off her backpack, and ran upstairs crying, "I hate that stupid school. I'm never going to go there again."

She was fifteen, halfway through tenth grade, and hated everything about school; the bus, the gym classes, her insensitive art teacher, the stupid rules, and an entire student body that dressed alike and made fun of anyone who didn't. Emily and her small circle of friends were bright young people capable of great success but they were also dangerously close to the edge of failure and I worried which way she would go. Every day was a roll of the dice. Would she succeed? Would she connect with some teacher or friend who would make things work, or would she fail, drop out of school, or just take off with some other dreamer and disappear down the road to nowhere?

The phone rang; it was the vice principal, Mr. M., the burly disciplinarian whom I knew was on her hate list. He sputtered and fumed. Emily had walked out of the school in direct defiance of his order not to. He had followed her out to the parking lot but she had accepted a ride from a friend, hopped in the car, and drove away before he could catch up with her.

Wearied by daily efforts to keep her going, I was also dealing with my recent divorce and relocation. I was a displaced homemaker with little hope of jumping back into the career I had left five years earlier, when helping Emily navigate adolescence had seemed more important than a second income.

An incident like this could be the one to push her over the edge. I had visions of watching her wheel away on the back seat of someone's motorcycle while I stood there watching, as powerless as big Mr. M. had been. She didn't look back in those visions, and she didn't return.

With a determination that came from desperation, I refused to let the tears out. I donned my armor and listened sympathetically to Mr. M.'s litany of Emily's offenses while my mind raced through possibilities of how I might both placate him and convince her to react in a way that was somewhat consistent with the world's perspective. In another life-time, I had been a director of human resources, so I knew the value of letting people tell their stories. It often deflated their anger and it worked this time as well. With pleas of hardship, given our situation and prom-ises of better discipline, I was able to convince Mr. M. to diminish her sentence from suspension to detention. When I hung up, I cried.

We had been lucky, but I knew that something needed to be done. She was really a good person and had been identified as a gifted student. She was just different and determined to be who she was and not hide it.

I hatched a plan to focus her attention on college, hoping she would see success in high school as the path to the future, with academic chal-lenges and an independent lifestyle ahead. I didn't even think about how we might pay for it, but went to the library, looked up schools that I thought might interest her, and planned a road trip during Easter weekend. Unconvinced of the wisdom of this idea, she buried her at-tention in books she had brought along while I drove.

During this adventure, we learned of early-admission programs that accepted students after completion of their junior year in high school. Could she survive another year? I wondered, but wasn't sure. She seemed pretty sure she didn't want to. Exhausted by hundreds of miles of driving and the tension of her disinterest, I headed skeptically into Massachusetts late in the evening on our last day out. There was one more place to consider. It was only 300 students, but it sounded very special.

The wooded campus at Simon's Rock College twinkled with lamp-light when we arrived well after dark. An array of students walked and played along the paths, fields, and low-slung buildings nestled among the trees. Astonished, I looked over at her and saw the same reaction on her face. These were Emily's kind of people: boys with scarves on their heads, girls with all manner of individual dress and hairdos ranging from unruly manes to barely brush cut. There were no two alike, except for the fact that each one was different. She sat up and stared, not even trying to feign disinterest. She realized that here was a place she would fit in simply by being different.

We learned that Simon's Rock was unique when it came to early admission. They took students in at age sixteen, citing many famous Americans who began their studies at age thirteen. They pointed to the encouraging successes of their students, and noted a fact I knew well: special students can be stifled in public schools. By September, we had rushed through the process of applications for admission, for scholarships, and for school loans. At sixteen, she was off to college after finishing only tenth grade.

Now, my independent daughter would be far more independent than others her age. I could stop worrying about how she fit in at school, but there were other things to worry about. Simon's Rock took a very proprietary interest in their young charges. There was a required series of lectures on surviving college, and strict attendance rules for classes, with no more than three cuts allowed per semester and dismissal for dropping below the required number of courses. They were isolated on this little campus three miles from the closest town, a benign little New England village.

What would happen if she didn't succeed there? Was she ready for this risk? Was I? I worried about her being on her own, 350 miles from home at an age when most parents still imposed a pre-midnight curfew on their daughters. I worried about sex. I worried about drugs. I worried about everything that first year except for what actually happened her senior year, just two days before Christmas break, one semester before her graduation.

I woke at 12:11 A.M. with the phone screaming. Something had to be wrong.

Emily! I bounded out of bed and raced across the cold living room floor. It had to be her.

I fumbled for the phone.

"Mom?" she was crying. I lowered myself onto the couch under the weight of her words. "There's somebody on campus with a gun. He is shooting people." She began to sob. "Two are dead and some others wounded. We don't even know who they are."

Stunned speechless, I shuddered. My baby, my only child, the one I had nursed and nurtured, was in mortal danger, and I couldn't protect her.

"Where are you? Are you OK?" Meaningless questions poured out of me at the same time that I heard voices in the background. Of course she wasn't OK, but she was alive.

She responded, "They got him. It's over. I'll call you back."

I was in total darkness. There was nothing I could do. Was it really over? Was there someone else out there? I had heard her voice and her distress. Could this possibly be true? Was she really safe? I waited second by second.

Emily called back around 3:00 A.M. but could barely speak. One of her beloved professors, a promising young Argentinean loved by all his students, was dead. She had been writing a paper for his class at the very time that he drove toward the gatehouse and met the shooter head on. A student who had run out of the library was also dead. Others had been taken to the local hospital.

I said, "I'm coming."

That night began the journey that would end with a basic philosophical shift in how I looked at life. The five-hour drive was a lifelong nightmare. Every minute of the trip I hated the distance between me and my daughter. Even above the speed limit, the car seemed to move in slow motion. When I finally got to the campus, the entrance was roped off and traffic was being turned away.

I knew a back entrance and drove the dirt road through the woods. The students were being encouraged to congregate at the dining hall, where teams of psychologists had been brought in to help them cope. The sight of those young faces, terrorized and sleep-deprived, will haunt me forever. They had all been damaged by this and I knew it would be a long, long time before any of us would ever feel safe again. Emily wasn't there with the group. I found her huddled in her room on her bed. All she could do was cry.

The school closed prematurely for winter recess and we drove home in silence. We went through the motions of celebrating the holidays.

We cried, we had nightmares, and we created ceremonies to let go of our anger, throwing small stones across the ice on the lake in front of our home. We wrote hateful things on wood shingles and burned them in the fireplace.

As the break period wore on, there were letters from the school addressing what became known by the students as "the tragedy at our school." By the end of January, pain and anger were still our predominant feelings, but it was time to go back. Some students had chosen not to return, but Emily wanted to.

I drove her there preoccupied with painful possibilities: *Could it happen again?* As I passed the places where people had been shot, I reached new heights of anxiety. Back home, tears were ever near and sleep was always fleeting. All I could think was that she could die at any minute far from home in what was apparently a dangerous place. I turned my anger into action, writing essays and a screenplay about violence.

Emily feeds swans who glide by in the tranquil waters beside the towering pink classical columns at the Palace of Fine Arts in Golden Gate Park. Or rather, she does that in the framed snapshot on my bureau. There is another photo next to it. In it, she grins, waves, and strides boldly across the tarmac toward the small plane outside Gate Number Seven at the airport, the first leg of her journey to Hungary. That day, I watched the plane gain speed and lift off, then fade and dwindle in size to a tiny dot in the sky. After it was gone, I watched where the dot had been for a while, seeing my daughter disappear before my eyes. Two weeks earlier, the newspapers had been full of stories about a similar plane full of young people bound for Paris that left New York and dissolved in the sky.

The smiling photo of Emily might have been the last I had of her, but it wasn't. She went on to walk alone through the dark streets of Budapest, to survive an avalanche in Switzerland, and a flood in Costa Rica. In the years that have passed since the tragedy, something has changed. Every time I catch myself starting to worry because I think she may be in danger, I remind myself that she once went to school in what was probably the safest place in the world. That taught me there is no such thing as security.

Helen Isolde, New York

It's hard to think of beauty as a liability. When I received the story that follows I was initially skeptical, wishing I had the problem of Ellen being *too* accomplished and attractive. Yet, as I reread the author's words, I realized her pain was no different than mine and that we both suffered because we had daughters who paid a price for being unique.

The Worst Summer

There are lots of movies about how hard it is to be the "dork," but I've never seen a movie about how hard it is to be beautiful. Beautiful girls in the movies are usually snobs or mean, picking on someone less fortunate. My daughter isn't ordinary in that she is a professional model, a background dancer for a professional singer who performs locally, Student Council president, and an aspiring actress who just signed with an agent.

At this point you're probably thinking I'm a stage mom, but I've only supported her, not pushed. Madison takes advantage of any opportunities that come her way. Yes, I know I could say "no" to her; however, if you saw the passion in her eyes, you would know I'd be hurting her if I did not help her follow what's in her heart.

The result of all this has turned out to be jealousy, and few friends. She tiptoes around the friends she does have and is careful not to share her success stories or mention any new endeavor in hopes they won't end up envious of her. Mothers are just as bad. When you're proud of your daughter's accomplishments, you want to shout it out to the world. Instead I keep it inside, afraid I, too, will not be liked.

Madison's last summer didn't go as planned. She went from having two best friends to having two enemies. They made my daughter's life a living hell by betraying her and lying about their friendship. I'd never seen Madison go through pain like this: betrayed, emotionally hurt, and feeling less confident with herself. As a mother I just didn't know how to help her get through it.

It all started after Madison won a local beauty contest. Her two friends would not return her phone calls, or they were never home. As a mother and adult, I knew they were avoiding her. We tried to tell her, but she would always stick up for them. One time Madison called from a different phone. Without Caller ID, Shannon answered the phone, but said she couldn't do anything because she had to help her dad clean the barbecue grill. Madison believed her.

They not only attacked her but they attacked our family. They accused her father of being an alcoholic, and me of loving only her brothers. She ran in my room crying, but all I could do was hold her and tell her she knew none of that was true.

I was boiling inside. I wanted revenge for the hurt these two girls had caused my daughter. My husband and I had been so nice to them—how could they do this? The next day Madison had an e-mail letter. This time I printed it out and decided to show it to the girls' parents, sure they would have their daughters apologize and that would be the end of it. They heard me out, but the apologies never came.

When I saw my daughter lose her two best friends in the whole world, I saw her loneliness and pain. Should I have left it alone? Was I interfering? Was I being childish? They didn't have to be Madison's friend, they didn't even have to like her, but they could have just left her alone like they had been doing. Instead, they sent her an e-mail letter that was timed at 3:08 A.M.

She was going to be starting a different school in a few short weeks so I hoped all this would soon be behind us. She became very depressed, moody, and bored. As the summer months came to an end, the whole family was fighting. Madison would fight with her dad, I would fight with the both of them, and take it out on my boys. There was so much tension in the house sometimes I didn't even want to go home.

When school started, things got back on track. Madison was making new friends, smiling again, and having a lot of auditions. I loved telling her that her agent called because her whole face lit up. It gave her something to look forward to and the whole family was happy again, because she was happy. It's funny how one person can affect the whole household.

Time heals all wounds. Right?

One Saturday afternoon we were watching a movie where the best friends killed the pretty, popular friend.

Madison turned to me and asked "Do you think Shannon and Donna will do that to me?"

I had to tell her "No, of course not." Afterwards, I thought about the girls—contemplating in my mind if they were capable of such an act. What's really horrible is that I had to give it a second thought.

Halloween was approaching and Madison received a phone call. Her first and last names were on the bathroom wall at her old school, along with "If you want to have sex call 123-4567" (her number). Remember Madison no longer went to this school, but guess who did?

My husband was furious and got on the phone to Shannon and Donna's parents, but there was no answer, which was probably for the best since they probably wouldn't have done anything about it. Again, I lost sleep. How was I going to handle this situation? I just couldn't leave her name there.

I was confused about the proper way to handle the situation. It had already gotten way out of hand and had me worried. I decided to go to the police officer stationed at the school. I explained to him the events that transpired over the summer and the bathroom graffiti. I even mentioned the comment Madison made to me about the movie. I wanted the officer to know who the two girls were, to keep an eye on them, and also to have some formal record of them harassing Madison, in case their cruel obsession went a step farther.

One of the mothers called me, furious, because I went to the school. That's the reaction I expected. She never once called about the harassing letter her daughter sent to my daughter but I guess she got upset that she had to go to the school. The way I look at it, she may thank me later. Hopefully, the talk with the officer may have prevented something more serious from happening.

It's been a few weeks now. Madison performs in her school musical tomorrow night and things seem to be "quiet." I know I should be forgiving, and I am trying in my heart, because they are still so young. But they hurt my little girl.

Sim Sulecki, Florida

Like my Ellen, the girl in the following story struggled to come to terms with her strengths, questioning whether it was really worth it to be smarter than most of her peers. Her mother was able to empathize with the situation because her school experience had been similar, but ultimately, it was her daughter's job to come to terms with a choice between sacrificing her values to conform and be accepted or continue being her genuine self.

Grading Oneself

It all began with the report card. Historically, my twelve-year-old, Hope, got high grades, but this time she was disgusted.

"I'm the only one to make all A's," she lamented. "My friends all make B's and C's. They think I'm weird. Only the real prissy, snobby girls make all A's."

I realized more than grades were at issue. Hope was thinking about choosing between doing well in school and fitting in with her group of friends, and that troubled me. Until then, she hadn't cared about fitting in and had marched to her own drumbeat.

"It feels like I belong nowhere," she told me.

Belonging is important. We all need to feel a sense of belonging. Hope had always been content to find her oasis, her identity, her place of belonging with our family, but now she needed more. How was she to find a place of belonging when she saw so few choices?

"Do you think if you started making bad grades you'd fit in?" I asked, wondering what my role was in all of this. I too did not belong to any group, especially in our small town where woman professionals were as rare as a silver dime. I could relate to Hope's sense of wondering, of knowing herself but having no soul mate to embrace. It was not a fun place to be at forty-two years of age and a real painful place to be at twelve.

"Maybe, but I like learning. I like knowing stuff."

"Sometimes life is hard, huh?"

"Yes, like right now."

"So, what are you going to do?"

"Don't know."

Days, then weeks passed. Hope and I talked endlessly about how girls tend to give in to the pressures of conformity in order to fit in, in order not to stand out or threaten the "way things have always been."

Hope was the only girl selected for a math honors team. That didn't make her many friends, with either girls or boys. Eventually, she slipped into a depression, feeling that no matter what she did, nothing would work.

I was with her, listening and encouraging. I shared stories of my childhood: being the girl to sign up for "boy" things like shop, liking sports, and being smarter than boys in math and science. Although I could walk beside her during that dark time, she had to make her own path.

After a few months of being on the margins socially, Hope decided it was not worth being a part of a group to sacrifice herself and her own values. She made friends with some older girls, a few boys, and tried to find a place of belonging within herself. Still, I know there is a longing deep within her for a heart friend, one with whom she can share her interests and her secrets.

Although family is still her place to be accepted unconditionally, it isn't easy. She struggles with being different, and yet wanting to be like everyone else at the same time. Adolescence is not fatal, but it can feel that way at times.

Malinda Fillingim, North Carolina

6

The Power of Mother's Intuition: Making Mistakes, Bullies, Lack of Trust, and Starting Over

When Ellen was in the second grade, my husband took a new job that required a lengthy commute in the opposite direction of my own lengthy commute. Although our children were quite happy in the small town where we lived, our living arrangements began to take their toll. At least once a week, doctor's appointments for allergy shots and ear infections required either Paul or me to take half a day off work. After a few close calls on the playground prompted emergency trips home by one or both of us, I was convinced we should move. The town where I worked had better schools and more opportunities, so it seemed the logical choice. Paul's commute was such that he could spend two or three nights during the week and all weekend at our new home.

As we carried in the first box and began to unpack, Matt, who was then thirteen; Ellen, who was eight; and Joe, age six, set off to meet the neighbors. They returned minutes later, claiming they'd been told to "go away" and "move back where you came from." Caught up in the moving process, I shooed them off, sure their reports were exaggerations. In the days that followed, the complaints continued, and it wasn't long before I noticed that it did indeed seem that the children in our new neighborhood really disliked my kids. Why this might be so was a mystery to me.

During the next year, all three struggled to fit in. I was stunned, since this had never been a problem; usually there were more kids at my house than I could handle. When Ellen's teacher called Paul and me in at the end of third grade and said our daughter wasn't getting along with the other children in her class, I was upset but not surprised. Based on what we saw in our neighborhood, no one liked her, or her brothers. When I asked the teacher if she could see anything Ellen did that irritated the other children, she said no.

Later that night, Ellen and Joe told us that since the beginning of school, all the kids on the bus had been singing songs they made up to tease them on the ride to and from school. There was one song for Ellen and one for Joe. Paul and I went back to the school to ask the principal to put a stop to the behavior, only to be told it was our children's fault. When we asked how this could be so, the principal shrugged and didn't answer us.

What had seemed like such a positive move and felt so right to me was clearly a huge mistake. We ended up transferring Ellen to a private Quaker school; Joe joined her there two years later, but that only addressed part of the problem. Summers were torture: All the neighborhood children would gather to play games or hang out, informing my three they weren't allowed to participate. "Go home," the ringleader would say, and that was the end of it. No reason was ever given. Finally, defeated, we moved out of the neighborhood, this time relocating closer to Paul's job.

Most people's faces light up when I mention the name of the town where we lived during that time, proclaiming it a great place to raise a family. Even after we left, the situation seemed so unreal I was sure either Paul or I had been overly sensitive. It was only when our new neighborhood turned out to be a completely different experience that I realized our perceptions were accurate. Now I'm sorry we didn't get out sooner.

Long before the situation with Ellen occurred, a minister had told me about a daughter of one of his parishioners who was picked on by her peers for no apparent reason.

"After two years of trying everything they knew how to do to make the situation better, I finally advised her parents to relocate," he concluded. "I'll never know what it was about that little girl no one liked, but it was torment for her to deal with."

His words came back to haunt me years later when my own children went through a similar situation. Like him, I'll never know for sure to what extent the behavior of the neighborhood kids made Ellen begin to see herself as worthless. The experience does make it easy for me to understand the helpless and confused feelings of the mother who wrote the following story.

Bullies

Imagine that you are in middle school and very much alone. Every day you dread tomorrow and have to drag yourself to class where children tease and taunt and point at you. The more you squirm, the sweeter the chase. There is no escape and hardly anyone ever comes to your assistance. Sometimes a child does not have to have a particular physical trait for other children to hone in on, sometimes they just pick on someone for the heck of it and the hate becomes infectious with group leaders and their followers within a school.

My daughter was targeted by children in her school of both genders, who ranged from mostly middle- to upper-middle-class families. They threatened her, saying they were going to jump her after school because they knew she walked home. They cornered her in the bathrooms and hit her in the halls.

When my daughter was instructed to write a personal essay for her English literature high-school class this year, she wrote about a time when she was walking out of the locker room from gym class in middle school. Several girls formed a circle around her, then one of the girls came up to her, yelling and cursing. They pulled her shorts down, and when she reached down to lift them back up, one girl punched her while another girl held her. She finally got away from the circle, but the hate in their eyes and faces haunted her for a long time after. I was told by school officials that two of the girls received three days' internal suspension, but my daughter told me it was only one day.

Her essay indicated, "A few days later, I was on my way to class when two boys shoved me against a wall. One of them started punching me very hard in my stomach. After a few punches I fell to the floor, then the other boy kicked me and yelled, telling me to get up. I could not stand, so I was yanked up. One of the boys repeatedly punched me. They left and I went to class and got in trouble for being late."

I never knew about this incident until I read her essay this year.

My daughter wrote, "There was a very popular, smart, and handsome boy I had a crush on, but I found out he was just like most of the other students." After poking her in the eye with his pen, he received a total of two hours after-school detention and eventually became one of her worst tormentors at the school because he had many followers. His mother was the president of the PTA and I was told by one of the teachers that he felt he could get away with anything.

My husband and I discussed placing her in a new school, but he felt she had to learn how to deal with the problems. I shouldn't have given in because too many groups of children disliked her, and most friends abandoned her due to peer pressure. I don't blame my husband. I blame myself.

The school officials always seemed to shut their eyes to what was happening and the students knew this. We spoke to the administrators and teachers several times. Once I asked them what would have happened if we (as parents) had treated our daughter as badly as some of the students did? One teacher said that they would probably accuse us of abuse. I will always feel I abused my daughter by leaving her in that school. She was never hit or spanked at home, so she probably did not understand why others hit her.

My daughter continued in her essay, "These incidents kept happening. Some of them turned into sex threats and mostly death threats. I did not tell my parents about these occurrences because I felt they could do nothing."

I changed jobs and worked part-time so I could drive her to and from school. My husband and I only learned of the sex and death threats after we moved away from the area and our daughter was more open with us. She told us every time we visited the school about the problems, the children made it worse for her.

When she was born, my husband and I decided I would stay at home with her for the first four to five years to give her a sound, safe upbringing during that young impressionable time. We had great fun together, going to the library, park, McDonald's, and any other activity offered out there for small children, including those "Mommy and Me" classes. I taught her all about goodness and treating others fairly.

We really had a kind of old-fashioned Donna Reed existence, while in reality, living in a world of Rambo and Terminator Men. I thought most other moms were teaching their kids the same things. Instead of teaching her self-defense and offense, I taught her kindness, which was a mistake. I was the parent who would never let her watch anything but G-rated movies, another mistake.

Her essay states, "Acting is my salvation. By becoming various characters, I understand wickedness and comprehend kindness. Understanding the human spirit and its flaws motivates me to become a better person . . . My experiences have taught me not to hate or become violent. When hate has a hold on you, it drains you and unleashes misery, therefore, I will let it pass by me like a simple breeze."

Although my daughter was welcomed by the students in her new high school, the two years of trauma in middle school had left scars. Luckily, we found a therapist who worked hard to reverse the damage that was done, with success.

I look at my little girl now and see a beautiful young woman who wants to be an actress and has already been offered modeling opportunities. Her attitude about people has helped her grow stronger, and I am hoping that soon I will let the hate pass by me, too. Perhaps then we will both be totally healed.

Mary Marcel, Florida

There are other mistakes that hurt just as deeply as inadvertently exposing our children to harm: well-intentioned actions we take hoping to make a situation better, but ending with the exact opposite effect. Here are two stories of how mothers erred and what happened to get their relationships with their teenage daughters back on track.

Nothing but the Truth

My daughter Katie has always seemed like the typical teenager. She is funny, innovative, and always the first in her circle of friends willing to try new things. Her eagerness to grow up often left me wondering if she was really old enough to take on all the responsibilities that she might encounter.

One day Katie came home from school, happy and ready to take on whatever challenges life had to offer. Like always, we sat at the kitchen table talking about what her friends were doing, who liked whom, etc.

She was only home a short time when the telephone rang. As I went to pick up the receiver, Katie went downstairs into her room. I remember feeling apprehensive about the voice on the other end. A "concerned friend" wanted to talk to Katie's mother. I calmly waited while the caller told me Katie was pregnant.

I was hurt and dumbstruck, thinking, "Could this be true?" Could my fourteen-year-old princess really have done this? Could this child of mine have taken that big of a step into what she perceived adulthood to be? In addition, was it at all possible that I could not have known that she snuck out with a boy?

I always thought of myself as having a tight rein on my children. I went everywhere with them, took them to movies, stayed up late with them, laughed, and cried with them. I was a parent that wanted to be involved, not only for the reason of being a good parent but because I really enjoyed spending time with them and their friends.

I was hurt and very angry. I had trusted Katie with all my heart. Could she, would she, have betrayed me like this?

I reacted in pure anger, calling Katie upstairs to discuss the telephone call. In my mind, as much as I did not want to believe that this notion could be true, I found myself doubting my own daughter's word. I sat impatiently and listened as she told me how she knew someone at school was trying to set her up.

She screamed, "Mom, I am still a virgin, I would never!" The whole time I listened, I did not believe her.

The next day I did what I felt I had to do. I took my fourteen-year-old to our family doctor to check the status of her virginity. When the exam was over, Katie came out of the exam room glaring at me with hatred in her eyes. We then went into the doctor's conference area for a chat, and there I discovered that Katie had nothing to be ashamed of— but I certainly did. Katie was, in fact, still a virgin.

I was deeply ashamed of myself; ashamed that I allowed an anonymous caller to disrupt our lives, ashamed that I did not believe my own daughter, and ashamed at the realization that I broke the infallible bond of trust. Could I ever get it back?

I spent many a sleepless night, not over Katie's actions but over my own. How could I make this right? How could I gain back her trust, something I had worked so hard at obtaining in the first place?

For what seemed like an eternity Katie wouldn't speak to me in more than short one-word answers. The times when we had sat around for hours talking seemed to be gone. Not a day passed when I didn't long for the relationship we had once shared, one filled with laughter and tears that only a mother and daughter could have and appreciate. Frustration was building, and one weekend after not being able to deal with it anymore, Katie and I jumped in the car and drove endless miles, at first with no talking.

I finally pulled the car over and stopped. We sat quietly, neither one quite knowing what to say to the other. There, on a little country road, we yelled and screamed at each other until we both broke down in a sea of tears. I told Katie how sorry I was for putting her through the embarrassment and humiliation I am sure my actions caused her, and she told me how disappointed she was in me for not believing her.

Katie and I seem to be doing fine now. It has taken a long time to forgive myself and to build the trust back in our relationship. We did this by listening and talking to each other. Not just talking about trivial things but by talking about things like my relationship with her father and about my experiences as a teenager. Although there are decades between us, I don't think that teenagers' feelings have changed much from when I was one.

Katie has agreed that she won't have sex until she feels she is ready emotionally to handle it, and when the time comes, she will act responsibly. I have agreed to never accuse her of anything based on an anonymous phone call, and to never live in a house without Caller ID again.

Pamela Colwell, Tennessee

Brandy Is Fourteen

Where do I begin? Four years ago we moved to a location not far from where we used to live for eleven years. Although we did not move very far, our children had to attend new schools since we were in a different county. This is where my story begins.

Between a new house, a new school, and feeling like she left the only world she fit into, Brandy, age ten at the time, slipped into a very deep depression. The old neighborhood seemed to be as far away from her as the other side of the world. The new neighborhood was a world she never knew before. There is always that one mean bully, and we happened to move right across the street from him. Brandy, in the fifth grade at the time, was in desperate need of a friend. I tried very hard to have her visit the old neighborhood and allow the kids to come to our new home. Unfortunately this didn't help. Brandy wanted desperately to be accepted by the kids in the new neighborhood.

Now, I'm the parent of two girls: one doing just fine and being accepted in the neighborhood, the other being teased, harassed, and downright bullied on a daily basis. Brandy was crying all the time and telling me constantly she wanted to die. I couldn't handle this! How could a child who was so dearly loved be going through this horrible difficult time? I mean this is what children from broken homes with awful parents go through, *right*? How could this be happening to my baby girl?

I realized my daughter was struggling with change. My husband's aunt had passed away right after our move and this was devastating to Brandy. Her friends were gone; people she cared about were leaving her. She was also realizing that others don't always accept you, and you can't change it.

All I could do was hold her in my arms and tell her how much we loved her, how special she was, and cry with her, until we fell asleep out of pure exhaustion.

Going to school was particularly challenging since she was with the very kids who harassed her, not to mention the new bully she encountered. She barely made it through sixth grade. Seventh was just as difficult; we had to pull her out and have her tutored in the last quarter so she could finish.

For eighth grade, my husband and I felt it in her best interest to home school. Thanks to my husband's contribution, not only as a wonderful father but also as a patient teacher, Brandy finished eighth grade. We got her involved in basketball and poured out every bit of love a family could possibly give. We are a very spiritually involved family, going to Bible meetings three times a week and praying to our Creator on a regular basis. I know this is truly the key to what pulled us through this difficult time.

We also went to both a psychologist and a psychiatrist, as we desperately wanted to help our child get better. My husband, our older daughter, and I went through a lot as well. There is a strain so intense you feel you just can't take anymore.

How did I feel during this period? *"Guilty."* I was the one who wanted the new big house. I felt selfish and horrible, so much so I wanted to sell the new house and beg the woman who bought our old house to sell it back to us. I needed to fix what I felt was my fault. I was even willing to pay thousands of dollars to get her back into her old school so she could be back with the kids she knew. I felt responsible for Brandy's feelings.

With the help of my husband and family, and counselors, I came to understand that I needed to stop blaming myself, and beating myself up. I needed to concentrate on helping Brandy work through the changes. By working through problems as they arose and not trying to fix everything, I'd be helping her become a stronger person able to adapt to life's unfair changes.

It has been a very hard and difficult four years, but I can honestly say Brandy has come a long way. She will be attending public school for ninth grade this school year, and I hope and pray she will be able to handle what lies ahead of her as she continues on the road to good mental health.

I may have spent countless sleepless nights crying until there wasn't a tear left in me, but I think I was able to show my daughter how much I really loved her and that I would always be there for her. I believe that through this we have built a loving relationship, and a bond between us that nothing can break. Sure, we still have our problems to work through, as do most mothers and daughters, but those are normal teenage issues. What a welcome change.

Lauren Fowler, East Coast

The next story is a bittersweet commentary on how one mother saw her daughter making the same mistakes she had. For the sake of her grandchild, Mary hopes her daughter will have more confidence than she did and will choose to pursue a different path in life before it's too late.

In My Footsteps

It's always assumed you want your kids to walk in your footsteps. For me, it's the last thing I want. My oldest child, Annie, was born outgoing, sociable, full of life and energy. I used to wonder, where did this child come from? She wore me out, but I loved her personality and spunk. Unlike me, she was magnetic to her peers and was surrounded by boys. From the age of twelve, she was never without a boyfriend. If things were looking bleak in the relationship, she'd strike up another before breaking off the first one.

But like me, she wanted and needed love. Her inability to be without a boyfriend was a sign of insecurity, fed by the same man who fed mine—her father. I believe now that he, unlike me, saw a resemblance in Annie and me. In her, he saw what I was, and could have been, and the traits he always fought so hard to discourage—individuality, independence, self-confidence.

There is much written about the mother-daughter relationship. While it is a very close, important, and complicated bond at times, we can't underestimate the role a father plays in his daughter's life. It's interesting to note that no matter how attentive and loving a mother is to her daughter, no matter how wonderful a role model she is for her, a young girl still requires the acceptance and love and adoration of her father. Without this attention, an adolescent girl would look for it in another man or boy. And so, at an early age, Annie wanted to get married and have children. She needed to fill the void where her father's love should have been.

Her first engagement was broken off when she joined the marines to try once again to make her father proud of her. Even though I knew her choice to join the military was not personal but rather to gain the love of her father, I welcomed the chance for her to have a few years of life experiences on her own before she settled down. Maybe she would walk down a different path than the one I had traveled.

Still, she kept falling for men and there was no shortage of them in the marines. She fell for one man in particular when they were stationed together and ended up marrying him even though I begged her not to do it. I told her the usual: you're too young, you haven't known him long enough, etc. I even told her to look at me. I tried to show her how she was following right in my footsteps.

They ended up eloping and now have a beautiful baby who at one year shows all the spunk and independence her mother did, and that I may have had as well. And since the marriage, she has had all the same complaints as I did, as her husband is very much like her father. He doesn't encourage her strength and independence and does not admire or support her. If history repeats itself, he will also work to discourage all the unique qualities in this child, ones handed down from generation to generation. Or, maybe, my granddaughter will be the strongest of us all, the one who walks bravely through the wilderness, forging her own path.

Annie told me today she wanted a divorce. When she told her husband, he laughed because he didn't believe her. I don't think she has the courage (yet) to go through with it, as I didn't for twenty years. But then again, she might surprise me. Maybe she'll give her daughter the chance I didn't give her. Maybe there is hope.

Mary O'Brien, Massachusetts

It astounds me that mothers have an intuitive understanding of their children's needs at any given moment that is almost always accurate. Like many of my friends, I can usually tell with a look how the day has gone for Ellen, Joe, or Matt. When they are away, I still feel a connection with them that is almost physical, even now when my oldest is twenty-one and on the opposite side of the country in the navy!

Ellen and I have been separated frequently because of numerous hospitalizations for her eating disorder. On one such occasion about two years into her illness, I woke up in the night, sure I had heard her calling for me. She was in a hospital two hours away, and I couldn't get back to sleep because of worry.

I telephoned the nurses as early as possible the next morning and was assured she was fine. That afternoon, I drove to visit and described my "dream" to her. Tears came to her eyes as she told me the event had really happened: hundreds of miles away, at 3 A.M., she had indeed wakened and cried out my name, and I had heard.

The next story describes a similar psychic link between another mother and daughter.

Timed Connection

October 31, 1998. The sounds of happy trick-or-treaters had subsided. Angela, my baby at age nineteen and the child with whom I am most connected, telephoned with a brief, "I-am-almost-grown" message. She was going to hang out with Erica, a longtime friend, until her older sister Katie got off work.

"Don't wait up," she added before assuring me that she and Erica were safely inside Erica's house—where they would stay until Katie called. "We are going to catch a movie and veg. I will probably just stay here, tonight."

I had no reason to doubt her words, and armed with the sense of security that this type of phone call brings, my spouse and I settled back against a mound of pillows to share a bag of popcorn and a movie of our own. For the next few hours, there was no conversation, yet suddenly I felt an overwhelming need to make contact with Angie.

"Something's wrong," I said, trying to stay calm as I picked up the phone and paged her. I already knew that she wouldn't be calling back; she was hurt and she needed me. Although Angie always answered my pages immediately, there was no response on this night.

Close to an hour after I had first tried to make contact, the phone rang. It was Erica, and she was so close to hysterics she could hardly breathe.

My husband and I were already pulling on clothing, but I don't think I was aware of anything else that happened until we dashed into the emergency room. My youngest daughter, shaking and confused, was lying on a gurney in the middle of the hospital corridor. Our eyes met. We spoke silently—words that could never be articulated to another.

"It hurts," she said through tears and chattering teeth.

"I know it does, baby girl," I answered, stroking her long soft hair. "I'm sorry."

"I'm sorry, too. It was supposed to be safe. It happened so fast."

"It always does," I whispered, "It always does."

Erica and Angie had decided to accompany several friends to a party at the beach. When it was time for Katie to get off work, they headed to the car to leave. A young boy who had been turned away from the party because he was underage and drunk was just returning with his friends.

The young man who had originally turned the intoxicated boy away asked him to leave. Instead, he produced a loaded gun and fired a single shot into the party giver's chest, then emptied the gun into the crowd. Every bullet found the flesh of a child.

Five young people were hit—all under the age of twenty-one. All survived, but they carry external and internal scars, and fear many things that no child should have to fear.

As my husband and I waited for Angie to come out of X-ray, we talked about my sense that something was wrong, and how I had felt my daughter reaching out to me.

"The first shot was recorded as occurring at 11:05 P.M.," the police officer told me.

"What time?" I asked him, goose bumps covering my entire body.

"11:05," he repeated.

I turned to Erica. "Where is Angela's pager?"

She fished it out of her purse and handed it to me. In an instant, the truth behind the words "A mom just knows," which I had spoken so many times, rang truer than ever we could have guessed.

My first page was recorded as going through at 11:05 P.M.

Tammy Bird, Virginia

PART THREE

Interventions:
On Our Own and with Others

7

Combating Depression, Eating Disorders, and Rebellion: Professional Therapists and Mother Therapy

A few months into the fourth-grade school year, Ellen's teacher took me aside. I can still hear the cautious tone in her voice as she addressed me, her eyes avoiding mine.

"I can't put my finger on exactly what it is, Cheryl, but I think some counseling would really benefit Ellen."

Third grade and our new neighborhood had been rough, but nothing I *saw* in Ellen's behavior at the time led me to think she was troubled enough to need therapy. She seemed happy at home and with the friends she had made at her new school. Still, I trusted this teacher and wanted to do what was best for my child. I searched diligently before making an appointment with a highly recommended child psychologist, Dr. J.

Dr. J. didn't tell me much initially, but after several sessions with Ellen, she informed me that we (Paul and I) needed to make a point of being completely honest with our daughter. At the end of her next appointment with Ellen, she called me into the office. Ellen sat between us, feet dangling over the edge of the chair and hands resting primly on her lap.

"Ellen, do you believe in Santa Claus?" Dr. J. asked.

"Yes," Ellen answered, her face suddenly animated.

"Well, there is no Santa Claus," Dr. J. said bluntly. I was as shocked as Ellen, and angry, since I hadn't been told about the plan ahead of time. New to the world of child therapy and unsure of myself, I said nothing. After all, my child's teacher had thought she was having problems, and I hadn't even realized it.

Shortly after that, I ended the sessions with Dr. J. It had been a battle to get Ellen to go back to therapy after the Santa Claus disaster and her teacher told me things were better at school, so I didn't bother finding another counselor or pursuing the Prozac Dr. J. insisted Ellen needed. Now I wish I'd believed in my own intuitive sense that nothing was wrong and had avoided the experience completely.

To this day, Ellen distrusts therapists, and, of the dozens of social workers, nurses, and psychiatrists she has seen (sometimes for extended periods), she has bonded with very few.

"They only act like they care about people because they're paid," she's told me on more than one occasion. She has also shared that opinion repeatedly and forcefully with her psychiatrist, Dr. B., who has been one of Ellen's kindest and most staunch supporters over the last three years.

While our frequent contacts with the mental-health system have made it easier for me to recite the "facts" of her illness, it's still hard to share the most intimate aspects of our life with strangers. Under the calculating gaze of professionals who have the power to point a finger and place blame for a daughter's pain, my past struggle with depression, her older half-brother's departure to live with his father for two years, and the death of Ellen's best friend in fifth grade all take on ominous significance.

Thankfully, Dr. B. has never suggested any person or event is to blame for Ellen's illness. She has cared not only for Ellen but for me, too—I know if I called her tomorrow with a concern about my daughter, she would answer promptly, always offering some hope of help. She is truly a gem—and unfortunately, atypical. For every bit of good advice she has given me, there have been dozens of others who steered me in the wrong direction.

One family therapist informed Paul and me that we allowed Ellen to manipulate us. We were to set firm limits with her and not allow her to interrupt or control us. Our opportunity to test this theory came when Ellen insisted we drive her to the mall on a Saturday afternoon when we were watching a Penn State football game on television.

"Not now, Ellen. Dad and I are doing something. Later," I told her, remembering the therapist's words. Ellen disappeared, returning in five minutes to announce she'd taken an overdose of Tylenol. It turned out she hadn't, but a previous suicidal gesture forced us to take her seriously.

Then there was another family therapist who assured me Ellen could be left to reap the consequences of her own behavior. If my daughter acted out, she told me, I was to leave.

"But what if she's standing out on the lawn screaming?" I asked, thinking of a time when this had actually happened. "Our neighbors will call the police."

"Then Ellen will have to deal with the police," the therapist replied confidently.

"She's a minor," I reminded her. "The first thing the police will do is track me down!"

The therapist had no answer for that.

As I read the following stories and thought back on Dr. J. and others I've encountered like her, I have to wonder: Do therapists hurt more than they help?

Excerpt from "Losing Time"

We sat around my daughter Allie's dining room table, less than two days after my phone conversation with her boyfriend, Steven. Allie seemed sullen, almost angry, and wouldn't look at me. Steven insisted that she speak.

"Things got really bad last night," Allie said. She wouldn't say any more.

I looked at Steven, and he told me: Allie had been agitated and crying the day before. He canceled their dinner plans with friends. Allie became more anxious and angry and took down all the posters in her room. She told Steven to go away, but he wouldn't. They argued. Her mood worsened. There was more agitation and crying. This went on for several hours. Steven sought advice from Leslie, the psychologist who was helping Allie sort through what I thought were the normal questionings of college life.

"Allie cut herself last night" Steven said. "She took my razor and cut her arms twice. I had to take her to the emergency room."

Part of me died then. I sat very still and looked at my beautiful daughter who would not look back at me.

"Allie, let me see your arms," I said softly. Allie rolled up the sleeves of her white blouse and there, across the top of both of her forearms, were a series of shallow red cuts.

"I love you, Allie." That was all I could say.

I didn't know it that night, but Allie was in the midst of what is called rapid cycling, a manifestation of bipolar mood disorder. She had been taking an antidepressant prescribed by a psychiatrist at the university health center two months ago. A few days earlier, she had called and told me she felt her condition was changing: sometimes she was so energetic and restless she cleaned her room in the middle of the night, but other days, she couldn't get out of bed. She said thoughts raced through her head and she couldn't seem to slow down. Sometimes she heard voices she called "drones" just talking at her, on and on. Allie had tried to contact the university psychiatrist, leaving messages asking for help. His response had been long in coming, but the two had never made actual contact. Now that psychiatrist was out of town.

Leslie, Allie's psychologist, was alarmed by the changes she observed in my daughter and had located the psychiatrist's replacement, but he wouldn't change the medication, even though he was sure that was the cause of her distress. He would accept Allie for a patient and switch her medication, he said, only if she changed psychologists and worked with someone on his staff. Allie did not want to leave Leslie, so she had lingered, untreated, waiting for me to arrive.

Now, sitting with Allie and her boyfriend, I tried to cuddle with her, like I did when she was little. I stroked her hair, telling her that I loved her and that I would fix this. After all, mothers are the ultimate fixers. But I had no idea what needed to be fixed.

The next morning we met with Leslie.

"Everybody has their monkey and this is yours," the therapist told us. "Did you have a swooper yesterday?" she asked Allie.

Swooper, I gathered, meant a low mood.

"Two or three," Allie answered.

Leslie was certain Allie needed different medication. I listened but kept asking her about Allie cutting herself, trying to understand what it meant. The act was incomprehensible to me, but nothing about Allie's condition made sense. How did things get so bad so fast?

Leslie reassured me that Allie was not suicidal and suggested we talk to a psychiatrist experienced in mood disorders. She was as appalled as I at the negligence of the first psychiatrist and the callousness of the second but knew of a new doctor who was knowledgeable and very responsive to his patients. There was, however, a two-week wait to see him. Allie could not stop the present medication without a doctor's orders and would linger in an agitated state until then. When I insisted the delay was unacceptable, Leslie suggested that I personally call the new doctor and try to get an earlier appointment.

"Sometimes mothers can get the doctor's attention," she said.

I took notes during my meeting with Leslie. Perhaps writing everything down would give reality to all of the talk, and besides, I didn't trust my memory. This must have seemed odd to Leslie, because before we left, she asked how I was doing. She said it must be terrible for a mother to see her daughter so distressed.

I lied and told her I was fine.

How could I tell her the truth? I was inexperienced in dealing with mental illness and distrustful of psychiatry. I was numb with fear for my daughter, lost in a foreign country where I didn't speak the language.

I wanted to lash out at both the medical system that treated an obviously depressed college student without consulting her parents and the doctor whose misjudgment and failure to follow through put Allie into this crisis. I was disgusted by the second psychiatrist, who hid behind rules and refused her emergency treatment. I dreaded putting

Allie's future in the hands of still another psychiatrist, but there was no alternative.

At home I would have had a network of contacts within the medical community. I could have sought out recommendations, talked to friends. Instead, I was alone and without resources, forced to rely on Leslie, who was still an unknown quantity to me.

"I'll talk to the new doctor myself," I told her.

The new psychiatrist was a godsend, a man whose compassion and expertise with the newest medications was exactly what Allie needed. Had she found this doctor initially, the worst days of her illness could have been avoided and the course of her treatment might have been shortened.

I stayed with my daughter for several weeks until both she and the new doctor said it was okay for me to return home, but I kept in close touch for the next few months. Allie's medications were changed, her symptoms decreased, and she worked extraordinarily hard to put her life back together. It was very difficult for me, as a mother, to be at a distance, but Allie wanted and needed to heal on her own. I knew that she or the doctor would contact me if I was needed.

This year, Allie graduated from college, aspiring to graduate school, a professional career helping other young women, and a chance to "go for the gold" in athletics. She is in very good health psychologically, and the doctor expects she can begin to decrease her medication in the near future.

My daughter's illness and the time I spent with her have created a special bond between us. I know her in a way and at a depth that only an experience like this could bring. At the same time, Allie's struggle tested me to my depths as a mother. Until she became ill, I thought depression couldn't—wouldn't—happen to my child. I had innocently believed that if I loved my children, pain wouldn't touch them. I assumed that if I tried hard enough, my children wouldn't experience suffering.

Now I see how naïve those beliefs were. I never imagined this would be my greatest challenge as a mother, and perhaps my real reason for being in my daughter's life: not only to help her survive the unexpected and unanticipated rough times but also to dig deep into the pain alongside her to find our joint salvation.

Sophia Rodgers, Midwest

It's no surprise that most mothers will do anything they can to help their children, but I was amazed by the creativity, persistence, love, and energy the women who wrote to me displayed in trying to help their daughters survive troubled times. The situations ranged greatly; the care and devotion did not. Read on to see for yourself.

Another Mother's Story

Most moms think their children are angels, and I am no different. It came as a great shock and distress to find out they are not. Horror of horrors! *My children are human!* Worst of all, I am not a perfect parent!

It was a Sunday evening and our little family was watching *Who Wants to Be a Millionaire?* A question came up that we didn't know the answer to. Our fifteen-year-old daughter, Marie, and nineteen-year-old son, Earl, got into a debate on the answer. The debate quickly turned into a contest of wills, with Marie shouting at the top of her substantial lungs and cursing to boot. As I sat there in amazement, all I could think to do was send her to her room to cool off.

Immediately, her stereo assaulted our peace. The all-too-familiar smell of cigarette smoke wafted from beneath her door into the living room. When my husband, Bob, went to investigate, he found her door locked. Marie refused to open it.

I quickly joined the cause, pounding on her door and screaming, until she finally let us in. The room reeked of cigarettes and she was looking at me like I was a demon from hell. *I lost it!* Before I even knew what I was doing, my palm connected with her face.

Then my body seemed to take over where my brain left town. Five minutes later, her drawers were empty on the floor and her mattress up-ended. We found enough contraband to make any parent sick: empty packs of cigarettes, condoms, diet pills, and her journal. I crumbled on her bed in tears. I had never been tempted to read her personal thoughts until that night, but read I did, right in front of her. The arrogance left her eyes, replaced by the fear of a girl found out.

All the familiar questions went through my mind: Where did we go wrong? What are we to do with her? Where is the nearest girl's boarding school?

We decided to restrict Marie. She needed to be separated from those "friends" who supported her bad choices. From that time on, we checked up on everything she did or said. It was hard, and I realized during those months why some parents just turn the other cheek and look the other way.

"*I hate you!*" she spat one time. "*You don't even know me!*" and "*I'm moving out as soon as I'm eighteen!*"

Any hurtful thing she could think of came flying my way. Many days I felt like just giving up and either running away or simply abandoning her to her own devices. Much time was spent on my knees crying out to God for help, guidance, wisdom, and strength. How thankful I am that we persevered through that time. Today, we still have our little skirmishes, but she is now repentant and trying to walk right. The "friends" she clung to so desperately have been revealed for who they are, and she walked away from them of her own volition. We have a long way to go yet, but we have come so far.

My mother-in-law once said, "When they are little they step on your toes. When they are big they step on your heart." I have come to realize that every teenager has to spread her wings at some point. They need to become their own person and to do that they will stretch the limits of sensibility. That is when a parent must be very careful. Go too far one way and they rebel completely and you lose control. Go too far the other way and you never get control to begin with. Bob and I walk the tightrope, loving our daughter enough to be hard on her but also to forgive her.

When you discover the awful truth—your kids are human—get on your knees and pray. Pray for the grace to get through it all, for yourself and for them.

Sharon M. McCampbell, Florida

Losing Control

Our problems began with my notion that our family ought to move. The six of us had been attending a church where my husband played the organ for two services every week, the children attended Sunday school, Vacation Bible School, and, until that point, day school. If we moved, the kids could walk to the new school, and the time I spent driving them places would be cut in half.

"But Mom! I don't know *how* to ice-skate. I don't even *know* those kids!" My fifteen-year-old, Diana, objected before the first youth outing at the new church.

What better way to get acquainted—a nice church group where she would be safe? I hadn't thought about the other people who might be at the rink, like J.W.: handsome, laid back, over twenty-one, lurking on the sidelines, eyeing her. Showing up at the house next week to take her on a date.

"No," we said, "she's too young for you."

After a multitude of tears and dramatic protestations, we made an effort to console Diana by promising to let her visit her godparents for a few weeks in the summer. Not exactly J.W.-exciting, but her first plane trip.

Summer turned to fall. Diana, a Scottish Lassie, went to do a half-time Scottish sword dance, kilts and smiles flashing. A nice, safe activity—or so we thought. When she failed to return, we called the police. A call from them informed us she was found necking with an older male in the bushes on the U.C. campus. J.W., of course. How long had this been going on?

My husband confronted him: "We have nothing against you personally, but you're just too old for our daughter. If you promise not to see her anymore, we won't press charges. If our wishes are disregarded, we will take action against you."

There are steps that lead from our front door to the street. Each night a spider spins a web across them. Diana used to be the first one out to break through. No more. After the incident with J.W., I chauffeured her to and from school and rehearsals. I was in the driver's seat, but I had lost control.

Cherise Wyneken, Florida

Feeling Through the Fog

The summer of 1997 was supposed to be the summer of firsts for Sara—getting her first car and thinking about where to attend college. This was the time when my daughter was supposed to be looking ahead to life with challenges and opportunities at her doorstep. It was also to be a time of firsts for me. As a single mom, I had raised Sara for fifteen years. My challenges were supposed to be relating to an adult child and finishing graduate school. The experts would say this was the time I should be worrying about drugs, alcohol, pregnancy, or eating disorders. When Sara started having rectal bleeding, the "supposed-to-be's" took on a whole new meaning.

As summer moved into the fall, Sara continued to bleed. We went from doctor to doctor as we attempted to find explanations for the physical symptoms she was experiencing. She sat as the dutiful patient, listening to a variety of reasons why she was having horrific abdominal pain and bloody diarrhea. Months went by as I watched helplessly while my darling daughter dealt with fatigue, weight and appetite loss, and anemia.

Our lives took on the feeling of living in a fog as we began to learn more about ulcerative colitis. Doctors matter-of-factly told us that it causes ulceration and inflammation of the inner lining of the colon and rectum. The depth of our comprehension was minimal when we were told that the cause is unknown and there is no cure at this time, except through surgical removal of the colon. Up until this point in life, neither of us had given much day-to-day thought of our colons. Now we learned that diet and stress management changes needed to be instituted in Sara's life, without any guarantee of improvement.

Fall moved into winter. The fog continued to thicken. Sara was put on a small dose of prednisone and rowasa enemas, with no improvement. In early December, she was hospitalized because of the severe pains and bleeding. Little did we understand that our lives were moving like a train out of control.

The treatment of choice in the hospital was 120 mg of IV prednisone. No one told us how crazy it would make Sara feel when she returned home. No one warned us of the possible horrific side effects of this medication. No one prepared us for the depths of her depression. No one taught me how to comfort my daughter when she reached the depths of despair from this medication. Since no one taught me, I learned by trial and error. I drove Sara in the car for hours when she could not control her mind. I rocked her in bed when she became too distraught to think. Most of the time I prayed that something would give me the wisdom and the strength to be there for her.

Sara slowly retrieved her mind as she was weaned from the prednisone. Now the treatment option being offered to her was Imuran, a medication with very serious side effects such as loss of hair and thrush in the mouth. It might prevent her symptoms from recurring, but she had an 80-percent chance of bleeding again and being rehospitalized. Once she came off Imuran, we learned, she might return to prednisone and still lose her colon in the long run.

My moment of crisis came when I stood in the drugstore with the Imuran in my hand. How could I go home and tell my child to put this medication in her mouth? I thought of how the word "crisis" is described by the Chinese: the symbols for "danger" and "opportunity." I knew I was in danger. Where was the opportunity? I was feeling my way through the fog, but it was too thick to see anything hopeful.

Over the years, I had come to trust my senses and instincts, especially in the face of what appeared to be insurmountable obstacles. Was I willing to trust my belief system with this life that I considered more precious than my own? Was I willing to trust my sense that there had to be a better way other than encouraging my child to put something in her body that could, in the long run, cause her more pain?

The decision was no longer fully mine. Day by day, Sara made the decision. She did not take the Imuran. We connected with a physician who exposed us to the first of many alternative medical treatments. Sara drastically changed her diet by moving more toward macrobiotic foods. She began an intense regime of vitamins, supplements, enemas, vegetable juices, and stress reduction techniques. We were both scared. What if this did not work? Time and again we came to the conclusion that the traditional medical alternative was always available. We continued down this road.

The surreal existence continued during the first five months of 1998. I had experienced major life changes in the past, but nothing like this. By mid-January of 1998, we were on the path of changing habits. Purchasing, cooking, and eating food became a new way of life. Reading labels and learning new recipes was a daily challenge.

Preparing fresh vegetable juices was time consuming. Sara, who always loved food, began to find eating a chore. She struggled with refraining from eating pizza, chips, and soda when she was out with her friends. Packing lunches and eating differently than her peers drew unwanted attention to her illness. Thankfully, she became more accepting of the changes when her friends expressed envy over the interesting foods she ate.

I started to feel as if I was making my way through the fog as each day passed. We started to look toward the future again. There were actually glimmers of light through the darkness. Sara thought about colleges. I began dating the man I eventually married. However, all the changes that had happened required Sara and me to spend more time together. Her enemas put us in intimate situations a number of times each day. I jokingly told her she did not want to leave me because she always had me in the bathroom with her. Our humor degenerated to bathroom experiences and "butt" jokes.

The most intimate connections took place at the end of the day when we would flood the room with candlelight and meditate with music. I called it our time to slow down and heal, and it became a soothing ritual that helped reduce the heightened anxiety we were experiencing.

Moving through the fog involved navigating who was responsible for Sara's health. I knew it was imperative for me to move further from the caretaker role. Sara learned to portion out all her medications and take them at the prescribed times. She became more involved in meal preparations. Her biggest leap came when she attended medical appointments alone, asked questions, and understood the answers. All of these steps required her to take a proactive role in her heath. She began to formulate her own belief system to balance the best of the traditional and the alternative medical communities. She became outspoken in regard to what worked for her.

As the months passed, Sara's depression began to lift as she weaned from the prednisone without taking the Imuran. We approached the turning point in April and May of 1998. We held our breath as she did not bleed when she went from 25 to 20 to 15 to 10 to 5 mg of prednisone. By mid-May, she was completely off and not bleeding. Needless to say, we were both elated. Sara's gastroenterologist encouraged her to continue doing what she was doing. He described her progress as "miraculous—not as a result of his treatment."

By the end of 1998, she was bleeding again, but we had come through the fog with more knowledge to draw from. Sara was now in control of how she chose to view the disease.

Sara is now a sophomore in college. Her disease has become a part of her everyday living, but it is not who she is. It is easy to see the real person who remains kind, loving, and caring amidst the day-to-day struggles. The possibility that colon cancer could erupt within six years is always looming in the background. The last three years have given her reserves of resiliency never dreamed possible.

I have learned to trust my instincts more and more. This trust involves stepping back as Sara takes on new responsibility for her life. I am able to appreciate the level of energy she must use every day to live. Her courage and determination leave me in awe. Would I have traded her illness for drug, alcohol, eating disorders or pregnancy? Probably not. As the fog has lifted, we have been blessed with the ability to clearly see the meaning of the colitis that has touched both of our lives.

Barbara Miller, Pennsylvania

I was so inundated with poems about mothering I have decided to create a second book containing only poetry. A few, however, seemed right for this book. Perhaps I was moved by the one that follows because it captures so perfectly the desperate need to intervene that I experienced when Ellen was at her anorexic worst.

1981: Sprite Lost, Sprite Found

Liberty. In God we trust. Or distrust.
This penny is dangerous. Minted the year my daughter was lost.
Beware of tube tops, lug-soled boots. Beware of ear piercing:
The more holes, the more trouble leaks out.
Trouble was the blue hair. The pink. The aubergine.
Fashion pages. Mirrors. Bikinis. Dope.
The boy with dreadlocks. The river guide. Magic mushrooms.

Lincoln's looking on in profile. His lips thin as is he.
As thin as she was. Honest Abe thought I could not tell a lie,
But I did, for when she began to starve herself,
I lost all liberty, all God-trust. There was no God.
In 1981, nothing was real but her skeletal hands
And coppery metallic breath upon my neck. Each night, in secret,
I poured out liters of saccharined diet drink
And refilled them with sugared Sprite to bring her—
My hardest, brightest, thinnest penny—back alive.

Susan Terris, California

(This poem appeared in the April 2001 issue of *Sun* magazine.)

8

Institutions:
Strangers Take Over Our Lives

During Ellen's initial hospitalization for anorexia in May 1998, I was like the mother in the first story of this chapter: an observer, stiff and uncomfortable in psychiatric units. By December of that same year, Ellen had returned to the hospital three more times, spending the better part of six months in various institutions as her weight dropped lower and lower.

Then, at the beginning of 1999, something changed for no reason I could identify. With weekly visits to her therapist, nutritionist, physician, and support groups, she was able to stay in school and work during the summer, although her anorexia continued and getting her to eat was a daily struggle. Compared to what followed, this was a relatively happy time.

In the fall of 1999, she entered tenth grade and began what has been one of the worst periods of our lives. Ellen's eating disorder took over again, only now she was considered to have anorexia: binge-purge type, because she ate and threw up, still managing to lose dramatic amounts of weight. Converting to bulimic behavior was very common in anorexics, her doctor told me, and in a way, I was relieved. At least she was eating. Much later, I discovered bulimia was more life threatening than anorexia due to the sudden electrolyte imbalances that can occur.

Within a week of beginning tenth grade, Ellen was suspended for smoking on school property, an infraction that cost her a month of grounding at home as well. Not long after, I was at home, working on the computer, when my son Joe handed me the phone.

"Mrs. Dellasega?" an unfamiliar male voice asked. "This is Detective Smith."

My hands froze over the keyboard, and the shoulder I was using to balance the phone against my ear cramped as he spoke: Ellen had been accused of stealing money from her employer and had to take a lie detector test that Saturday. The only contact I'd ever had with the police was decades earlier, when my car overheated on the New Jersey turnpike, and a cute policeman escorted me to a gas station, trying to impress me with all the different sounds his siren could make. I sat at my desk for a long time after hanging up, stunned into a state of shock.

Ellen went to the police station directly after taking her pre-SATs at the high school the following Saturday. Although the polygraph was negative, I was upset with her for putting herself in the position of even being accused. She had walked off work several times and left early on her last day, right when the missing money was discovered, behavior that made her suspect.

There were many more distressing events during that time, but certain positive aspects of her personality didn't change. She continued calling me at work every day when she arrived home from school, just to report in. Most days, she told me she loved me, and on the weekends when she went out with friends, she was always home on time. Every Sunday morning she went with us to Quaker Meeting, claiming we would ground her if she didn't, but once there, a peace would come to her that I rarely saw elsewhere. Although she often slept through the service, it was the one time when I knew she was safe and in a place surrounded by love. By then, the fights at our house had changed the environment there from one of comfortable coexistence to constant conflict.

In rapid succession throughout the end of 1999 and beginning of 2000, Ellen was in a partial outpatient program, state hospital, two private eating-disorder facilities, and another partial program. The diagnoses accumulated: bipolar disorder, oppositional defiant disorder, and borderline personality disorder. The only class she completed in tenth grade was honors math; she got an A.

During the summer of 2000, she was able to hold down a job she liked—largely because of a very kind boss—but within two months of beginning eleventh grade, her eating habits and behavior were again out of control. Our house was in a regular state of chaos, and at times her anger frightened us. One day, on the way to an appointment with Dr. B., she tried to jump out of our moving car on a major highway. Things were getting more dangerous, but attempts to find a therapeutic placement that would address her problems fell through again and again.

The stories in this chapter touched me because as our family got drawn deeper and deeper into the mental-health system, I changed from being like Adelheid—a onetime visitor—to become like Mary, all too familiar with psychiatric institutions. I grew to hate surrendering my purse and coat when I visited my daughter and to envy the nurses who got to tuck her in bed at night. Driven by loneliness, I spent many early mornings in Ellen's empty room, sleeping in her bed, my face pressed into her pillow to recapture the smell of her.

Although I resented being told when I could and could not see Ellen during her hospital stays and chafed at the fact that other adults were in control of her life, I complied with nearly all the recommendations I was given by professionals. I believed they knew what was best for her recovery, but as each new treatment failed, I began to wonder if anyone really knew how to help my daughter. When I consulted one of my lifelines, her psychiatrist Dr. B was honest enough to tell me that she, too, wasn't sure exactly what was going on with Ellen beyond the eating disorder.

One day as I sat in the waiting room outside the psychiatric ward with another mother, she nodded her head at the locked door separating us from our children and said: "Having my daughter locked away from me is gonna make me crazy, too."

I knew exactly what she meant.

School Security

My first thought is: "An accident. She's hurt."

The cop assures she is okay, but they still need me at school, immediately. I wash off the garden dirt, find the car keys.

Not an accident—then what? She doesn't cheat on tests. It must be worse than that, anyway. Does she have secrets I can't even imagine? Maybe drugs?

I am relieved when I see the printout of her e-mail: "What exactly is wrong with walking into a school and shooting people?"

I understand why the cop is alarmed, but have dealt with her questions for months. Why did you set five children into the world? Don't you care about overpopulation? Why are there still wars? Why doesn't anybody do something about global warming?

She would tear my answers to shreds, then run to her room. I would cry when I had to, yell when I couldn't help it, and remember that growing up is difficult business. It wouldn't last forever. She isn't the first teenager I have raised.

When she came to ask: "What is depression? When you hear voices, is that schizophrenia?" I talked with a psychologist. She refused to see him.

The cop actually knows the difference between a question and a threat, but he hesitates before leaving. The vice principal proposes a psychological evaluation. Fine, I wanted that all along, but I refuse to search her backpack before school every day. Or do I have to? She loves this school, the only one in town to offer a special program for motivated students.

The vice principal says my daughter sometimes dreams of shooting people who exist only in her dreams. How did he find out? And why has she never told me? She also admitted that some students at her school sometimes irritate her. She gave him names (under great pressure, she tells me later).

The vice principal proposes "a few days off," in his soft opaque voice. I remind him she has not violated any school rules, but he has the authority.

The way home feels almost good: we share the same anger.

The psychologist I trust is out of town. My daughter wants to be back in school, badly, in time for the big end-of-year concert. The mental hospital could admit her and do an evaluation, so that is where we go.

"I am placing a hold on you," says the nurse who greets us. "If you run, I'll call the police. They'll get you within hours."

Nobody is trying to run. Both of us are frozen with terror.

"You may wear your own clothes, but first you must strip, under a gown, and empty your pockets. You may bring your toothbrush, cosmetics in plastic bottles only, no floss. No scissors, no pencil, no string; books need to be approved."

The unit looks like a daycare center: pale wood a little scratched, finger-painted windows. Bullet-proof. Teenagers laying a jigsaw puzzle. The door locks automatically.

I can't stop crying. The nurse has read the patients' rights to me without even trying to make me understand. Somehow I managed to ask for a copy. She had me sign some agreements. I told her I was not in a state to sign anything, but was too weak to insist.

They let my child's stuffed cat pass, and the *Dogs for Dummies* book. I don't try her fantasy novel. She wants me to bring her flute, still hoping to play in the concert tomorrow night. I have packed some cheerful T-shirts, not her favorite black ones. She smiles.

She can be held for seventy-two hours "on suspicion." During this time, a psychiatrist must see her and can order a longer stay if warranted.

What freaked the nurse out was my daughter's refusal to see the world in black and white. If this is considered sick, what will they do to make her "well"? If she refuses treatment, will they never let her out?

And what if she really is schizophrenic?

I bite my fist in frustration that night. No use to wake my husband. I am afraid to fall asleep, though for the first time in years, I have locked the front door. If they can take my child away, what else can happen? Police searching my computer?

I am almost glad when my eight-year-old wiggles into my bed, my body the only security I can offer her. I listen to her breath.

I call my sister, then my best friend. Both can't hold back their advice. Could an attorney help? How to find a good one? Just how expensive are they? I am in no state to listen.

At thirteen years, she is the smallest patient in the teen unit. Easy gestures, suntanned. She outplays everyone in basketball because they are all medicated.

"Did you see the rain last night? And I could not go outside. The social worker is cool, but the psychologist is so stupid. That one schizophrenic guy, he is a genius, but nobody listens to him. The psychiatrist said he'll examine me tomorrow. He looked at me as if I were a science experiment," she tells me.

In another state, a student shoots his teacher. He is thirteen, has straight A's, plays the flute. My first thought is: Did he have to do it right now?

A thousand dollars a day. So far our insurance seems willing to pay— up to fifteen days per year.

My daughter did get out after three days, on condition of another psychological evaluation. After that, the school wanted her back, but she refused to return. She is also more firmly opposed to professional counseling than ever.

I have begun my graduate studies and am home schooling my daughter. We get along quite well at this time, but I can't tell if she changed her behavior, I changed my perception, or this is just the quiet before the next storm. Her teens won't be over for another five years, but having seen the faces of adolescent mental illness, I have lost all my fears about her mental health.

Adelheid Deyke, Colorado

Child Retreating

Waitressing had never been easy work, but I was good at it and it paid the bills. The hours were long but flexible and gave me the freedom to attend classes during the day. I was thirty-five and still struggling to get my degree in applied sciences. It didn't leave me a whole lot of time for my five children.

We had moved several times because I couldn't keep up with the rising cost of housing. It was hard on the kids, and I knew education was the only solution. I was forced to go on welfare when I left my addict husband and found I couldn't survive on welfare. Friends and family thought I was cutting my nose off to spite my face.

I worked the graveyard shift (6:00 P.M. to 6:00 A.M.), five or six nights a week. Once home I would set out bowls of cold cereal and paper cups of milk next to them. The kids could pour their own milk into the cereal once they got up so it wouldn't get soggy. I brought home little packets of sugar from work and put one next to each bowl so they wouldn't use too much.

They tried to be quiet and let me nap until it was time for them to leave. No easy task since I slept on a couch in the living room. They'd wake me when they were ready to go out to the bus and kiss me goodbye. I'd check their clothes and hair and fall right back to sleep if they passed inspection. More often than not someone would be missing a shoe or unable to locate a book bag. I would get up, snap at them, and rush them out the door once I found what they needed.

On Tuesday and Thursdays I would attend classes from 9:00 A.M. to 3:00 P.M., racing home just in time to meet the bus. I'd fix them a snack and have dinner prepared and ready for my oldest to microwave. Some days I would doze in a chair until it was time to go to work. On days I wasn't in class, I would sleep and do housework. I tried to spend some quality time with the children but was always tired and overwhelmed. Not much of a family life for these poor kids, but they tolerated my inadequacy and worshiped their flawed mother.

My middle child was depressed since birth. I enrolled her in a child developmental program on the advice of the county psychologist when she was three years old. She hated it and cried every day for a year. I was torn but thought the professionals knew best. Looking back, I'm sure it did more harm than good. She felt betrayed by me and her anger found root in those early days of treatment. The following year, I enrolled her in preschool and that began a career of visits to the principal's office. I lavished more attention on her because she needed it and that did not go unnoticed by my other children.

Somehow, we all survived those early years. My middle child was a loner and kept to herself a lot. I knew there was a problem, but as long as there were no outbursts or calls from the school, I was able to lull myself into a false sense of security. I fooled myself into believing she was outgrowing her troubles. I call this my ostrich reflex: bury my head in the sand and pretend nothing is wrong.

If you bury your head in the sand long enough you can't breathe. Soon I was forced to recognize some very disturbing facts. The first one was finding diet pills and marijuana roaches in her knapsack. I tried not to overreact but was filled with panic. I had had my share of dealings with alcohol and drug abuse through my brothers, my parents, and of course, both my ex-husbands. It was probably normal adolescent experimentation on my daughter's part, but I quickly enrolled her in a drug treatment program. My 20-20 hindsight leads me to believe this was another huge faux pas on my part, but at the time I thought it was the right thing to do.

Eventually I allowed her to talk me into letting her leave the treatment program, another huge flaw of my parenting skills. Things seemed to get a little better for a while. She found a part-time job after school, had less free time to get into trouble, and was making her own spending money. Her boss was a man my age and I thought he was a stabilizing influence on her; a father figure. Perhaps he was at first, but within a year he was sleeping with my fourteen-year-old daughter. I'm sure the signs were there, but I didn't see the truth until it hit me in the face.

She eventually found him cheating on her with another fourteen-year-old girl. I still didn't have a clue what was wrong with her. She was so distraught she couldn't eat, couldn't sleep, and refused to go to school. She dropped an alarming amount of weight, and I feared as much for her physical state as I did her mental well-being. Once I realized what was really going on, I had murder in my heart. I probably should have had her employer/lover arrested, but at that point I was afraid it would just create a bigger rift between me and this stranger who was my daughter. I tried to be supportive. I allowed her to quit school, knowing she was on the verge of a breakdown. I gave her as much attention as I could, but it was nowhere near enough. I hoped that time would heal her. In the meantime, I still had to work.

I was in the middle of the dinner shift one Tuesday night, with a full station and most of the orders in the works while I served drinks and salads. There was someone on the phone for me, and I was surprised the manager allowed me to accept it—usually they won't let us take calls during dinner shift. It was my oldest daughter, crying hysterically. There was a lot of noise in the restaurant and I couldn't make out what she was saying. Slowly it began to sink in. Her sister had slashed her wrist.

I dropped my order book and ran out the door. The faces of my customers were startled, and my boss called after me, but I never even looked back. There would be chaos trying to figure out who ordered what, but that was their problem.

I knew I should have spent more time with my daughter. I knew I should have called in sick. *Please God, let me get there in time, let her be all right. Don't punish her for my mistakes. Oh God, Oh God, Pleeeease!* My old station wagon nearly fell apart at the speeds I was traveling; it is a miracle I didn't kill someone else or myself on the way home. The fifteen-minute drive took five and I jumped the curb, leaving the car running, parked half in the street and half on the lawn.

I took the narrow steps up the steep staircase two at a time and saw blood splashed all over the hallway. Her shirt was in a heap at the top of the stairs, drenched in blood, and another large puddle of blood seeped under the peeling kitchen linoleum in our cramped attic apartment. So much blood everywhere! My oldest, still in hysterics, told me the neighbors had taken her sister to the hospital.

I made the twenty-minute drive to the hospital in seven, running into the emergency room as if I were on fire. Nurses tried to stop me but I blew past them and started searching cubicles for my little girl until I spotted my neighbor and froze in my tracks. Did her eyes hold news of the death of my child?

She hurried over to me, a worried smile on her face, and told me my daughter was okay. I nearly collapsed on the floor but she helped me to my daughter's gurney.

My child, so small and pale, was almost lost in the hospital bed. Her eyes were sunken and filled with tears. Her arm looked like a white club; wrapped in so much gauze it dwarfed her head. That image has etched itself into my brain forever. My poor, sweet baby. I gathered her into my arms, buried my face in her beautiful, long auburn hair, and cried out a lifetime of guilt and shame.

"Thank God you're okay," I finally choked out. "Everything will be all right. I am so sorry, honey."

A hospital social worker approached me with a clipboard and a condescending smile. There were forms to be filled out and questions to be answered. I tried to dismiss her so I could hold my daughter. She persisted and explained that my child was at risk and they were going to commit her. Oh God.

"Hasn't she been through enough? Leave us in peace." I had no choice in the matter; they were going to do it with or without my consent.

"Won't you please make it easier on everyone and help keep your daughter calm?" one of the hospital staff asked me. I knew in my heart it was wrong to do this to her, but my hands were tied. My inadequacy as a parent and guilt over all my past mistakes led me to doubt my own judgment. I held my daughter's hand, smiled a fake smile, and reassured her everything would be all right as the orderly strapped her down to the gurney.

She cried and begged me to bring her home, promising to be good. "Please don't make me go!"

"Soon, honey," I told her. "We just have to go here first, for a little while, then I'll bring you home," I lied. I followed behind the ambulance with its lights flashing and siren screeching as the dark night closed in on my entire world.

We approached a place not far from where I lived. Tall steel fencing spiked at the top enclosed a huge building of imposing brick and stone. It seemed to have no end to it and grew a new wing at each turn or corner. A dim light bled through the small window above the large door at the main entrance.

The paramedic pressed a buzzer and a voice crackled over the intercom with instructions to enter the facility. My blood ran cold and I felt more trapped than I ever felt before. I wanted to grab my daughter's gurney and flee. Instead, I accepted the clipboard handed to me by the overtired nurse in a faded smock too tight for her large frame and began filling out yet another volume of forms.

It took several hours to get my daughter admitted, which included a brief tour of the psychiatric center, as if they were proud of the place. The current residents all had the same glazed look in their eyes as they did the Thorazine shuffle from room to room like animals in a cage. Green spiked hair, piercings on every place visible, along with scars and tattoos, belied the ages of these young victims. I felt as though I had entered the twilight zone.

All too soon, visiting hours were over and I was ordered to leave. My daughter panicked and begged me not to go, pleading to go home with me. Attendants restrained her as the tired old nurse shot my child full of something that would make her sleep. I promised to be back in the morning. The fear in her eyes was so haunting I cried all night: for her, for me, and for the way things should have been.

Morning light did not find the situation improved, in fact, it seemed to cast shadows on the long road ahead for my daughter and me. The staff searched the bag of clothes I had brought and checked my pocketbook as well. Unbelievable as it may seem, they had caught parents smuggling drugs and alcohol in to their children. I waited more than an hour before the doctor was available to see me. He explained to me that my daughter was severely depressed and suicidal. They would keep her here for several *months* (did I hear right?), put her on antidepressants, and give her intensive therapy. I was free to visit twice a week and call every other day.

What was he talking about? She couldn't stay here for months. I argued with the professional, and he pointed out that my expertise landed my daughter in this place with a slashed wrist. The blow he dealt was low and knocked all the wind out of my sails. I surrendered and meekly asked to see my child.

The transformation overnight was frightening. A girl resembling my daughter had fallen in step with the rest of the inmates, sporting that same glazed look and drugged shuffle. Her mouth was lined with a dry white crust—residue of the drugs she had been given. She stared at me with a blank look, as if she didn't recognize me. Although she whimpered a little and asked me to take her home, there was no fight in her, no strength. She no longer wanted to die, nor did she want to live.

We fell into a bizarre pattern. I visited twice a week and called every other day. She asked to go home each time we met or spoke, knowing the answer in advance and not really caring. Easter came and I brought her brothers and sisters to see her. The staff rummaged through the

Easter basket we carried with us, extracting the chocolate under the guise of too much caffeine.

Week after week, I argued with the doctor to release my daughter. Week after week, he explained she wasn't ready to be released. It is amazing that her recovery occurred on the ninetieth day, just as state funding expired.

She was ordered to attend a school for problem children. If we refused to cooperate, authorities had the ability to remove her from my home and place her permanently in a residential facility. For her own good of course, or until the money ran out, whichever came first. My daughter highly resented the hospitalization and hated her new school. Though I had no choice in the matter, she blamed me. I had failed to protect her.

It was two long years in that facility with family counseling, one-on-one therapy, and antidepressants that kept her from leading a normal life because she was too tired to participate in sports and constantly nauseated. Eventually, I weaned her off the drug.

I continued to fight to have her mainstreamed back into the regular school, but it wasn't until I learned of a woman who advocated for children's legal rights that I was able to extract my daughter from the system. She attended her regular high school for senior year, but mostly in small special classes. She hated it and dropped out months before graduation, but the authorities invoked a Person in Need of Supervision petition against her. If she did not do what the state thought she should— finish high school—they could terminate my parental rights and institutionalize her.

One bright June day in the summer of 1997, I packed everything I owned into a tiny rented truck and left the small town of my upbringing. I drove as far as my budget would allow, found a job, and rented an apartment. My two older children remained behind to finish college.

Although her treatment wasn't all bad, I firmly believe it did more harm than good. Money was the deciding factor in all of this, not her welfare. Our relationship has been irreparably damaged because she blames me for allowing it to happen to her. Still, we coexist, trying to rebuild our lives. We have our good days and our bad days. She may never forgive me for the mistakes I've made, but I've finally forgiven myself. My best may not have been enough, but it was all I had to give, and better than the professionals, who were paid to help her.

Mary Hoehmann Galgano, Georgia

Although this mother had a brief encounter with an institution, it was a dramatic one that would color her relationship with her daughter for years to come.

Lost Shoes

We are eating fat, crusty sandwiches in the food court at the Carousel Mall. I find myself adjusting to, rather than relishing, Annie's changing looks. Her hair is dyed from chestnut streaked with red and gold to almost black. Her nails have grown, and her tongue-post (last year's news) is barely noticeable as we talk.

A college freshman, Annie is telling me that she has made a discovery which will eventually clarify a career choice. Over her left shoulder looms the orange-red Hooters sign; over her right, pink and blue jewel-eyed horses carry small girls and boys away, then quickly back again.

"I know one thing for sure," she says, "I want to help people."

We eventually begin to discuss the stages of Alzheimer's disease. My father has recently been diagnosed, and according to Annie's information from her gerontology class, he is most likely in the early middle stages. She tells me that he will probably forget how to dress himself, that he will forget the meaning behind objects he now holds dear. The bread and vegetables and smoked turkey I'm chewing suddenly won't go down.

I am overcome with emotion at the knowledge that this loss of my father will be steady and excruciatingly painful. For a moment I think I will need to run from the table, but my daughter's voice holds me. She doesn't look away.

As I struggle to keep the food in my mouth, she says in a voice at once both changed and more familiar, *"It's okay, Mom."*

Those words and her voice take me back to a January night the winter she turned sixteen. My husband was away, and my son, a high school senior, had decided to take his first trip to visit some friends at the college he wanted to attend. After he called to let me know he had arrived safely, I spoke with Annie and felt satisfied with her plans for the evening.

My daughter was generally a good kid, and happy. She did well in school, had many caring friends, and was class president all four years of high school. Occasionally, though, a red flag would go up that would cause me to wonder whether she was in pain inside. One such incident occurred in sixth grade, when she scratched a boy's initial into her arm with a paper clip after watching her friend do this.

Annie always seemed to be on the front edge of those kids in her class who were testing the limits and experimenting. With each transition she had to make a statement of some sort, it seemed—some more serious than others. For example, upon entering middle school she decided to dress in extremely sloppy, oversized clothes completely unlike what the other girls were wearing. Within two weeks of entering high school in ninth grade, she began dating a senior boy; the boy she dated for years did not truly value her, but Annie seemed devoted to him in ways that proved painful. He betrayed her by "hooking up with" several of her girlfriends. I have always wondered whether a small, cigarette-burn-sized scar near her navel was in some way connected to the emotional hurt he inflicted.

One evening of her junior year, I settled in for the night, sure she was safe. Robe. Slippers. Book. Tea. When the doorbell rang a short time later, I was startled to find a friend whom I hadn't seen in quite some time standing there in the cold, and even more shocked to hear her say Annie was in her car, semiconscious. Some boys had brought my daughter to her—one of their mothers—because they were worried.

It turned out Annie had ingested four or five shots of vodka very fast. Though another adult the boys had consulted advised them to let her "sleep it off," they were afraid. I was terrified by the rag doll look of her when they carried her in; when I shouted into her ear, her eyes could not focus; coordinating her voice with the movement of her lips seemed too much for her.

In the emergency room, I could not stop myself from touching her. A plastic bag of sodium chloride poured into her vein to flush out the alcohol. It chilled her, and her violent shaking reminded me of my own legs' wild quivering those first moments after birthing her. Sixteen years later, reeking of vomit and vodka, Annie made a slow return from a different, slippery darkness, blinking into florescence, crying, asking me to hug her and apologizing.

Annie had lost her shoes, and as I steadied her down the hall and away from the emergency room, I was entirely absorbed by the movement of her pale bare feet. Her toenails, painted midnight blue and iridescent, swept along as we walked, as if torn bits of what had been the sky were blowing in slow gusts across the dirty tiles. When I looked up, the large E-X-I-T sign on the swinging door lost its meaning, and in that stark corridor, I felt I had lost my way. I remembered then that it was night and it was snowing. My car was parked in a lot far away. I wanted to be large enough to carry my daughter across, but it was Annie, her head somewhat cleared of vodka, whose words guided me.

"It's okay, Mom."

Linda Tomol Pennisi, New York

9

Change of Struggles, Change of Scene

"I think your daughter should try a wilderness program," the voice on the other end of the phone told me. "They can really make a difference for kids who haven't responded to hospitals."

Sending my daughter to a wilderness program was a choice I felt I simply could not make. I had read too many sensationalized reports on the boot-camp atmosphere of these places and how parents often used them as "dumping grounds" for their difficult teenagers. I was convinced that I would be harming my daughter more than helping her by sending her to such a place.

However, a short time after making this decision, Ellen was expelled from the private school for "at-risk" youth where we had placed her in eleventh grade, along with a second recommendation that she go to a wilderness program. By then, I had read a lot (including two of the stories that follow) and talked to many parents who had sent their children to these camps. Not one of them impressed me as eager to get rid of their kids, or uncaring, or inadequate. Still, it was with great trepidation that I arranged for her to go to Utah for a month of hiking in the snow.

"I can't do it. I can't send her so far away, especially for the holidays," I sobbed to my husband as I told him of the plans.

"How can we not try and help her in any way possible?" he asked.

At this point, Ellen had been through fifteen hospitalizations for her eating disorder and depression, sometimes in luxurious facilities that looked like resorts, other times in private or state hospitals. After each stay, we would bring her home only to see her crash, despite weekly visits to both her therapist and medical doctor.

Each year, she seemed to become progressively sicker, and we were running out of solutions, so I spent my forty-seventh birthday researching wilderness programs on the Internet. Although Ellen's weight was in a healthy range and she was medically stable at that point, many of the places I called refused to take a girl with any history of eating disorders.

Finally, I found a program that sounded ideal, and after grilling the admissions director, counselor, and case manager as well as talking to six other parents who'd sent children there, we arranged for Ellen to go. Surprisingly, she ended up benefiting far more from the thirty days there than I would have thought possible.

"Mom, I'm eating Spam out of a can!" she boasted, during our first phone contact. Her frequent letters astonished me—she was happy, taking pride in her ability to lead some hikes and enjoying therapy from a cliff top. Not washing her hair for three weeks didn't bother her—"I can make it stand up by itself in a Mohawk," she wrote.

"Stay in touch. We've really grown to care about Ellen," Sheila B., one of the directors of the program and a mother herself, told me when Ellen left. Not only had Sheila and other staff at the program coached me through many worries, they now had given me something equally precious: a sense that they actually liked my daughter—and would take her back if needed. That was a first.

I owe a special thanks to the mothers who wrote the following stories. They made it possible for me to be a little less terrified that fateful day Ellen got on a plane for Salt Lake City.

Hiking Boots

I didn't like the way my daughter was making her way through adolescence. She was enslaved by the cult of her own hair and body. She woke up at 5:30 A.M. and went straight to the mirror. Then she got in the shower and, for forty-five minutes, shampooed with balsam, chamomile, and nettle.

"Ma, could you bring me the egg timer?" she called one morning.

When it went off, she rinsed out her conditioner (she wanted her curly hair to be sleek and straight), and then, using a variety of brushes, tugged for an hour to blow it dry. She put beige foundation on her face, outlined her eyes and lips, and got dressed. She came into the kitchen in a red see-through baby doll nightgown top over a black bodysuit and a three-tiered ruffled skirt. It was exotic, but decent.

"Your breakfast is ready," I said.

"In a sec," she answered, on the way back to her room.

A few minutes later, I heard the school bus wheeze to a stop.

"Here's the bus!" I cried.

She came out in a pair of cowboy boots over gaucho pants and a striped bolero.

"You missed the bus," I said.

"That's all right. I'll take a cab with my own money. I have to change. This outfit doesn't look right together."

By the time she left for school, she hadn't touched her breakfast and had already missed French. Until then, she had written poems, sculpted clay figurines, read the classics, played Chopin on the piano.

"She'll grow out of it," friends assured me, but I was unwilling to take that risk. A friend who was a psychologist told me about rigorous wilderness expedition programs available for teens. After careful research, I chose a few of them to present to my daughter.

I made a long distance call to Wyoming. "All of her supplies, tent included, have to be carried on her back," the wilderness guy said. "And there are no showers. Sometimes a two-week stretch between baths."

It was music to my ears, but she didn't want to go.

"There's twice as many boys as girls," I told her.

She was convinced. When she stuffed hair conditioners and makeup into her backpack, I didn't argue that these things would be a burden to her. The desert would tell her itself.

All summer I quaked at images of her coming down with Rocky Mountain fever, getting bitten by a tarantula, or losing her canteen and dying of thirst.

"Our truck nearly turned over," she wrote in a postcard. I got one call that she had lost her pouch with all the money she had brought for the trip.

After six weeks, when I picked her up at the airport, she strode towards me in hiking boots. She was tall and muscular, her knees scraped under her cut-off jeans, her hair a tent of ringlets, a goddess awakened to her own power. I blinked back my tears.

During the car ride home, she talked about animal rights, recycling, and saving water.

"I'm going to take very short showers from now on," she announced. "And I'm not going to use any makeup that was developed by experimenting on animals."

For the rest of the summer, she padded around in Birkenstocks and the same pair of cut-off jeans that she had been wearing at the airport. Her hair was free of gel, mousse, and sprays. She wrote in her journal, read a book on Native American culture, and went out with her camera, taking pictures of the neighborhood.

She developed a desire to help others. She served Easter dinner at a soup kitchen in Hempstead, volunteered as a counselor at a camp for the developmentally disabled, and tutored children. Her true nature shone through like her face without the makeup.

I don't take credit. It was the earth that had healed her, drawing her into its own mirror of lake and sky.

Rochelle Jewel Shapiro, New York

Out of the Woods

A mother I'd never met called me recently and asked if I'd join her and another mother for tea. A few days later, I sat across a restaurant table from these pale, weary women whom I recognized right away as loving parents caught in the middle of terrible trouble with their teenagers. They had heard that several years ago I went through difficulties with my own children, and they wanted some advice.

In our discussion, we each admitted that, yes, our families had experienced challenges and painful confrontations, as every family does. None of us, though, could have ever imagined that our cared-for, well-loved teenagers could fall in with a group of street kids and become so infatuated with promises of freedom that they'd walk away one day and disappear from our lives, but that's what happened. Now they wanted my input on what to do if their children were found. I advised a wilderness program, which appalled them, given reports of abuse in such places.

It's not just the programs that are scrutinized by others—so are the parents. People wonder what could possibly be so horrible at home that parents would resort to the wild to teach their children a lesson. Why would any good mom or dad put a child in such danger?

Four years ago on a bitterly cold January day, I sat in a small, crowded office in Albany with my sullen, angry sixteen-year-old at my side. This was the first I'd seen of her in several weeks, since the day she and her fourteen-year-old sister—both of whom had been sneaking out of the house and skipping school so they could be with their street friends—had disappeared.

After long days of crazed and distraught searching and nights of no sleep, I'd hired a retired cop to search the streets to find them. He did, transporting them to Albany, where I'd enrolled them in a wilderness therapy program. Before I signed the girls up, I asked many questions and researched several wilderness expeditions, calling parents whose kids had been on a trek and asking local counselors their professional opinions. Even in crisis, I made myself check out the program before I signed on.

I was to send the older daughter off on a trek that Sunday, then the second daughter hours later on a different journey. For three weeks they'd live in the woods with trained counselors and confront trials offered naturally by the outdoors.

The five kids in each of my daughters' groups—who ranged from fourteen to eighteen years old—would take responsibility for their own actions in the woods, while gaining physical strength and emotional stability. Along with the others, my girls would carry their own food, build their own shelters at night, gather their own firewood and start the flames with a piece of flint, not matches. For three days near the end of the trek they'd live alone in the woods, speaking to no one—a journal and a pen their only companions.

The cost of the two trips was much more than their father, who lived in a different state, or I could manage. We turned to our extended families and got our insurance companies to cover a portion since each program was state-licensed.

Anguish marked the face of every parent around me the Sunday when we gathered to send our children off into the woods. As we told our stories during the morning family meeting, it became clear that each child in the room was dearly loved and supported. Neglect by these parents was not an issue, nor was juvenile delinquency of the children. We were families locked in a circle in this little room because we'd temporarily lost our way. What we each wanted, desperately, was to be reunited with our children. We yearned to believe a wilderness trek would help accomplish this.

For three weeks, our kids would be guaranteed a life free from drugs and other more frightening threats from dangerous peers. Professional counselors, whom I'd interviewed the preceding week, would guide the teenagers to reflect on their day-to-day decisions and help them rediscover a commitment to family as the group traveled miles over public land in eastern Oregon. One of the counselors, trained in emergency medicine, would watch out for any mishaps. Back home, with time to breathe, parents could make some much-needed long-term plans for their children.

But, oh, how hard it was to step into. At the meeting, as the head counselor was describing the bags of beans and lentils that would be stuffed into each child's pack as her main source of food, my daughter leaned over and scowled at me.

"You want me to die," she said. "You want to send me out there to kill me."

Not true. I longed for her and my other daughter to have healthy, happy lives. I'm sure neither would have believed that I was more saddened than they over my choice of wilderness therapy.

It was snowing in the Cascade Mountains, with a huge dump forecast for the weekend around Waldo Lake, where they were headed. My daughters were not in good physical shape, having long ago dropped out of their dance classes and sports. I felt like the world's worst mother for sending them into the wild.

Over and over I asked the counselors to describe the risks. Again and again they helped me remember that if I took the girls home, they'd run right back to the cluster of friends who promised utter freedom from authority, drugs, alcohol, and late-night leaps onto freight trains.

Sitting in the wilderness program's offices that day, I wished it was a different kind of world, one I could call upon to help my children and me out of trouble. But the reality is that aid for families in trouble is extremely rare—in fact, our culture has become decidedly anti-parent. When my girls were missing and I'd gone to the police, the officer I spoke to sympathized with my plight but told me it's not against the law in Oregon to run away. He said there was nothing law enforcement could do to get my daughters home. The girls' high school informed me the only individual liable for punishment when a child is truant is the parent.

I wanted to do most of the work of tending to my family myself, but I was astonished at the lack of societal support for parents who want their kids back. I'm not at all surprised that the quaint saying that it takes a village to raise a child has disappeared from our vernacular so quickly. Most of us realized immediately what a fallacy it represents. There is no village. There is no tight, loving system that comes into play when families—not individual children, but entire families—are in trouble.

Instead, our communities are much more apt to view kids on the street or arrested for juvenile crime as products of poor parenting and then push those families to the edge of society's consciousness. Parents like us are judged when our kids make poor choices and judged again when we resort to a solution as drastic as wilderness therapy.

But I, for one, stand by my decision. I was alone, every resource exhausted, and my daughters seemingly irretrievable. I had to do something to separate my children from the crowd they were so enamored of, or I had to give up. I was down to those two choices. How could I have done anything different?

I won't claim three weeks of wilderness therapy fixed my family. In fact, our troubles got worse before they got better, but the treks put us back on level ground at a time of chaos, and the experience cemented deeply held values in both daughters, helping them make healthful choices for their lives.

My daughters are strong and inquisitive; striving in their own ways to make the world better. I place part of the credit for that attitude squarely on the fine men and women who led them through their treks, who fed them with confidence and with the consistent message that they could take care of themselves, and who awakened them to the knowledge that they could achieve independence and still honor family.

Of course, I'd prefer to go back and find a way to make my family function so we didn't get to the point of wilderness therapy at all. Yet, I can't deny that two of the happiest moments of my life came at the conclusion of my daughters' three-week journeys. That Sunday in early February, I waited in a drippy campground deep in the Cascades for my children to return from the woods. The other moms and dads and I paced restlessly around the campfire, anxious, peering out in the crisp air for any sign of movement, for any squeal of teenagers.

Then, there they were. Our wool-clad, grimy kids, hats pulled tight over their crunchy hair, empty packs bouncing on their backs as they ran toward us. We threaded together, parents and children, pressing into each other like soft metal.

I took one daughter's face in my hands—as I would the other daughter's in a matter of hours—and started to cry. It had been so very long since I'd seen those bright eyes, that brilliant smile. So long since she'd said, "Mom, I love you."

Finally, I had my daughters back.

Debra Gwartney, Oregon

A Miracle for Two

Karen was a difficult child; as she neared adolescence, her problems steadily escalated from worrisome to alarming to frighteningly dangerous. By the time she was sixteen, she had developed an addiction to alcohol, used drugs, been sexually promiscuous, stolen from stores, damaged property, engaged in fights, abandoned schoolwork, had no respect for authority, abused me, practiced self-mutilation, and showed suicidal tendencies to the point of jumping out of a moving car.

Attempts to prevent her downward spiral would sometimes bring a glimmer of hope but quickly prove to be futile. Karen was removed from school and tutored for the last few months of eighth grade, barely passing. Her high school career began at a structured school for learning-disabled children. After one semester, she was sent home and then attended the local high school. After less than a month there, she was sentenced to nine days of out-of-school suspension. The school then hired a behavior specialist who followed her throughout the school day, but she finished her freshman year in an adolescent day treatment center at a nearby psychiatric hospital. She continued there throughout the summer and into her sophomore year. No real change was evident, but supervision was optimum and Karen miraculously avoided legal involvement and total self-destruction.

Up to this time, as a single parent, I had endured the horrors of needing to pay constant, vigilant attention to the behavior, activities, and whereabouts of my child. Like most parents of our society's "problem children," I had boxes full of reports, evaluations, correspondence, meeting notes, legal documents, applications for programs, insurance claims, and bills. One crisis after another was wearing me down to a totally beaten woman. I constantly feared for my daughter's safety. Then I found a residential emotional growth school for troubled teens a year ago and got her admitted. Finding this school and getting her there was like leaping over a precipice. Finally, I thought, there might be an answer for her. In any case, she would be safe.

Since the day before Christmas Eve 2000, I've had a lot to think about (as if I didn't before) regarding my daughter's situation. This would be my second holiday season in a row without my only child. I had been planning to be at her school for a visit Christmas week when a phone message on Friday evening assured me that that was not an option. I was told to call one of the school officials, who started our conversation with a question: "Has anyone ever talked to you about a wilderness program?" My answer was "no."

The pictures in my mind were vague images of hiking and camping and living simply off the land. I had heard of teenagers whose lives had changed as a result of such programs, but I didn't really understand how that might happen. A life-changing experience was certainly in order, but

I had never considered sending Karen to a wilderness program because it seemed like just one more Band-Aid that would be too expensive.

The counselor from Karen's school said we would see how things developed after the holidays, but that I should be prepared to send her to a wilderness program by doing some research and serious consideration. That's just what I did. The Internet proved to be my source of information; I requested materials from several programs and talked online to other parents who had sent their children to wilderness experiences. It all sounded great, but I resisted the overwhelming thought of arranging for her to go 3,000 miles away to a place with people whom I had never met and where she knew no one. I tended to think that this too might be one more futile attempt to "fix" my hurting child.

Ever optimistic, I still prayed and hoped that Karen would change and begin to show the effort needed at her school so the suggestion of a wilderness program would magically disappear. However, after the holidays, it became clearer that she wasn't even trying to comply with what the school expected of her. She was stuck in negativity and dreaming of her old lifestyle. If I was wishy-washy for a few days about what to do, two things caused my vision to become crystal clear.

An older girl walked away from Karen's school after being there for over two years and seemed to be ready to pick right back up with the destructive behaviors she had engaged in before going away to school. The other girl had been stuck, too, and was just filling time until she was eighteen. I realized that this could be my story ten months down the road when Karen became old enough to sign herself out of the school.

The other thing that made a lightbulb turn on over my head was the report that my daughter quit the basketball team. This was part of her pattern, deliberately sabotaging herself from possible success. Looking back, I could remember many times when something would be achieved only to be immediately followed by a self-designed failure. It was almost as if Karen wants and expects to be doomed for the rest of her life. An inner voice was shouting to me, "Do something! Your adorable child is sinking in nowhere-land!"

I decided. Wilderness, here we come. The thought of spending more money I didn't have and taking days off work to travel seemed like insurmountable problems, but at least I had direction, another option to help her, and the relief that a decision made brings. I used the information and recommendations I had gathered and found a program that felt right to me. Everything fell into place from that point on.

At the end of the wilderness trek, I went to Oregon to pick up my daughter and attend the traditional culminating all-day family event. I can't say I was particularly excited or happy about the prospect of traveling across the country. It seemed like a somewhat frightening, long, and lonely adventure that would probably end up being for nothing anyway, just like all the other times. I was also worried about the two days it would take to return Karen to school and the possibility that she might try to run away from me at some airport or street corner. This was just something I had to do whether I liked it or not.

Though the travel was grueling, the reason for the trip and the glowing girl I retrieved made me forget the hmm, let's see, twenty-one hours it took me to get there. When I arrived at the site, I was met at my car by a man who, upon finding out who I was, broke into a big smile and said that my girl had worked hard and come a long way and that she was beside herself with joy that I was coming. My dubious attitude immediately melted into near rapture. I felt like after so many years of stumbling along the road going nowhere, I had just hopped a train and was zooming off to some wonderful place.

Hugs never came easily at home, but the hug I got from Karen that day made up for any we missed in the past. A radiant, composed, and beautiful young woman entered the yurt (large tent) and walked toward me. No words yet, just a long, sincere hug. My tears began. She said, "I'm so glad you're here. I have so much to tell you." I told her she looked wonderful and that I was all ears. I saw the bright eyes of my little girl, looking just as excited and happy as she did on her first trip to the zoo when she was two years old.

During the family session that followed, I quickly got the sense that my daughter had been a shining light throughout the trek. The other members of her group considered her a leader. I was beaming as much as she was. Was it a dream? Could this be the same girl I had to leave work and retrieve after she punched and scratched a classmate at school? I wished the teacher who had told Karen: "Everything is fine in math class whenever you're absent" was there to see my daughter, the one everyone looked up to. It was a new and wonderful development!

Each participant spoke for a half hour to forty-five minutes and shared what they had learned and what their plans were for the future. I used half a roll of toilet paper as I cried for almost six hours straight. My tears were happy ones for all of the kids, but mostly mine, of course. All of the others mentioned what a help Karen had been to them. This role in itself must have been a turning point for my daughter, as she was usually the one who caused the problems, not solved them.

Karen has discovered many things about herself during the program and learned to focus on one problem at a time. In the past, she had become so overwhelmed by her many difficulties that she gave up easily, but the wilderness program, with its concentrated 24/7, almost one-on-one assistance, helped her strengths emerge. They wrote in journals constantly and had to spend four days and three nights completely alone with written assignments to complete. She had four notebooks full of good stuff, and for the first time since her waywardness started, she seemed to realize what a dangerous path she had chosen.

She often mentioned her love for me, calling me "her hero," and apologized in front of everyone for all the things she could remember she had done to hurt me. She cried when she said she was sorry for ridiculing me, screaming at me, and accusing me of things that were not true. She wanted to fix the door she broke and all the dents in the walls. It was hard for her to mention the times she threatened to kill me with a knife in hand. I had never seen a hint of remorse for these things before. She even stated that she wanted to take care of me when I'm old. Karen never wanted to cry, as she thought it was a sign of weakness. Her only outlet for emotions of almost any kind was anger. Just seeing her cry in front of those six families was, to me, a miracle. Choking with tears, she told what her biggest fear was: "My mom won't want me back."

Well, I could go into many areas that were covered and strides she made in great detail, but I think the picture is painted. I will relay one incident that made her day and mine. One of the fathers, a sophisticated-looking guy who was a medical doctor, came up to her at the end and said, "I want to be the first customer at your hair salon (one of the dreams she shared) but not just for the haircut, I want some advice!"

Karen's participation in a wilderness program was definitely a valuable step in our lives. I have never seen my daughter glow in such a positive way, a sight that will last me a long time. As my friends and family will tell you, I came from the wilderness with a glow, too. I hope and pray that we can keep that glow. Sending her to Oregon was hard, but the hardest part is yet to come. Remembering what she learned and keeping the new commitments in normal everyday life will be the true challenge for Karen. No matter what lies ahead, I am confident that Karen and I will always have a piece of the mountaintop within us.

Trudy Nelson, New Jersey

PART FOUR

When Troubles Go On and On

10

Crazy Soup Emotions:
Love, Anger, and Frustration

When Ellen first became sick, I was overcome with worry, but I felt an ache of love that energized me to keep trying every possible approach to get her to eat. At the same time, I was frustrated by her blatant disregard for her health and upset over her apparent willingness to put her entire family through so much suffering on her behalf. I was reluctant to let her know how I felt, though, worried that any negative emotion from me would lead her to stop eating again. It was a very tense time.

As the years passed and her condition worsened, it was harder to continue being patient. My sons commented on the amount of time and attention I gave Ellen, and Paul and I often squabbled about what to do next for her. More and more, I felt angry with our situation—and with her.

One night I woke to discover her crying with leg cramps and knew instantly her blood potassium level was probably too low due to repeated purging. A trip to the doctor's revealed I was right, but instead of feeling relieved, I was distressed. How could Ellen place herself in danger again and again?

"Righteous indignation is a far healthier response than depression," one of her counselors advised me. Certainly, it's easier in some ways when I can distance myself from Ellen by being angry, but at the same time, no matter how much she upsets me, she is still the daughter I love. Her problems terrify, demoralize, and depress me.

Love—anger—frustration—even rage. Just as I sense she feels all these things toward me, I feel the same toward her, sometimes in a matter of minutes or hours. Other mothers wrote about a similar response.

History of Chelsea

Chelsea, my fifteen-year-old daughter, is, as we speak, locked up in a youth detention center. Our troubles began when her dad and I divorced when she was five. She and I began counseling because I felt she wasn't clear as to what was going on and why.

That seemed to help—things went well until the middle of fifth grade, when she began lying a great deal. By middle school, her grades did a nosedive from exceptional to failing, and she was spending most of her time in the principal's office or ditching school. Since I worked in her middle school, I knew everything that was going on.

Again, she and I went to counseling, which was expensive for a single parent, especially when there was such a lack of results. Much to my surprise, I received my monthly phone bill not long after this— $1,600.00. When I questioned Chelsea about it, she blamed the man I had been seeing for a short time, but he had no access to my apartment or phone. I was confused because I never thought my daughter would do anything like that, but spent the next several weeks calling telephone companies trying to explain the situation. Finally, I sent proof of her age, copies of the phone bill, and a letter stating that I refused to pay the debt. Within six months all but $300 was cleared off my bill.

Chelsea told me she wanted to go live with her father because he "could take better care of her than I could." I called her dad and asked him to supply the ticket, which he did, to my surprise. She left the second week of June 1998, with the agreement she would stay with him for a year. Three weeks later, I received a phone call from Chelsea, telling me how great and wonderful I was and could she come home? Before long, her dad began calling frequently to complain about what a spoiled brat she was. "And your point is—?" was the only thing I could think of to say. (Working in a middle school does wonders for one's vocabulary.)

In April 1999, her dad called to say Chelsea would be on the next plane home, which happened to be the following day. I took two days off work to pick her up and help her acclimate and get reregistered in school. Not much changed. Chelsea got back with her old crowd, only the drinking and drugging got gradually worse.

I found drug paraphernalia while "cleaning" her room, a parent's worst nightmare. I called the police, not knowing what to do. They sent out a couple of officers to the house. When I pulled the pot pipe, a bag of pot, and a Baggie of pills out of my pocket and presented them to the police, Chelsea was speechless. They handcuffed her, put her in the back of the patrol car, and took her to the station. I met them there, filed charges, and she was released to my custody. I thought I'd made a mistake, but these events soon became routine: arrest, release, arrest, release.

Chelsea began running away from home too, breaking back into the house when I wasn't there. She stole my personal checks and was using them to pay for her drug use. I discovered this fiasco when my bank told me I was overdrawn by $350! Later on that day I found checks in Chelsea's room between her mattresses, in her pillowcase, and under a rock just below her bedroom window. I called the police again, filed forgery charges, and this time made sure that social services was involved.

I had become a pit bull simply because I was running out of options and patience. Since Chelsea was on the run at the time, I reported her as a runaway as well. She was found, taken into custody, and I was told to take her home. I finally refused and asked the police to find another place for her to stay. It wasn't going to be with me anymore.

When the social service agency was notified, I didn't get much of a runaround. Reports were filed, paperwork was signed, and my daughter spent her first night in jail until a foster placement was found the next day. I kept getting told that I needed to take her home. It's a good thing that I was so angry because that's the only thing that kept me from caving in.

The first foster placement lasted all of ten days. She took off again and no one bothered to call me to inform me. Four days later she was found at her boyfriend's house—she'd been high for the entire time on anything that he would hand her.

She was placed in an adolescent treatment center for three days until a second foster home was found sixty miles away. When these foster parents brought Chelsea back for a court hearing, she casually walked away and was gone for two weeks. This time when she was found she was placed in the treatment center for five days. By now, the social service agency was involved full force, actively searching for something more effective than foster care. The caseworker placed Chelsea in a drug and alcohol treatment center.

During her stay she appeared to be making so much progress that when she asked for an overnight pass, it was granted. I did my dutiful mother thing and drove up, looking forward to a pleasant overnight visit with my daughter. The ride home was a little tense but nothing I hadn't gotten used to at this point. We arrived at the house around 10:30 P.M. I went to bed, thinking she would follow suit within an hour or so. I was so sound asleep that I didn't hear her when she took my car and disappeared, again, for four days. She also took all the money in my purse. Felony #2: car theft. I called the police, reported the car stolen, and pressed charges. I was getting really good at this sort of thing, but couldn't believe my fourteen-year-old daughter had two felonies.

When Chelsea was found driving around the local park with a friend, she didn't even deny who she was to the police. I went to the station, which was like my second home at this point. Chelsea was so blitzed she didn't even respond to my being there and chewing her out. When I got to the car, I got even madder—condoms were all over the front seat, and trash from the past four days, including but not limited to cigarettes and beer bottles. The car reeked of alcohol, sex, smoke, and God knows what else.

"Why?" was all I could say. What had I done to deserve this from an individual who claimed to love me? At this point, for the first time I felt true hatred for this person I had vowed to love unconditionally for all eternity. I'd had enough and ended up giving custody to social services.

Totally by the grace of God, a position at an all-girls drug and alcohol treatment center opened up. This place had, at the minimum, a six-month waiting list for admittance, but due to some connections with Chelsea's caseworker, they found a spot within two weeks.

Chelsea was admitted to that center but has run two or three times, in addition to an incident when she earned a six-hour pass with me. I had driven up to take her to the mall for a fun-filled afternoon/evening. At 5:50 P.M., I asked her to meet me out at the car, so we could get something to eat. When I got to the car and she wasn't there, I knew almost immediately what had occurred—she had taken off again.

I went back inside the mall to call the center and let them know what happened; they told me to go ahead and go home, which I did, under much duress. You can imagine how I was feeling. All the way back home, the mood inside of my car was as "blue" if not bluer than the outside of my twelve-year-old Plymouth. The rage reared its all-too-familiar head once again! Once again I had allowed her to use me.

I didn't hear anything regarding Chelsea for about five days. When I finally received a call, it was from her caseworker, who told me the police had found her living inside someone's car. She was arrested (for what I'm not quite sure) and taken to the place where my story began. She is trying to charm her way into a facility that is placed in the middle of nowhere in Utah—we'll see.

How have things turned out? In my world "things" are still turning. It's amazing how one of the most important people in my life has ripped me apart and never known it. I love my girl so much; I know that because she's the only one that can and has truly broken my heart. My only insight from a parental point of view is that regardless of your position in a child's life—whether it is one of a biological, foster or residential care provider—learn to take care of "you." So many of us place ourselves on the "back burner" physically, emotionally, socially in order to do what we feel is the "right thing" for our loved ones.

Don't stay at home or worse yet isolate yourself and beat yourself up. Find support through positive sources such as Al-Anon, Divorce Recovery Workshops, and parent groups. Realize that what is happening to your loved one is due to a personal choice on their part, not yours.

I don't claim to be a perfect parent, nor have I ever met one. We all make mistakes that we regret, but we need to take responsibility and move on! This last bit of advice is the hardest for any concerned parent—*let go!* It's the most difficult aspect of teaching our children about consequences for their actions; it's not your fault. I'm right in the middle of this one; case in point, every time I even speak my daughter's name, I cry. As angry as I may feel toward what she has done, I can't help but think back to better days—but most important of all, I'm learning to focus on a more positive future, for both of us. I know it will come.

Donna Houser, Colorado

On the Run

As I glance away from the computer screen, I see a reminder of my daughter's love: the desk plaque she gave me a few years ago. The words chide me now: *There's a bond between a mother and daughter made up of loving memories they share.* Where are those memories? I promise myself I will move ahead. My very survival relies on forgetting the past and protecting myself for the future.

My daughter ran away with a friend two years ago when they were seventeen. Funny how I sensed something was going to happen. Maybe it was her heavy sighs that I had learned to recognize as a signal she was lying or scheming or manipulating.

She and her friend Alice decided that they no longer wanted any adult supervision. They were going to prove to their parents that they were independent. My daughter planned the escape: figured out when no one would be home, armed herself with babysitting earnings, packed some clothing, cut classes, and left with Alice on the bus.

We didn't know she was gone until that evening when we found her note. No mention of destination was included, so we had to try and figure out where she would go. We called her friends, and frantically, my husband and I reread the note, hurt by the words each time. Finally, her boyfriend, whom we believed to be a decent, wholesome teenager, told us what he knew. We later found out that he was arrested.

In a cruel, perverted way, just knowing her plans calmed us. At least she wasn't kidnapped or languishing somewhere in the gutter. We contacted the bus lines and train station, but to no avail. No one was able to track two teenage girls on their way to a new life.

I'll never forget how this incident affected my husband and me. We started blaming each other for Patricia's destructive behavior.

"I should have done this."

"You should have done that."

We didn't realize she was dragging us down with her. We didn't see that the very survival of our marriage was threatened. Our love for each other was being squeezed—almost as if it were in a vise and she was the one who applied the pressure.

Finally, late in the evening the phone rang. It was Patricia. She was safe. No, she would not tell us where she was or where she was going. She was not coming home. There was no reason. We didn't understand her and she was tired of trying to be perfect for us. To me, she sounded lost, sad, and childlike.

We pleaded with her to tell us where she was so her dad could come to drive them home, but no amount of cajoling would change her mind. She knew that she would be suspended from school and probably not graduate, but didn't care. She and Alice had a plan: they would work in a restaurant and receive lots of tips. As soon as they had some food and a night's sleep, they would look for work. The call ended as abruptly as it had begun.

The next call came in the middle of the night. Having been startled out of a fitful sleep, my husband answered the phone. I listened to his conversation and decided to find another phone so I could hear her voice. The defiance was still there, but muted, as she repeated that she could make it on her own and that we were smothering her. I interrupted the conversation and begged her to tell us where she was. I can't remember what I said to change her mind, but she broke down and said she was at a bus depot, where some men had offered them their home for the evening.

I panicked, screaming, and trying to find the right words. Before she told even us that she was at the Greyhound bus terminal, my husband was already dressed and fumbling with his car keys. Imagine, two girls barely out of the bandage-on-the-knee stage thinking they could spend a night with derelicts who prey on children.

He and Alice's father drove for an hour and a half to rescue the girls. When Patricia returned home, she kissed me lightly—almost an afterthought—and went to sleep. She never mentioned the incident again.

Our relationship has deteriorated since that episode. She barely speaks to me except to manipulate or pit my husband against me. Most of the time the spurts of discussion are accusatory. I accuse her of lying for the sake of lying and she accuses me of not meeting her teenage needs. I look at the child I brought into this world and nurtured, and I see a girl poisoned by the very culture in which she lives.

She is drowning in her own deceit. Friends reinforce her destructive behavior while her family tries to save her, but there is so little strength left, and my marriage is in shambles. I try to understand her. I have even tried to change, but I am the only one who is willing to save my daughter when I can barely survive.

I once asked her why she lies and she wrote a perfunctory apology indicating that she really didn't know why. I have come to believe that her lying is her way of rebelling against demands to be perfect. Where do these demands come from? Unrelentlessly, the media accosts girls to be thin, beautiful, sexy, alluring. In short, to be *perfect*.

There are days when everything appears normal, but they lose out to her verbal abuse. It lashes out and burns my heart as I try desperately to revive a relationship that maybe never was. Still, I sometimes see a glimmer of hope, only to have it snuffed out by her destructive behavior. I am afraid that the mother-daughter relationship I once arrogantly bragged about is in danger of not surviving. The flames of "Ophelia" are consuming it as well as my relationship with the man I so need and once so loved.

Juliet R. Speare, Virginia

I have friends whose daughters aren't rebelling or in the midst of crisis who still experience that mixture of positive and negative feelings parenting inevitably involves. When problems occur with a daughter, these normal feelings seem to escalate: worry becomes intense fear, protectiveness becomes aggression, and frustration turns into anger at her behavior, as well as fury at our own inability to change the situation.

The following mothers describe what happens when they are unable to gain control of their daughters for various reasons.

Seven Years in Hell

I think of 1990 through 1997 as the years my daughter and I spent in hell. When I divorced her abusive stepfather, I did not expect our lives to go from bad to worse. I thought the joy we'd once shared would return and that my daughter would spend her teens in peace and safety, but that was not to be.

My daughter was thirteen when I began to notice symptoms of her pain. She couldn't get up in the morning, wept unceasingly, and dreaded going to school, claiming she was worried about me and didn't want to leave me alone. I'd eventually lose patience and demand she get up even if she had to go to school in her pajamas. This behavior persisted for close to three months before diminishing, only to be replaced by other signs of distress.

As friendships became more important to her, peer slights and cruelties caused hysterical reactions. She began setting small fires in my study, and her grades plummeted from perfect to failing. Family therapy sessions became a nightmare as she assaulted me with one accusation after another: I had thought only of my own happiness, had not listened to her or protected her from her stepfather's abuse. At first I let her rage wash over me and set no boundaries to what I believed was legitimate expression of the pain she'd endured as a child, but soon there was no controlling her assaults.

I dreaded returning home from work, never sure what I'd find—boys in the house, beer cans under the bed, knife slashes in the walls. Terrified, I tried to set tighter boundaries in an effort to stop the torrent of hurtful actions from destroying us. She defied my efforts and wouldn't tell me where she was going, disappearing at night and refusing to come home when I tracked her down. I lived in fear of what might happen to her and tried to keep her close without success. Putting on a brave front, I pretended to be in charge, but inwardly I knew the situation was out of control. Even my friends could not understand what was happening in our home. I felt ill with fear, alone without resources.

One day while showering, the enormity of what was happening crashed in on me. I could no longer pretend this was just a phase, an acting-out after years of repression. Feeling totally helpless, I collapsed sobbing in the shower.

While at work that afternoon, I had a presentiment that something was terribly wrong and rushed home. My daughter had attempted suicide. I found a note telling me she was too tired to live and that I should not feel sorry but should just pretend she had left on a journey. When I entered her room and found her curled in a fetal position on the bed, I actually hesitated before calling the police, wondering if it would be kinder to let her leave a life she found so painful. Then I dialed 911.

During the years that followed, she grew even more distant and hostile. I felt as if with each new day, another piece of her drifted away. Ongoing depression and psychotic episodes led her to be transferred from one institution to another.

The loss of my beautiful daughter tormented me and I longed to undo the past. My performance at work deteriorated to the point where I was told that unless I got myself together, I would lose my job. I seemed to be forever on the phone with doctors, social workers, and hospitals, but things kept getting worse. With crisis following upon crisis, I was finally forced to acknowledge that regrets were useless. I could not undo the past, nor could I save my daughter. That was her job. I had to let go.

The turning point occurred when she was sent to a juvenile detention center for mooning passing cars on a heavily traveled road (in another situation this might have been humorous). On visiting day, I tried to prepare myself for what I knew would be an ugly trip. I could see nothing ahead but a continually deteriorating situation, one in which I would ultimately be forced to accept what I most dreaded: the road my daughter was taking would lead to death. I knew I had to look into her coffin and accept the fact that I could not save her; and as I did, a furious, roaring, blessed anger surged through me.

The visit went much as I'd expected it would, with my daughter swinging between sweet childishness and ice maiden. When she threatened to kill herself if I didn't get her out of the detention center, the anger gave me the strength to tell her I knew she was quite capable of taking her life. If this was what she decided to do, I could not stop her. Although I loved her beyond her willingness to understand, I would no longer allow myself to feel responsible for her choices.

My daughter is now twenty-three, and we share a rather odd but loving relationship. She continues to struggle through life, sometimes managing colossal successes, sometimes making choices that send my heart plummeting into my shoes. It is then that I take a breath and repeat the words that helped me survive those years in hell:

"You, my precious daughter, are responsible for your own choices, for the direction your life will take, for your own happiness. No matter what those choices are, I am always here for you, to help but not to rescue. I will always love you."

Beryl Singleton Bissell, Minnesota

Out of Control

I feel tremendous love/guilt/love for my daughter, Raeleen. When she was younger and I was still actively mothering her, I got so tired of people meaning well when they said to me, "If you would just control your child—"

If I could control my child, then undoubtedly I would have! Does any parent willingly let their child be violent? I do not think so. My daughter's mental condition is real and beyond my being able to "control" her or take care of her. I have to acknowledge and accept daily that I cannot "actively mother" my own child.

When other mothers would blatantly ask me or give me the look of "control your child," I would sigh deeply (couldn't they see I was trying to discipline her?), wish for my own mother, and then ask, "Do you want to walk in my shoes for twenty-four hours and then judge me?" There was usually no reply from the mothers after that.

Raeleen is the true "pre-mother hero" here as she struggles through her life's experiences. She is the eldest sister, girl grandchild, and girl cousin. She is now learning to be the matriarch of the family. However, she has many obstacles to overcome. First and foremost she has survived and continues to thrive from being diagnosed at age six with epilepsy and a brain tumor. Raeleen underwent brain surgery at age nine and had the tumor removed, which dissipated the epilepsy. Also, she has had to see the only family she knew be disbanded by divorce and then the remaking of another family that includes half-sisters.

Going into her teen years, Raeleen has been diagnosed with attention deficit, oppositional, and bipolar disorders. In the twenty-four-hour care of her doctors, they are trying to find the correct medications for her chemical imbalances, as well as for her to learn life skills.

Raeleen looks and seems to act like any normal teenager. She wants her hair to be cut in the latest style and to wear the most current clothing. Of course, there is the typical haughty teenage demeanor coming from her—"Mom does not know a thing." When I look deeper I see my little girl who is trying so hard to be normal but just cannot quite get there. It breaks my heart to see this.

The guilt I have felt over the years and still feel could eat me alive. However, I have learned to put it into perspective. Sometimes one person, one mother, a single parent cannot fix everything for or about their child. That there is a time and a place for everything—and maybe at this time it is not my time to actively mother Raeleen. Also, I have learned that it is okay to reach out to others for help and to rely on those who are parenting/taking care of Raeleen during this interim.

I believe it takes an entire family's mothers to raise a child, starting with the matriarchs—grandmothers then following mother, aunts, nieces, girl cousins as well as good family women friends. It also takes the fathers of the family to make their life contributions to the raising of the child as well.

Until I lost my grandmother, mother, and aunt in the space of three years I did not fully understand their continual contribution to the raising of my own daughter. There have been days that I long for them to be just a telephone call away. Now, I walk as a lone mother and appreciate more and more the wisdom from the women of my family who touched my life and helped me with my daughter. At any given time since the deaths of these three important women in my life, I have turned to the fathers of the family to help me with my daughter—my father, her grandfather, my ex-husband, her father. However, I have learned that the support from these fathers may not always be forthcoming and I must once again step back and do the best I can on my own.

I admire Raeleen's courage and love her even more dearly for it. She gives me hope when she does little things: tells me that she does not want to burden anyone with a troubled teenager or gives me her long-sleeved shirt to wear even when she is cold from the air conditioning. These little sparkles of looking outside of herself and being able to contain her frustration level so she is not lashing out give me hope that she will conquer her disorders and thrive in her life.

Zana Gay Harvey, New Mexico

11

Grieving for Our Little Girl Lost: When Proms, Graduation, and College Fade Away

When someone dies, it's logical to grieve, sometimes for extended periods. Although the adrenaline of constant worry over the past three years has provided enough energy to keep me going physically during Ellen's crises, there are times when I feel devastated by sorrow for the losses accumulating in her life. I mourn for the proms she won't attend, the parties with girlfriends she's missed, and the graduation with her class she won't be part of.

My husband says: "She can always go to college," but that isn't what really bothers me. She has missed many experiences her high-school years could have provided and won't get the chance to relive them no matter what happens.

"She'll get back on track," friends tell me, but I wonder. With all she has gone through, can she ever find a place in life where she will feel comfortable and accepted?

Sometimes my grief over Ellen mixes in with worry and hurt and guilt, and sometimes it's as acute as if she were lost to me forever. Although several mothers of daughters without apparent problems wrote and told me they still worried something *might* go wrong, I think what separates me from them is grief. Here's how other mothers describe the sadness they experienced in relation to the struggles of their daughters.

Double Difficulties

Never in my worst nightmares did I ever imagine going through something as heart-wrenching, painful, and terrifying as I have with my daughters. My girls and I were very close until five years ago, but problems started in January 2000 when I was in the process of regaining custody of my then twelve-year-old daughter. She and her sister decided they wanted to dictate the way they would live with me, and would settle for nothing less. They both wanted no rules/responsibilities—just to do whatever, whenever. They resented the fact that I attempted to enforce some sense of normalcy in our lives.

Nancy (age thirteen) was sexually abused by her father and emotionally traumatized. Donna (age ten) was separated from me for about one year while I got things set up in a new place after going through a violent divorce. That is where the anger comes from. No matter what I say or do, they feel and express the need to hurt me for their hurt. They haven't always been angry, even when separated from me. It's only been in the last year that the anger has surfaced.

My (second) ex-husband made me choose between him and my children because he couldn't and wouldn't deal with their problems. He wasn't rejecting me, just the issues at hand. He had tried to help me with the girls by being their friend and showing them how to do some things, but they made false abuse allegations against him, which resulted in our eventually getting divorced, so I am now a single parent.

I love my girls so much and am at the point that I just don't know how to help them. I have tried everything I know to reach them: counseling, parenting classes, and a lot of heart-to-heart conversations. They tell me what they think I want to hear and continue to do what they want. I fear for their safety, as some of the things they do put them in jeopardy physically and emotionally. Nothing has worked.

I finally had to get the juvenile system to help when the violence started about three months ago. I know kids say things they don't really mean when they're mad at you, so I guess I played ostrich and thought it would go away. When my daughters told me they stood over me at night with a butcher knife, contemplating how to kill me, I knew I had reached the end of the line as far as what I was capable of doing to help them. I needed a professional to assist me.

When they were admitted to a juvenile treatment facility, they accused me of abuse. Now I am fighting for my own freedom from false allegations. I am at risk of losing my job, because my boss is very unsympathetic. I feel totally isolated since I live in an area where I have no friends or family around to help me, so I am working through my thoughts, feelings, and emotions as well as the trauma of dealing with the state officials on my own.

I deal with all this one day at a time and do a lot of praying. Some days are better than others, but I keep putting one foot in front of the other. I am scared *of* my girls, because of what they said; however, I am also scared *for* my girls because they are so young and I'm not sure they emotionally can handle the situation as it is evolving. My life is forever changed, and I will never see my girls the same way I once did. Their youth is gone and innocence is tarnished.

I am terrified: terrified for my life and the lives of my children. They are so young and yet have destroyed so much of their future already.

Renea Marx, Missouri

Tears from a Rose

What I do for a living, what my real name is, and where I live seem irrelevant. What defines me is the hell I've lived through, and what I've learned along the way. In the end, we are all the sum of our experiences *and* what use we've made of them. I'm trying to make use (and sense) of mine. I'd like to help other parents avoid some of the traps I fell into and find some of the helpful things I discovered.

I am forty-one years old, and married. My twin daughters are now seventeen years old, and we also have a nine-year-old daughter. I've always done the best I could for all of my children. The twins had more advantages than we could really afford. They had years in orchestra, and instruments, rented, borrowed or repaired for them to play. I made their clothes "in style" so they wouldn't look odd at school. I sewed fancy dresses, blue jeans and bell bottoms, better than any store made according to Twin B. They learned to stretch money because I was always stretching it, so in some ways they are very well-suited to managing their own lives now.

We all participated in upkeep on the house, and when I had to go to work, they knew why, and usually what bills I was paying off. I took parenting classes when I needed them, to learn about new stages of development. The advantage of working sporadically was that I made time for my children. We had fun. We camped, made things, painted pictures, played with clay, built our own swimming pool (now I understand why installation is so expensive!), pruned the big tree and cut the grass. We repainted the house and refloored the foyer. I taught Sunday school so there would be a class for them and taught chess to them and the neighbor kids in the summer.

The time spent with my children ranked over material things. This is what made their rebellion so heartbreaking. What happens when you do everything as right as you can, and it all goes wrong? The time I have invested in my children may not have been a waste, but in 1999 it sure felt like it.

My first contact with the Gothics were hoodlums from our hometown in Texas, that hung out with my twins. None of the ones I met through the twins have completed high school. Most (possibly all) used drugs. Some were self-destructive, carving their skin up with razor blades, piercing each other, etc. Some were into carving animals or other people up. Most, like the twins, just did the dropping-out scene, bumming sleeping quarters at friends' homes, begging or stealing for food or cigarettes, living in parks and cars, a little bit of self-mutilation, glorifying poverty and martyrdom. Their dress ranged from tight black vinyl pants and green hair to dark Jncos and black T-shirts, or slinky black dresses, burgundy- or black-dyed hair, and vampire-pale makeup with black or deep-red lipstick.

I figured the Goths were a passing phase for my girls and didn't worry about them a lot. I wouldn't buy the hair dye or the makeup, so my kids worked part-time jobs to buy them, but I didn't ban them either. I didn't go off the wall until the twins went over the wall. When they ran away and dropped out of school, a local police officer, our resident expert on Gothics, came to visit and took a look at Twin A's room. He provided much of the information that started the Gothic page on my web site. His encouragement helped me.

The running away started in August of 1998, at the beginning of tenth grade, and continued until May 22, 1999. The authorities did their best to find me at fault as a parent, accusing me of not handling discipline when they were younger, but the girls knew right from wrong, they knew about consequences, and those were as appropriate as I could make them.

I did not think Twin A would survive February 2000. She was losing five lbs. a week, depressed (despite the antidepressant our doctor put her on) and talking about suicide. I heard she was doing a mix of heroin and crack cocaine, smoking it, but I will probably never know the truth.

She denied doing any drugs to me and said her roommates weren't heroin junkies, but she came clean on that when one went in the hospital for liver failure. I knew from her weight loss and the phone calls I was getting that my little girl was lost, emotionally. She felt that she had to live at the heroin house to take care of her friends and was perpetually fund-raising to try to get the electricity turned back on. I couldn't sign her into a treatment center without her consent, and since she didn't think she had a problem, she refused treatment.

I finally located my ex-husband one terrifying morning when Twin A called, depressed because she'd tried to reach her paternal grandmother and the phone was disconnected. I tried grandma's number, and it worked (she must have misdialed). When I explained my fears to my ex-mother-in-law, she miraculously came up with a phone number for my ex-husband. Within two hours I was talking to him, and within three days Twin A had moved to New Mexico to be with him. It isn't all rosy out there. I'm sure marijuana is readily available, and I know he allows her to drink beer, but she's gaining weight, working, going to school, and to my knowledge, the stronger drugs aren't easy to find. This probably has saved her life, at least for now.

Twin B married in August 1999; she and her husband have their own jobs, an older car, apartment, and a two-month-old daughter. Oddly enough, when she married, and no one was attempting to force her to do anything, she hit *normal*. She talks to me, holds a job, drives her husband to work, and made the decision to take her GED. She is a good mother. This is the "bipolar" child that needed lithium?

I think what she really needed to do was make a commitment to managing her life. Some kids can do that without the crises that she put us through. Some can't. She had to be holding the rope on her own, with no one tugging at it, before she could face life on life's terms. Her husband also seems to be perfectly normal, and working toward a future, now that no one is attempting to control him. He works from forty to eighty hours a week, is a good father, husband, and son-in-law. So much for crazy teens.

Twin A never got formally diagnosed as bipolar. She is very moody, and swings up and down. She is genetically identical to Twin B, so I'm guessing that she isn't. She simply hasn't chosen to make a commitment to managing her life. It is still easier for her to be the "poor mistreated child" than to accept responsibility. She rents a trailer near her father and calls to complain about all the teenagers that she has let move in with her. I have a simple solution: if you don't like it, fix it.

Ideally, treatment for kids like my twins would offer education, counseling support, and medication *if needed*. It would also feature "thinking rooms" with padded walls, where my berserk Twin A could have pounded to her heart's content, released her anger, and not hurt herself or anyone else. Then someone to talk with her, one-to-one, afterward, to help her understand her part in the situation. My poor house (with holes in the walls), and I, did this job. It's a tough one.

The main thing that would have been helpful was a spot where there's no one to blame, no one to complain to, and essentially the teen is forced to confront herself (or himself) and *choose* what to do from there on. I'd have sent them to the moon for this if I could, because it looked like the only place out of reach of their Gothic and rebel friends, and the stay would have to have been long enough for them to hit bottom, because only then would they face themselves. For Twin B, her marriage, all the freedom in the world, and a place to call her own worked. For Twin A, she's basically got the freedom in the world and no place to call her own, filled with a new, less drugged, more drunk, bunch of teens of her choosing. Perhaps when they get on her nerves enough, she will face her part in it and commit to handling her life.

Throughout history, teenagers have rebelled. They try on different modes of behavior and dress to differentiate themselves from their parents. Since the parents hold power, teens need to rebel. (It is odd how many of the parents' values get incorporated later in life.) The question is, when does rebellion become mental illness? We have new diagnoses daily. Oppositional disorder and conduct disorder I find very humorous, in a dark way. They aren't fun for a parent to live through, but I am not sure that they are mental illnesses.

I started typing for therapy, to put down the facts I was learning, and to find a way through my own pain. I typed for about two months, roughly six hours a day. Thus my web site (http://www.tearsforarose .com) was born. I think what makes the Rosetears site work for me is its anonymity. If something bad happens, we feel ashamed: of our children, or of our humanness in making a mistake. On the web site we can honestly face what has happened, knowing there will be no re-crimination, no well-meant pats on the back from people that do not have the slightest clue as to how we feel. Having had coworkers, employers and others offer well-intentioned but totally inadequate advice and inflict extra pain trying to "fix" my situation, I know how unhelpful it can be.

Today is September 25, 2000. I'm weaning myself from Zoloft. It's been helpful, and probably was the only reason I survived 1999, but I do not wish to have my life revolving around the presence or absence of *any* drug. Painting or writing is more fun than taking a pill in the morning. Doing arts and crafts with my youngest will be easier without the drug. I look forward to that—we've had little time for fun, and communication and knowing one another. If I don't make time, in a few years, I may have another problem child. Blessing upon us all.

Rose, Texas

Christy Lynn, My Little Princess

My daughter's name is Christy Lynn. She is now eighteen years old. She was a beautiful blonde-haired baby so happy and full of life that I called her my "Little Princess."

In sixth grade Christy Lynn became really depressed. I tried reaching out to her in every way and began counseling to no avail. One day she arrived home three hours late. I was working as a private duty nurse and got permission from my patient to bring her along to work after that. It would do her good to see people less fortunate than her, or so I thought! As she sat on the couch across the room from my patient and me, she stared us down so hard that it felt like a knife cutting through my soul. I looked at her and wondered. Where are you now? Where is my Princess?

Things got progressively worse over the next few years. As a single mother, I worked two jobs and sometimes had to leave my son, Cody, who was eight, with Christy while I worked. One night I returned home at 11:00 P.M. and received a call from Cody that she had dragged him on the bus to the Ocean City Boardwalk to hang out with her friends. I am horrified when I think of the things she exposed him to. I felt like a failure of a mother at that time. I felt I had not only lost control of Christy but had now placed Cody in danger, too.

In June of 1998 I was handed Christy's eighth-grade diploma but told she could not walk with her graduating class. She had cursed out her teachers. I cried all the way home but managed to pull myself together, knowing that Cody was counting on a mom who was strong. I have wonderful friends but could not count on family support at that time. It was all up to me!

Christy entered high school in a new town that fall. I had given my house to my ex-husband and moved in an attempt to give Christy a new start, so Cody was forced to relocate, too.

Christy started running away when she didn't like my rules. I kept a police file on her runaway attempts. One night she called and said she would not be home until she was ready. She had given me a friend's pager number. The police called the pager number and when the girls returned the call, Christy brazenly informed the police she would return when she felt like it. They tracked her down and brought her home.

While I waited for her to return I entered her room, which was covered with garbage and dirty clothes. I took four large trash bags, filled them and took everything from her room. Left behind was a bed, a pillow, and a few articles of clothing. When she returned, she flipped out, screaming and cursing at me. I had reached my limit. Her father had skipped town without child support and she was telling me she wanted to live with him.

At the advice of my lawyer, I turned full custody over to her father. I was told that this would prevent me from being held responsible if she really got into big trouble. All it managed to do was to cut me out of any further decisionmaking in regard to her life and what was best for her. Looking back, I wish that I had gone with my first instinct and sent her to boot camp. Yet I feel it was important for her to see her father and to be able to ask him why he left her behind.

In the spring of 1999, I proceeded further in my attempts to get help for my daughter. I knew at that point she was involved with drugs and I was afraid of losing her completely. I was afraid she would end up dead. She had gotten herself into a situation where she was raped by a so-called friend. She was living a life of hell.

I wrote letters to all her past teachers, administrators, counselors and friends to put a file together for Boy's Town in Nebraska I had the chance to get her into. I spoke with Christy about this opportunity. At first she cried and objected, but after further discussion decided it would be best for her to go there. Unfortunately her father did not agree, and because I turned custody over to him, he had the final word.

Christy started talking about rehab to members of the church she was attending, and decided to go to the Walter Hoving Home in Garrison, NY. I was nervous about her doing it on her own.

December 27, two days after Christmas, Christy called me from New York City to tell me she had run away from the Poconos and was en route to the Walter Hoving Home. She arrived there safely and for once I felt like she was on the right track home, but her father didn't agree and located her a week later and went to bring her home.

Another year passed. Christy got involved with hard drugs, trying cocaine, heroin, and ecstasy. She watched friends overdose and almost lose their lives. She slept on the streets and ate dinner at the Salvation Army. My heart breaks when I think of this.

We did attempt to let her start a new life in our home after she turned eighteen. She brought a boyfriend along, and they stole money and jewelry from me and robbed her little brother's piggy bank, all for drugs, so we had to put her out on the street again.

I lost contact with Christy. She got in with a real bad crowd, living on the streets of Easton, PA. For six months, I did not know if she was alive or dead. I felt numb inside. I knew that no news was good news. I jumped every time the phone rang, wondering if it was going to be a call telling me they had found my daughter dead. I prayed to God every day that she would be O.K.

Again I turned to poetry, and wrote a poem called: "What Do You Say to Your Child Who's Lost?" I wanted to tell Christy that I loved her and I was waiting to listen with an open heart and open arms.

God must have heard my prayers. A month and a half ago I received a call from Christy. She told me she had been raped again by a street thug and that she needed to get her life in order. She went away for a few weeks to the safety of a friend's home and spent time reflecting on her life. She asked if we could get together.

Driving to Easton, PA, I was nervous that I would hear the same lines over that I had heard in the past. I was ready. I had my defenses up. When I saw Christy she looked like a scared, lost child. She was clean for the first time in a long time and had clear eyes and clear thoughts. Christy cried her eyes out telling me how sorry she was for all she had put me through. She asked for forgiveness and apologized for taking money and my jewelry as well as being such a bad influence on her brother. The thing that hurt me the most was hearing that she didn't really remember so much about the last few years of her life because she had been too stoned.

We have missed out on the proms, the graduations, the mother-daughter talks. We can't get any of that time back, but we can take our steps forward. We have made a vow to each other to take baby steps along the way. I don't expect the road to be smooth. I do expect her to attend Narcotics Anonymous or Alcoholics Anonymous meetings and to pursue her GED. I expect her to slip and fall along the road to success. I just hope she stays strong enough to pick herself back up and know that I will be there waiting to catch her with open arms. As long as she remains honest with herself and with me she will continue on her path to success.

Most of all, she needs to love herself.

What Do You Say to Your Child Who's Lost

What do you say to a child who's lost,
Lost in a world of drugs?
Living a life that's dangerous and wrong,
Out in a street full of thugs.
You have to stay strong and hold your ground,
Hoping that someday she'll come around.
Maybe she'll realize that life can be good,
If only she'll do the things that she should.
Keep loving your child, pray to God up above,
That she'll understand unconditional love.
Maybe someday she'll come to believe,
Without all the drugs, her dreams she'll achieve.
So, What do you say to a child who's lost,
Lost in a world of drugs?
Just tell her you're waiting to listen and love,
With an open heart and your hugs.

Dedicated to my daughter, Christy,
with my prayers that she is listening

I Love You, Christy

Sharon Lee Robinson, New Jersey

Even though the following stories are from stepmothers, the sense of grief these two women felt on behalf of their stepdaughters was no less powerful than that of birth mothers. The instinct to try and help, the sorrow over failure to "fix" problems, and the mourning of relationships lost are the constant mothers share, even absent blood ties with a struggling daughter.

Emma's Stepmother

I am Emma's "father's wife." This is how I introduce myself when I am in her presence. "I have a mother," she used to say, and made this clear in no uncertain terms.

Her father, Max, and I met two years after my first husband had died. Soon after, Max, then the divorced father of four-year-old Emma, moved in with me and my eight-year-old son, Jonathan. We married the following September, and he adopted Jonathan the next year.

For our wedding I made Emma a Raggedy Ann outfit in yellow flowered calico complete with a white apron and pantaloons. After the wedding, when we tried to drive away from the reception, she clung to the door handle on the passenger side of the car consumed with screams, her swollen face an angry red.

Her weekend and midweek "visits" to our house were miserable, and I came to dread them. She would glare at me without blinking, her stormy eyes warning me away. Rarely would she speak to me directly or acknowledge I was in the room. Even though I tried to please her, there was always something wrong with what I fixed for dinner or a speck of dried egg yolk found on the plate.

By adolescence she held all the cards. I did not know how to confront her, nor did her father. She talked about her mother constantly, inserting "my mom" into almost every sentence. Soon after arriving at our house, she disappeared upstairs, where she talked to her mother on the phone, crouched into the corner of the hide-a-bed sofa, whispering and giggling into the receiver held tightly in her hand.

As a teenager she performed in a number of musicals at her school, and often played a brassy leading lady, like Lola in *Damn Yankees*. After it was over, my husband and son, and her mother and grandmother, would gather in the lobby waiting for her to emerge. I felt intimidated and wanted to fade away even more than I already did.

On one such occasion a teacher approached asking if I was "Emma's stepmother." She looked at me as I tripped on my words saying something like, "No, she has a mother. I'm married to her father."

Around her I felt mute, censored, erased, and invisible. Yet she was a child and I the adult. Looking back, it's hard to know just how this happened, but she came to control the territory where I had once thought I belonged. I came to understand that I had no place in her life. There simply was no room, and for her I did not exist. For her thirteenth birthday she requested her mother and father take her to dinner and they did. My husband was not enthusiastic about doing this, but felt he couldn't say no. I was furious and said nothing.

Shortly afterwards, I announced he would have to see her outside our home. It was probably exactly what she wanted, and this arrangement went on for some time. They went to dinner with him as her escort. In essence he was a single parent, and I was out of the picture.

Today she is twenty-seven and for the most part a stranger to me. We have had a few interactions over the years. I sense she sees me as someone more than just her father's wife; she has expressed sincere acknowledgment of my teaching and writing. She no longer glares at me, but we do not share an authentic relationship because the gap between us is so unfathomably wide and deep.

I would like to change this, but it seems impossible. She has no desire to explore or try to understand the past we shared. She and her mother continue to be close, and I assume neither one of them is aware of the way it is for me in relation to her.

If it could have been different I would have tried to make it so, but silence and the inability to interrupt a story that felt as fated as a Greek tragedy kept me from action. When I think of myself in relationship to Emma, my central feeling is one of loss, but not the loss of anything I ever knew. Rather, it is an empty space where I might have stood to speak with her and where I could have found a name.

Joan Fiset, Washington

Being Kelly's Stepmother

When I first met Kelly, she was nine years old, a little girl with beautiful red hair and green eyes, but one who didn't smile much because she was embarrassed. She'd been in a car accident with her mother and, with no seat belt on, had hit the dashboard and lost a front tooth. Her alcoholic mother signed off on any claim to the insurance company and gave Kelly five dollars for the missing tooth, an indication of their relationship.

I was serious about Kelly's father, Mike, at the time; when he moved in with me and my two children, Kelly began to visit every other weekend. Slowly, the story of her emotionally impoverished life unfolded: she had grown up in a poor area of the city where there were rats in her apartment but little food. She was always hungry when she came, and the fact that she could eat anything in our refrigerator was an alien idea. I was brought up in a household where the thought of not having a full fridge is a disgrace. Each weekend when she was due to visit, I bought special foods I knew she liked.

I had survived a difficult childhood and thrived due to some kind people along the way, so I had hope for Kelly. As someone who had been a child-care worker for two years after college, I spotted her problems very quickly. I had the gut feeling that no amount of my intervention could help Kelly, but I would not be at peace unless I gave it my best shot.

When Kelly came to visit, I noticed that her clothes were cheap and worn, so I started buying her shoes and new outfits. After spending two weeks at home, she would always return with her old worn-out shoes. Finally I asked her what happened to the new ones, and she said: "My mom took them. We have the same size feet and she liked them." Mike told me this probably was true, but he was afraid to confront his ex-wife about it for fear visitation would be cut off.

I solved the problem by keeping the new things I bought her at our house. Whenever I took my children shopping, I always bought Kelly something, but she appeared surprised that I would think she deserved new clothing.

There was an underlying sadness about Kelly that bothered me. When I questioned her, she responded by saying that her mother always fought with her brothers and was returning to an abusive relationship with a man to escape the poverty they lived in.

I took Kelly to my children's dentist to repair her tooth. The dentist informed me he had never seen such neglected teeth in a child her age—she had a mouthful of cavities and her teeth had never been cleaned. After the repair of the cavities, I took her to an orthodontist to repair the missing tooth.

Although I was doing all the right things for Kelly, sometimes I felt overwhelmed. I told myself: "She is doomed, anyway." The damage to her young life was far more than a matter of one tooth, it was the matter of a broken spirit. My daughter told me Kelly cried herself to sleep every night, which confirmed my sense of how deep her wounds really were. Even if I tried with all my heart, could I repair them? I had to keep trying, believing there might be hope somewhere.

When Mike and I became married and pregnant, my children Sandra and Victor were excited, but I could tell Kelly was frightened. Although she smiled at the news, I sensed she felt she would become lost in the maze. It appeared that I was the only port of peace in her deprived life and would now be taken from her. After the birth of my second daughter, I found Kelly hunched in a closet, crying. She reminded me of a wounded bird with no wings.

Unfortunately, our infant daughter caught whooping cough from Kelly and almost died. I knew her mother had not taken her for the regular childhood vaccinations because my other two children did not become ill.

My anger toward Kelly's mother grew. I wanted to confront her, but Mike said no. He was the kind of person who wanted peace at all costs and turned out to have a problem with alcohol himself. That led to our divorce after a short marriage. The pressure of a job, three children, his substance abuse, and trying to save Kelly was far too stressful for me.

The person I felt the most sorrow for was Kelly, who now was left with two alcoholic parents. I encouraged her to visit as often as she wanted, since I still cared for her and wanted to help. She and my oldest daughter, Sandra, got along well. When Kelly stole clothing from her, I explained to Sandra that Kelly wasn't really a bad child, just a sad victim of circumstances.

Kelly's mother beat her so badly one night she begged to live with Mike, and he consented. I knew things weren't going to be much better for her with him, as he was still drinking and had a job that required travel far away. Kelly, now a teenager, began missing a lot of school and doing drugs. To his credit, Mike quit his job and stayed home to keep an eye on things.

One day I took Kelly to lunch. I tried to explain that school was a necessity for a better life and drugs would only hurt her. She listened, but was beyond reach. Right after that she decided to return to her mother's and dropped out without even completing her first year of high school.

The next time she visited, she brought a new boyfriend, a young, unemployed man she clung to for dear life. I asked her to lunch again and attempted to explain the importance of school and self-esteem to her. My youngest daughter was with us, and she paid more attention than Kelly, who said she loved this man and could not be alone. I knew the relationship was not going to end well and felt great sorrow for this lost little girl.

The next time I heard from Kelly she was seventeen, back at her father's, and pregnant. She had a new boyfriend, who was in jail for attempted murder, but Kelly assured me he was a man "with a past" and had been framed. There was no way she would consider giving up her baby; she considered it a "love child" and was determined to keep it at any cost.

My sister, who lived near the city where Kelly came from, told me the newspaper had run a story on the new boyfriend. He was being held for the beating of Kelly's half brother, who lay in a near-death coma at the local hospital. Apparently Kelly had watched the event, and it was her mother who called the police.

Kelly left Mike's abruptly, but returned to steal a large sum of money that belonged to the business he was supervising. He called the police to try and find her based on her long-distance telephone bill. I know since then Kelly had her baby and took the infant to jail to visit her boyfriend, but she hasn't contacted me.

I cry for the red-haired girl that I met years ago. At times, guilt hits me hard. Could I have intervened in some manner to save her? I mourn her lost childhood and womanhood, and the baby destined to relive her life. It seems her life will consist of poverty, pain, and perhaps a young death. I hope I am wrong.

No one ever really loved Kelly enough to make her whole. I tried, but her wings were broken far beyond repair when I met her. All I was able to fix was her tooth, and to send her to camp, and give her some shelter from the storm.

Sally Sutton, Canada

12

Trying to Survive:
Getting Through a Day,
an Afternoon, or an Hour

How do you hold your life together when your child is falling apart? What do you do to stop her crisis from destroying your other family members, who are just as precious to you as she is? Is there ever an end to the turmoil?

I only have my own answers to those questions, and they all relate to keeping myself functional. When I fall apart, it seems everyone else does, too. During the years of enduring Ellen's problems, I've learned, somehow, ways to avoid collapsing, although I can't say they always work. Sometimes I simply have to recognize the difficulty of that day, knowing I've survived before and can do so again. I've even come to make a game of it—classifying my days by my mood.

My "nightmare days" are the most benign. Did you ever have a really bad dream that woke you with a start and gave you a chill each time you remembered it? That's how those days feel to me, except the things that scare me really happened. The most notable one I remember was when Ellen first got restrained in the hospital. I didn't see it, but the nurses told me about it. For the rest of that day, the image of her bound up and immobile kept coming back to me, making me shiver with horror.

Then there are the "hangover days" when I feel so physically and emotionally sick I can barely function. Lots of sad things prompt the grief and disappointment that underlie those days. I'm guaranteed a hangover day when I get a dreaded call from a treatment facility saying Ellen can't stay.

"If you don't get her out of here immediately, I'm calling the police," the director of a famous eating-disorder clinic informed me once, even though she knew I lived two hours away. Again, my hope for Ellen's recovery at yet another hospital was dashed, and for the rest of the day I felt ill with sorrow.

The other kind of day I can recognize and classify is a "falling-apart-completely" day. These are days when I truly can't function. Usually, I seclude myself and cry my way through the day, feeling that, as one woman told me, "a mother's tears never end." It takes a lot to rattle me this badly, mostly because I hate for my family to see me in such a state. Thankfully, there haven't been many of those times: One was when a nurse called and said Ellen had been punched in the face by another female patient. The thought of my daughter being hit caused me to dissolve completely, staying home from work to weep inconsolably.

There are other ways I try to tame the monster days. Talking to moms who understand helps, as does prayer. I also take great comfort from my sons, my extended family, faith community, volunteer work, and my job, where my mind is distracted from personal problems. Sometimes being around other girls is a good thing. Coaching swimmers has helped me remember that most teenagers aren't struggling as desperately as Ellen.

The following came to me in an e-mail inquiry that evolved into a story of one mother's attempt to survive her daughter's illness. Because it captured the flavor of emotions described in this chapter so well, Lori gave me permission to use it.

Struggling Through

Finding you is like an answer to a prayer. It's hard for anyone to understand what I am going through, or to know how much pain a mother feels when her child is hurting herself. My daughter is fourteen. She has always been quiet, even as a baby—I always said that God knew I had been through enough so he gave me Ally. Her father left us when I was six-months pregnant, so she never knew him.

Ally is the baby of four children. My other children always had me at home with them, but being newly single and responsible for the welfare of four children, I was forced out of the home and into the workforce. Unfortunately, my Ally spent a lot of time at daycare. I didn't get to see her first step, hear her first word, or spend the time with her that I had my other children.

At three, I noticed that she held her books very close to her face, so I took her to an ophthalmologist. It turned out she hadn't been able to see up to this point. It broke my heart to watch her see birds for the first time. She had a difficult time in school but tried so hard I never got upset with her grades.

She was teased a lot because of her "coke bottle" eyeglasses, Shirley Temple curls, and feet that turned inward, but she never showed her pain. Then, at age eleven, she got contact lenses, and blossomed. She was such a beautiful child. She also got interested in music, started taking piano lessons, and playing softball.

She finally found things she could do better than anyone else. I was so proud of her. She jumped from beginning band to stage band in one year and plowed through every piano book I got for her. She loved softball. She played catcher, and was tougher than any boy I had ever seen play the game.

Now my beautiful, talented daughter has been hospitalized for the last five weeks for hurting herself. She says the pain she causes herself hurts less than the pain she feels inside. I found her journals, and she talks of killing herself daily. She has suffered silently, and I never even knew she was depressed. What happened to my little girl?

I had to take her to a facility in another state, because my insurance wouldn't pay for her to stay where she was. Two days later, they called me from an emergency room. She had cut each forearm ten to fifteen times with a razor blade. She had to be moved again.

I spoke to my daughter last night, and she sounded hopeful that the new facility where she is going will help her. She says that everyone tells

her that she cuts to manipulate me, which is also what her case manager
at the insurance company says, but she and I both know that is not true.

I keep hoping that this is a bad dream, and I will wake up soon. I
have never experienced this kind of pain in my life, and I can only
imagine what she must be feeling. Where do we go for help?

Lori Lappin-Keeley, Nevada

The following poem captures some of the emotions we experience
on bad days: Fear that our daughter is really lost, panic at the thought
of our families falling apart, and a loss of hope for the future. None
of this stops us from loving her and praying that things will somehow
get better.

Breakdown

Fall

Three times today, and every day for weeks,
I am on the phone with my anguished daughter
on the other coast, her voice in my ear so
close, I can see the childhood scar beneath her left
eyebrow grow red as a curled lip, the fragile skin
under her swimming eyes mottled blue and bruised.
But she is hurtling away from me into the darkest
spaces between stars and my ears are radar
dishes; my heart lunges forward
like a telescope searching out the faintest
glimmers. I need to give her a story
that will bring her back, a story
of light.

Winter

Months now, since all the lights went out,
the biochemical storm of anxiety descended.
Our blithe adventurer—who used to
leap before she looked, land, teeter, spring
into the next lucky step, say

watch me watch me as she led us up
steep cliffs, who didn't need the roots
that hold, always skidded into home
safe, and saved again—arrives for
winter break, head bowed, every fiber
willed into tense composure for the trip.
We hunker down in the bunker of family,
to survive.
Like battlements, we flank her
on the couch, take turns, or even together, stroke
her hair and face, focused and holy as lovers,
and terrified that she needs us so much—
terror soothed only by our response,
stroking and smoothing. But when she writhes,
beats her fist on the floor, spittle hanging from her
sputtering chin, I look on, refusing
to acquiesce that her life is over, then I long
for the sweet fevered heat of her against my chest—ill
at one or two with something familiar—the pleasure
of hospital visits, predictable pink fizz of liquid
penicillin.
And I go into mourning for my daughter
of throwaway grace. She who seemed to calm
the nervousness of my own mother that flutters
within me—my mother whose hands continually
straightened collars, picked at
lint, wet a finger to rub a smudge off
a cheek, wrung each other.

Spring

After the freak storm, the chemical calm,
a guest we don't know but welcome with open arms
like a child's friend from another country, and the child, too,
back from a long journey to some place we can never
visit, a place that has changed her in ways we will never fully
understand—though we can hear the alteration

in the timbre of her voice, feel the new
cavernous space within her—and whose dust
on her shoes she'll always carry.

Another Fall

And after this, how quickly she recedes
into the glamorous scrapbook of parental pride,
caught in flashes, leaping again from pinnacle
to pinnacle, my remote heroine of
independence—greater-than-mine until
she calls from a foreign
city after many months and before
I quite realize who it is
I am speaking to my alter-soul.
We are together, inside an aura—
like the nimbus around one's own full
name, suddenly stumbled on, in print—
inside an atmosphere palpable
in the mouth and tongue
as the return to one's own language
after exile.
But the next time she calls
I am shy, at a loss for
what to say.

A Previous Winter

In Cairo, a city we visited her in, on a whim,
at her urging, long before the storm,
there is, even in the dark, a background
hum, a living vibrancy in the air, which you at first
take as the subdued roar of traffic, street vendors,
crowds, until you realize it is the almost continual chant
of prayer or call to prayer. That air alive
with vivid reverberation—that is my heart
for her.

Julia Kasdan, West Coast

I can only imagine what advice I might give Ellen if she got pregnant. However, I can understand the loss of dreams that occurs when a crisis comes into a daughter's life, as well as the terrible weight of being asked about abortion in a life-threatening situation.

A Very Special Relationship

My nineteen-year-old daughter and I have always had a very special relationship. She has had many struggles throughout her entire life because she is the older sister to a brother with special needs, and we live in a very dysfunctional household. I think some of her problems are because of our living situation. We are one of four families living in my mother's three-bedroom house.

My fifteen-year-old son is emotionally disturbed (ED). I have separated from the family in the past because they refused to accept him as having a disability, but his problems have made it very difficult for me to afford my own housing. I have constantly missed work because I am called away for him. My daughter has lived through this and has been very supportive. It was very difficult for her, because as a single parent, I didn't have a lot of time to devote to her.

She has been a scholar student for most of her school years, never asking for much and *always* understanding. My daughter learned to overcome adversity during the years she attended a majority white high school. During her last year of high school, she got into trouble for the first time with another student she had some difficulties with in middle school. Trying to do the right thing, I told her to make the office aware that she was having problems with this student and let them intervene. That never happened, and the day came when she could not take any more, so she had a fight with the other student. She was in such a rage that the police were called in. In the midst of the fight, she hit the police officer. That caused her to get suspended for thirty days, and she lost all of her opportunities for scholarships from the school.

She was sent to an alternative school and, thank the good Lord, her grades were not compromised. This taught her that you have to pick and choose your battles and that this one was not worth the outcome.

I still stuck by her because I knew it had to be bad for her to get to that point. She had to do some volunteer work for community services, which made her a stronger person. Sometimes we have to go through things to get to where we are.

For the first four months of her pregnancy, she kept this to herself. All her life she has argued against abortion, but in the situation she was so torn. This is a child that has carried a 3.5 GPA all through school and was determined to get a college education. The hardest part was feeling she had disappointed me, but I wasn't upset with her regarding the pregnancy because she had guts. She stuck with her beliefs on abortion and was determined to face whatever came her way.

My two children were born out of wedlock, so I know her inner turmoil, but I admire my daughter because I didn't have what it takes to do what she's doing. I try to keep her on a positive note and let her know that I will support her and that I will be there for her when she goes back to school.

My daughter developed some complications due to the size of the baby. She was put on complete bed rest with bathroom privileges only. It was a lot to swallow at one time. She didn't know just how dangerous it was until they asked her if the choice had to be made to save her life or her child's, what did she want them to do? She immediately turned to me and asked me what would I do. That was the hardest question I've ever been asked. Naturally I said I would save my child's life, but that was like telling her to put the baby first. I then told her that I couldn't answer that question for her but please don't take *my* baby from me. It is very tense now, and I don't want her out of my sight. We have both become so attached to each other that it's scary.

Through it all, I continue to admire her. She has courage and strength.

Patrice Somerville, Virginia

Many mothers have told me that like Patrice, confronting the potential death of their daughter was a necessary step for their own survival. The following letter illustrates this point.

Letter to a Friend

In thinking about Michele's patterns and behavior and her current attitude, I am not at all sure she will make it. I mean, at some stage, at some time, in some time, in some situation, I think she will manage to kill herself. It appears to me that she is hell-bent on self-destruction. There is no logic in her whatsoever. No rational thinking. Not a glimpse of it.

So just what am I doing trying so hard? I am not equipped for this. I don't want to get ill or go down with her, I really don't. I don't want to obsess over my daughter's destructive life.

I am now angry that she came here, but of course I can't tell her that because that will really drive her to something drastic. I am damned if I will let her mope around without taking any responsibility for her own recovery or facing the reality of what is happening/has happened to her. I am feeling ill and without any energy or enthusiasm for anything, and depressed—this is ridiculous.

In fact I think I am counterproductive to her recovery. By always being here for her whenever she decides to turn her life around—she takes me and this home for granted and even dislikes me for it. You see, it's a losing battle. She has nowhere else to go, but doesn't want to be here. She won't go to a hospital, into therapy—and hates me for speaking the reality of her situation. She is really managing to alienate me, on a deep level. I want to rage and scream at her, but can't. I'm fed up, really fed up. I *want* to help, I just don't know how, or if I can.

Maureen Earl, California

(Maureen's note to me: "I wrote this letter to a friend who is a doctor in August 1998, just a while before Michele truly decided to get straight. I send it to show there is hope.")

Surviving can mean many things. The following pieces were written by mothers who literally needed to find a way to continue going on with life after their daughters died.

Some Notes About a Mom

Recently I attended a three-day workshop on loss. Most of the participants were licensed clinicians, one or two RNs like myself. Throughout those three days, personal stories were shared, continually reminding us of bonds we have in common and those we don't.

One woman, a clinician, spoke frequently about the traumatic death of her teenager. She was articulate and I found myself drawn to her, wanting to know more details about how she was able to cope. She said that her child had been smart, successful, popular, and handsome. He had so many friends that on the day of his funeral, the church was so packed, young people, friends, spilled into the street. When she returned home, her house was filled with mourners, that day and for many more to come.

I cannot claim to know what the pain of that woman was like, but I know my own, which has been silent. The day of the conference it was more than seven years since my daughter's death. Those nights after the workshop I wrote in my journal, talked with my partner, and looked at pictures of my own dead daughter, remembering as if watching the blur of rewind on the VCR. I had tried so hard to forget. I felt sorry for myself and angry with this woman I did not know for all the support I imagined she received, and for her ability to speak so freely of her loss.

I didn't like that I was still so angry and full of grief. I was ashamed to be resentful of a woman, a mother, I did not know. I was angry with the room of therapists and "professionals" at the conference who symbolized the ones who had failed to help me when I was so lost. As I sat with my terrible feelings, I realized what was happening to me. There was so much I had never been able to tell!

Our family was poor. I was a lesbian mother living openly with my partner. We were trying to raise five teenage girls and a young son.

Life as the mother of young daughters had been easier. From about six to ten or eleven they charmed me with their tenderness, generosity, open nature, playfulness and inhibition. Their wild sweetness was indescribable. The world of other mothers back then was friendlier and kinder, too. We enjoyed simple, benign interactions, discussing our children's development, comparing notes, commiserating about missed time for ourselves, watching our children play.

As my first daughter entered her teens, the lay of the land changed, and I began to lose my way. When my second daughter began late pre-teens, I stumbled and fell, losing my way completely. My often grandiose, oppositional ideas of how I would not be a mother like my mother were forgotten one by one.

By the time my daughter died from the complications of AIDS, our family had been under siege and "at risk" for a long, long time. I began to disappear from my job, friends, and social activities into grief and survivor's guilt. My fourteen-year-old daughter spent time on a locked psych unit for adolescents. Once when I visited her there I remember my numbness and my helplessness when she showed me a self-carved word on her stomach: It said "b-i-t-c-h."

Four of my girls survived their years as adolescents; feral, mysterious, changelings. Their sister did not. She too was pretty, bright, and funny. She was never able to be popular, struggling with addiction at fifteen. Her social skills became the skills by which she stayed alive on the streets for long, terrible years that ironically ended up being too short. After she died, I found a medical report in a box of her personal papers. The attending physician's report stated, "This deeply depressed, sad, very unfortunate twenty-one-year-old white female . . ." What mother can tolerate such a description? The words expressed a truth I would have given anything to change. How could I not have felt the torture of guilt? Where had all those teen years gone and what had I been doing?

At her funeral she had no peers. Most were dead or lost to the streets, addiction, and AIDS. Her ill husband could barely walk. At that time there was so much AIDS phobia and ignorance it was impossible to get support for my daughter, myself, or my family throughout her illness and death; her sisters and little brother were not offered any counseling.

In the long, long weeks after her death, only one person that knew her in our community left us a remembrance. One morning sitting on the front stairs, in the sun, was a note. It was written by a teacher who said she remembered a sweet, smiling little girl out on the playground and that she truly was sorry for our loss. For me it was a simple gesture of profound kindness and support.

This is how I started to write my story. Tired to the bone, mad as hell. There have been safe havens along this journey into the wilderness, a steadfast, fierce and loving partner and co-parent, a compassionate, radical therapist, who remained patient and human with me. Today, thankfully, some things (attitudes, ignorance) have changed as HIV, addiction, and violence have impacted more young women's lives. I still am angry and sad. I regret it was not different for my daughters. I regret it was not different for me. Yet struggling with this strange letter telling this to someone who cares so deeply about all of us is truly a remarkable thing.

Sunni Rose, California

Prone

Tasting the bitter stick
There I lie
Prone on the forest
Floor, sun shut
Out by tangled
Branches, cheek against
Moss as cold damp
Seeps through
My thin yellow dress.
Shivering I know
Your absence.
Alone, bones
Pressed against
Wet earth, mind reels
Against the blow.
Fearing animals
In the wood, I tremble,
Animal now myself.
Sometimes like faith
Brings me to petition,

(I hear Barbara say:
I have done it for myself.)
But I could not.
Help me rise, I asked. Or
Let me die.
And something
Brought me to
My feet.

Bettie Anne Doebler, Arizona

13

Discovering Boundaries: Saving Our Daughters, Saving Ourselves

We try and we try. We try when everyone else gives up, and we try when professionals tell us we should turn our energies elsewhere. Despite consistent recommendations to place Ellen in residential care, it was another thing I refused to do, sure she wasn't that sick. It was only in the fall of eleventh grade, when the physician who had cared for her over the entire three years of her illness spoke honestly to me, that I realized I could no longer fight the battle *for* Ellen.

"How's it going?" Dr. L. asked, as he always did at the beginning of our clinic visits. This time, he had come out to the waiting room where I sat alone, which I knew meant something was on his mind.

"Not too well." He'd heard that from me before; knew all the reasons that might be so: Ellen's school troubles, weight loss, worsening depression—I'm sure he had the list of her problems memorized as well as I did. Further, like me, he could sense when she was going downhill long before her weight dropped to life-threatening levels.

"What's going on?"

"Her rages are out of control. I'm afraid of her—we all are." I went on to describe her escalating anger and depression as well as the danger I felt we faced because of it. His eyes stayed neutral, even when I asked: "What do you think I should do?"

"I think it's time," was his answer. Usually, when I asked that question, he would shrug his shoulders and explain away my latest concern or come up with a plan: It was summer, and Ellen's life was unstructured; she would do better once her routine was in place, or the new medication hadn't started working yet, or, she was in an unfamiliar setting, and anxious. He had a way of normalizing her behavior that always helped me believe she would get better and that I could be the one to help make it happen. This day was different, though.

"She really needs something more," he continued. "I think she needs a long-term program. You've tried everything else possible for her."

It was hard to hear this from him, one of Ellen's strongest supporters, but I knew he was right. Somehow, an answer came to me through a trusted woman friend whose situation shared an eerie similarity to my own. There was a boarding school not far from our home in Hershey, Pennsylvania, that offered a strong academic program for "at-risk" youth and dealt with eating disorders, among other addictions. Paul and I went to visit and were told we had to make an eighteen-month commitment to keeping Ellen in the school, which was tough.

"If we make this commitment," I asked the admissions director, "will you commit to keeping Ellen?"

"We can handle her," he assured me. Still, I persisted, offering to share her medical records with him, but he said there was no need. They were more than capable of dealing with my daughter.

Paul and I were impressed by the kids we met during our tour of the school, which seemed far better than the residential care facilities we had been offered. Ellen would have a chance to graduate on time if she went to this school. Maybe the chance to do well academically, something she was more than capable of, would boost her self-esteem. Although she initially balked at the idea, within a week she agreed she needed more help and was willing to go.

Our entire family took her to be admitted. We could have been on our way to a vacation, the mood in our car was so hopeful. Once there, Ellen cried and begged us not to leave her. Sad to say, I was used to that behavior, but it still took some firm reminders from Paul about what a great opportunity this was for her to get me out the door and on the way home.

Two days later we got a call from the school informing us Ellen was being escorted back home. She was not cooperating, and had to be carried by other students to classes and meals. Her counselor was also worried about her weight and said the school wouldn't take her back until she gained at least ten pounds, even though she was thirty pounds heavier than she'd been the year before.

I took this decline worse than any other, because of the school's stated commitment to helping her recover, and realized I didn't have it in me to continue on the same path much longer. Ellen was admitted to a hospital in Philadelphia where she had spent several months during the first year of her illness. As I drove on the Pennsylvania Turnpike to visit her, I was overwhelmed by total despair, defeat, and hopelessness. I knew the road she was taking could lead to her death.

Don't cry when you see her, I warned myself, **tears won't help the situation any.** Yet when I arrived at the psychiatric unit and sat across from my daughter, I couldn't stop weeping. I was tired of "psych ward" talk: How's the new medicine working? Anything interesting happen in group this morning? How's the food? Did you sleep okay last night?

In that moment of not caring if she saw me sob, I realized I had no other choice but to set her free. I cried for her, for myself, and her father and brothers, sobbing uncontrollably because I had tried so very hard and failed so very badly. I had come to the point where I had to admit, for the first time, that I could not save her. If she was as determined to destroy herself as it appeared she was, I couldn't even get her committed to an institution where she would be safe: In our home state of Pennsylvania, children can sign themselves in and out of psychiatric facilities at age fourteen.

It was crushing to admit to myself there was nothing more I could do for my daughter—no new medicine I could suggest to her doctors, no new treatment facility, no new therapist, and no new approach at home. Despite all my attempts, none of it had worked, and now I was beginning to feel the threat of depression press in on me. The other members of our family were also starting to crack under the strain of living with Ellen. If something didn't change soon, there would be four sick people at our house instead of just one.

I can't say I gave up on Ellen at that point or that I stopped trying to find places for her to get help (she returned to the boarding school, was expelled again, and went on to the wilderness program). What did change were the things I told myself inside. Instead of chanting "She will get better," I tried to substitute "It's her choice." I began to think about how I could save the rest of our family, myself included, from going down with my daughter, if that was what was going to happen.

Not every mother who wrote to me reached the point of realizing she needed to begin taking care of herself and didn't have the ability to rescue her daughter, but many did. Some illustrations of this were more dramatic than others.

Grand Mother

"I am not raising another child!" is my visceral response to the announcement from my seventeen-year-old daughter and her boyfriend. Although the news of her pregnancy does not come as a total shock, given her irrational and rebellious behavior during the previous months, I am distraught. Their decision to have and keep this child seems rash and immature. They have known each other for four months. They have no idea.

My life is already stressful: I am working on a doctorate, anticipating a career in teaching. Throughout the past year I have wrestled with fears and personal issues related to codependency, relationships, and goals. Now I'm supposed to prepare a teenager for motherhood who has yet to learn to care for herself?

Breaking the news to her father, who is remarried and living in Arkansas, is hard. He is upset, and we talk long-distance many times, once breaking down and sobbing into the receiver over a shared sadness for our youngest child. Do we grieve over the loss of her innocence or our dreams? I only know that now we see her life as irrevocably changed, taking a direction that neither of us envisioned.

I am appalled to hear my daughter confer via telephone with teen friends who describe their experiences with pregnancy, labor, delivery, and child rearing. At the mall I see these child-mothers wheeling infants in strollers or balancing toddlers on jean-clad hips. I vent my dismay and fears openly to friends, family, and neighbors. At work, I end up talking with customers who reassure me that things will work out. Sometimes they let me hold a baby to test the feel of it in my arms.

My daughter tells me she intends to finish high school, but despite her good intentions, pregnancy leaves her feeling apathetic and sluggish. She begins missing classes and barely copes with her fast-food job. Eventually she drops out of school. She begins to physically and mentally anticipate the arrival of her baby, while her father and I are resigned to the situation.

Early one December morning I drive her to the hospital, and after an amazingly short labor, she gives birth to a son. In spite of the circumstances, I feel privileged to be present for Isaac Nathaniel's arrival into the world. I share the emotion of his shaken nineteen-year-old father, who is allowed to cut the umbilical cord as tears stream down his face.

From then on, my daughter begins to really understand the far-reaching effect of the birth of a child. She must drop the baby off at the sitter before work, but she's still, after all, a teenager. She doesn't always hang up wet towels or keep her bedroom floor clean, and at times dirty diapers pile to disgusting heights before she will take out the trash, but there are signs of progress. She wants to finish high school, get a better job, live in her own place, and attend college. Eventually, she will.

We experience bad patches, as well. A few weeks ago, after a sleepless night with the baby, my daughter says she can't handle it anymore, that she probably should give her son to someone who could take better care of him. She has even called her father and stepmother about it. This is not the first time she is torn between the life of a carefree eighteen-year-old and the weight of motherhood. Even mothers in the best of circumstances sometimes feel overwhelmed, I tell her, and believe me, all new parents go without sleep. We tough it out, and she hangs in.

Day by day, we move toward autonomy, my daughter and I. For the present, the biggest challenge lies in maintaining a balance between tending to my needs and encouraging my child to attend to hers; remaining available as helper, rather than doormat; serving as the baby's grandmother, not his primary caretaker; listening to my daughter more and nagging her less.

Sherry D. Engle, New York

How I Lost Control of My Daughter but Regained Control of My Life

It is impossible to love and be wise.
—FRANCIS BACON

Only a few times in our lives do we make a decision that has long-lasting effects—the kind of decision that changes our life, not for the moment, but for years ahead. Only when things go terribly awry do we realize just how much we have undertaken, and then it is too late.

Fifteen years ago, I decided to have a child on my own. A year after that, I decided to marry a man I had just met. I always joked that my daughter chose her father, and she did. She loved him from the beginning. I loved him too, but almost from the start of our relationship, I felt he needed to control me. Although we had violent, angry arguments for more than eleven years, I truly believed we had a "marriage," despite all the pain.

I was too caught up in my own survival to see what my children were learning from the violence. When he said that he would kill me, I knew things had gone too far. By this time, my daughter was nearly thirteen and our son was going on eleven. I asked my husband to leave, and thankfully, he agreed. But the damage had been done.

When he left, a great black cloud over our house left with him. Though things were better, all was not immediately well. It took nearly two years to get a divorce. He didn't want the children, yet he fought me over them all the way. During this time my daughter entered adolescence. At first it was mood swings, the usual "I love you" one day and "I hate you" the next. She was often angry with me—for cleaning her room, for "siding" with her brother, for allowing my boyfriend to move in. Then one day, at the worst point in the divorce proceedings and what I saw as a low point in my life, my daughter hit me.

I couldn't deal with this new problem: a year after my husband had left, I was still grieving the loss of my marriage, and the loss of any "normal" family life. I had lost my job, and the legal bills were mounting because the divorce that was supposed to have been final suddenly wasn't. And now, the violence I thought I'd escaped had returned, only my dear daughter was the perpetrator. I may not always know what I want or need, but I knew, after learning the hard way, what I could no longer tolerate: violence.

My mother had constantly offered to help, and while I had previously talked to my daughter about going to stay at her grandma's house for a while, she declined. She said she had friends and a life in our town and told me she loved me too much to leave.

All that changed when she put her fist in my face, and I reacted. Without further thought, believing I had no choice, I packed her up and sent her to my mother's house. When she realized she would not be returning home after a few days, she vowed never to forgive me for sending her away.

As when my husband left, life was instantly better. My son became an "only child" and his previous depression and self-esteem issues disappeared.

Immediately, I regretted my decision to send my daughter away. A month later, I asked her to return, but she said, "No, I'm doing well at grandma's house."

In the summer, she attended camp, and I assumed she would return in the fall, but it became apparent my daughter had made a commitment to staying angry. My mother was now unwilling to help me, she refused to acknowledge that I wanted my child back.

In September, against my wishes, my mother enrolled my daughter in the local high school. I still visited at least one weekend a month, but my daughter made it clear she wanted to stay where she was. Family members told me to leave well enough alone: if she was happy there (and she apparently was), why should I complain?

But I had much to complain about. My mother was making parenting decisions of which I did not approve. She allowed my fourteen-year-old daughter to work and drive a car, and refused to take her to a counselor.

One year after my daughter left, she suddenly decided she didn't want me to visit. When I asked, she was always "busy." I paid for her to participate in a sports league, but that activity prevented her from having time to spend with me. At the same time, she refused to tell me when or where she played so I could simply go and watch her. My mother conspired to keep me in the dark, under the guise of respecting my daughter's wishes.

By April, I was severely depressed again. It was bad enough having no control or involvement in my child's life, but having no opportunity to even see her was beyond comprehension. Why had this happened? How could I make it stop? I begged my mother to help, to send her home. My mother stopped talking with me then, and the one line I had for gaining information about my daughter's life was cut off.

I look back at this time as part of my own grieving. Elizabeth Kubler-Ross defined the five stages of loss as denial, anger, bargaining, depression, and acceptance. At different points during this two-year period, I went through every one of these emotions. It wasn't until "acceptance" that I realized that I needed to feel this pain and then move on with my life.

Six months after she cut me off, my daughter suddenly allowed me to see her. I spent a weekend with her and a friend, but she was in charge of what we did, just like she was in charge of her life. I gave her everything she wanted, and when she told me she was ready to return to grandma's house, I took her back—though I asked her repeatedly to return home (as I had every month since she left).

A week later, she called. She didn't want to live with grandma anymore, she said, but she didn't want to come home either. Of course, I went running. After I spent another weekend with her, she promised to move out of grandma's house, to go stay with a friend, and call me.

Then I lost her again: she never called. When I called my mother's house, no one answered. My phone calls were not returned. My mother's friends lied about my daughter's whereabouts.

I contacted the police. They weren't willing to pick her up, but they were willing to set up a meeting with a mental health counselor. When I went to this meeting, my daughter was in another room with "her attorney." Thus began a painful and draining legal battle.

By this time, I felt that I was experiencing the divorce all over again. The worst situation in my life was repeating itself—only this time, it was with my daughter. I could not understand how things had gotten to this point. I did not know how to stop the situation or control it.

I hired my own lawyer, who understood the juvenile law and began a proceeding in Washington state known as an "At Risk Youth" (ARY) petition. The ARY petition provides means for parents to regain control of their out-of-control youth. My daughter was exhibiting early at-risk behaviors: her grades had dropped from A's to C's and D's, she was skipping classes and was increasingly interested in boys and alcohol. She lied and refused help.

Based on these details, the judge granted me the petition and ordered my daughter home. I was elated, but on her first visit home in more than nine months, she became angry and hit me again. Then she left, refusing to visit again or to participate in joint counseling.

At this point, my mother hired her own attorney and filed suit for custody of my daughter. When she did this, she also asked for a restraining order, so that I would be prevented from picking up my daughter or seeking police intervention. My mother was granted an emergency order, and by the time I learned of it, it was too late to rescind. The court set a new hearing date.

The same judge returned to hear the request for temporary custody. It is here that I lost the war. My daughter had assaulted me, but because Washington state only has a mandatory arrest requirement for domestic violence offenders over the age of sixteen, as well as a "three strikes and you're out" rule, the judge let my daughter go. She gave my mother temporary custody, suggesting that we reconcile our differences before the trial date a year down the road. She set visitation and told my daughter if she didn't improve her grades, visit me, and go to counseling, she could be held accountable to the ARY. Then she closed the books on the case.

I cried for two days, then I accepted the situation. I never expected my daughter to visit—and she hasn't—but her grades have improved and she is apparently in individual counseling. I tried for weeks to work out a deal with my daughter's attorney, but to no avail (since she "won," she apparently had no more interest in legal proceedings). At this point my mother's suit is still pending, but my daughter will be nearly seventeen by the time that goes to trial.

Recently, my daughter and I have begun to talk through e-mail. In one month, we exchanged dozens of messages. Mostly I told her I loved her, and mostly she told me to "stop harassing" her. I am very thankful she is willing to write me, but cautious not to anger her. I don't want to be a victim again.

Violence is about control. My daughter and mother have tried to control me by forcing me to drop the ARY, by refusing visits, and so on, but no one can condemn, coerce, or control without permission. For years, I gave my husband permission to hurt me, and then I gave my daughter that power as well.

It was only when I accepted the fact that I have no control over the situation with her that I began to accept it. I have also learned that this loss in one part of my life has affected all parts of my life. My relationships with my partner, son, friends, and family, as well as my job, have all been affected by what happened with my daughter.

I know I have made mistakes and that I will continue to make mistakes, but I also know that taking responsibility for my mistakes and learning from them are what make me human. I have also learned that taking care of myself is paramount to recovery. I will recover from my failed marriage and more than a decade of violence and abuse, and the loss of my daughter by eating well, drinking a lot of water, working out, doing a job I love, walking every day, visiting with friends, getting support, and spending time with my son. I have felt my loss, I have experienced life without my daughter, and I have started working on myself.

I have accepted the choices I've made in this life and am letting go of control. If I don't want others to control me, then I cannot expect to control them. It's too late for me to "fix" my daughter's life, but she is strong and capable and I have faith in her ability to take care of her-self—she will have to do that, given the choices she has made. Still, I have hope for the future.

Melissa London, Washington

Change

Jenny will be seventeen this fall. She has failed her last three years of school, the last at an alternative school outside of our district. During this time, I have listened to countless teachers tell me that academically Jenny has no problem, but what she needs is to come to school and stay the whole day.

That isn't easy, because Jenny has a drug and alcohol addiction. She has been to a rehabilitation facility and tried outpatient therapy. Several physicians and psychologists have told her she has clinical depression and needs medication.

Both my former husband and I are recovering alcoholics. My mother committed suicide at the age of forty (I was twenty), and both of my children are chemically dependent. I mention this because I have a Master's Degree of Life in alcoholism and codependency. The truth is, our journey has been extremely painful, like surgery without anesthesia.

With Jenny, I yelled, screamed, threatened, tried to set boundaries and when I realized just how sick I was getting emotionally, physically and spiritually, I pulled myself out. When my thoughts of suicide were actually becoming a viable option, I knew things were *not good*.

Thanks to something more powerful than me, I realized that it was time for Jenny to reap the consequences of her behavior. I wrote to the State Board of Education, to see what alternatives there were since her school had said they were out of ideas and suggested I should be my child's advocate.

I pushed for her to be tested to rule out any learning disability. I offered her therapy and an appointment with her physician to make sure she got the appropriate medications. I did everything I could to help her succeed and try a different path. Then I just loved her up and watched. That is still the most difficult part.

I cannot fix Jenny or alter her path, so I simply give suggestions and keep on loving her. Jenny has mentioned getting her GED, works sporadically, and does not seem any happier. There's a saying: "If Nothing Changes, Nothing Changes."

Bonnie May Ostroski, Maine

All She Needs Is You

A friend told me last spring, "In all the time I have known you, the only time I have seen you truly happy is when you grabbed the bull by the balls and took control of your life."

This comment was made to me shortly after returning from Mexico, where my two teenagers and I had lived for six months. Upon our return I felt out of place in the United States, missing the sense of community that was ever-present in the small village in which we had lived. I missed the fact that it was okay for my kids to hang out with me, unlike here, where it is not cool to hang out with your mom.

The year leading up to our departure for Mexico had been full of painful and hard times with my daughter, then seventeen. She was by some standards acting out in a typical teenage fashion: lying, skipping school, and experimenting with drugs. However, to me it was much more than that: I was confused, and very frightened. My son, then fourteen, was concerned as well, and it seemed during this time that he and I bonded in a unique manner that was to be a pillar for us both in the weeks to come.

The first signs of trouble came during my daughter's sophomore year, when I noticed a drop in her grades, and more and more unexcused absences on her report cards. When I would confront her, she would either completely blow me off or give me such a logical explanation I couldn't say anything. Each time she would promise to change, I trusted her. Each time she told me it would never happen again, I believed her.

Once junior year rolled around, things began to get worse. I was receiving phone calls from the school on a regular basis with the message that my child had missed one or more periods that day. She could always convince me that everything was okay. Some weekends she would not come home at night but would show up the next day with loves and hugs, crawling into bed with me and each time assuring me that everything was fine.

There was more than one instance when I called the police and filed runaway charges, only to be told there was really nothing they could do. It was a frustrating dead end.

One thing that confused me the most was that when we were together, we got along beautifully. We communicated, laughed, and did fun things. It was only when we were apart that she made choices that ultimately came between us. It was because of the way we got along when we were together that made it impossible for me to follow through with any sort of discipline. When I did, things were catastrophic. There would be yelling and screaming and when I would attempt to keep her at home, it became physical more than once. She would threaten to call the police, claiming I was physically holding her. With all of the lawsuits children are bringing against parents anymore, I would back off, scared of being accused of child abuse. She knew just how to play me.

By this time, I suspected more than experimental drug use. I imagined that her drug of choice motivated all of her choices. I had a history of cocaine use during my marriage to her father, so I was familiar with the behaviors, the physical changes, and the various drugs available. My daughter had begun to lose weight drastically. She had always been heavier than many of her friends, but suddenly she was as thin or thinner than they were. It seemed as though her self-esteem had risen dramatically—on the outside. On the inside, however, I knew she was struggling like never before. Her actions were in direct opposition to her values and beliefs.

Early in the school year of her junior year, it became clear that I needed help. I am not sure what prompted it, but one day, I called her stepmother and one of my girlfriends who had worked at a drug treatment center. The three of us went to school, picked my daughter up, and took her to the local drug treatment facility. She was not at all surprised and was very cooperative. We spent several hours filling out the paperwork and evaluations, and after conferring with the doctors, came to the decision that she would participate in the outpatient program.

She attended and seemed to understand the magnitude of her choices. This went on for approximately six weeks, and then the rules changed, and she decided she didn't like the game anymore, so she stopped playing. We were back at square one.

The end of her junior year brought with it once again a report card with great grades, even in her advanced placement classes, but no credits due to unexcused absences. We met with her counselor and decided she would attend a full schedule of summer school, and night school first semester of senior year on top of her regular schedule. This would allow her to graduate with the friends she had grown up with, something she said was important to her.

The first month of summer school went great; she was attending classes and achieving her usual high marks. The semester ended the week prior to the Fourth of July bringing with it the beginning of the end.

My son and I left on Friday evening to attend a regatta approximately 100 miles north of us. My daughter and her girlfriend were to drive up the following day and camp with us. At the last minute, they decided not to come. It was a tough decision, but because she had been doing so well, I chose to trust her and continue with my plans.

When we arrived home on Monday, the house was trashed beyond belief. I don't mean destroyed, but garbage everywhere, and filthy. It was quite obvious she had had a major party. She was nowhere to be found, while a few of her not-so-close friends were hanging out on my front porch. She did not come home that night, or the next. I had been in contact with her best friend, who at this point was naturally very protective of her, but at the same time understanding my concern. Second semester of summer school was beginning, and she was missing classes. After several more days of her not coming home, I was to a point where I knew something drastic had to be done.

I found myself looking through the backs of magazines at the ads for camps for troubled teens. The previous year, a woman and her son had come into our office and told us about a program that he had gone to. It was a combination school and center for troubled teens. The curriculum included experiential workshops and events that focused on self-esteem. The school had three locations: Mexico, Jamaica, and Montana.

The thought of sending her away broke my heart, but the situation had gotten to a point where I feared for her life. Throughout the summer she didn't come home, but her friends would call me and let me know she was okay. They were all concerned as well and were a strong base of support for me.

In July I met with the young man who had participated in this program. He told me he normally didn't like to meet with the parents to discuss the school, but for some reason he was compelled to meet with me. He told me that while the program did get him on the right track, if there is any better way, find it. He also told me these unforgettable words: "All she needs right now is you." (Shortly after arriving in Mexico, I came upon an article in a magazine describing the horrors and abuse that took place in these programs.)

I realized after that conversation that he was right. I had been working full-time and available every day, all day, for my clients. In making myself available to this extent, I had been neglecting my family for at least three years. I had trusted that my mature, wise, trustworthy daughter (and son) could take care of themselves. They said they didn't need me or want me around, and I believed them. Unfortunately I have later realized that those words in "teen talk" actually mean, "We need you, we want you, we just don't want to know you are there."

During this period, a friend of mine had leased a house in the jungle just outside of a small fishing village north of Puerto Vallarta. He had offered to lend me the place several times, as he only went down two or three times a year. After hearing the words "All she needs is you" and having them hit home, I e-mailed my friend and asked him how long we could stay in his house. His reply, "As long as it takes."

For the next two weeks I researched what it would take to move to Mexico. The library was a great resource, as was the Internet. I read about working, traveling, visas, passports, eating/drinking, vehicle registration, bringing animals into the country (we took our Malamute-Wolf mix and our English Setter with us!), everything I thought I could possibly need to know to make this decision. I literally had no money for this adventure, as we had been going in the hole for the few months prior to this.

On August 5, I spoke the words clearly and confidently first to my coworkers, to classmates at my twenty-year high school reunion that evening, and the next morning to my mom and her husband: "We are moving to Mexico next month." Naturally, there were many questions, fear, and excitement.

On September 12, 1999, we packed our final belongings into the Trooper and pulled out of Boise at 6 P.M. That night, through tearful eyes, we watched the town we had called home for fifteen years go by in a blur, not knowing what was ahead of us and not having any definite plans. This was the end of all we had ever known, and the beginning of all we would come to know.

That was a little over a year ago. We stayed in Mexico for six months, and hated leaving, but due to visa limitations and obligations in the States, we packed our belongings and headed north. We arrived back in Idaho the first week in April—just in time for my daughter's eighteenth birthday. We had decided to let go of our house in Boise and move to a small tourist town in the mountains with a beautiful lake—my hometown. The plan was to stay for the summer and then go back to Mexico.

My daughter decided to stay and live in Boise. She was there until mid-June, when she moved back in with us, got a job, and began to show me through her actions that the choice I had made the previous summer had made a difference in her life as well as ours. She stayed with us for a couple of months before moving back to Boise and landing a terrific job. She is now drug free, a licensed child-care provider, and living a life that is creative, inspiring, and full of love.

Kim Hess, Idaho

PART FIVE

Part of the Picture:
Significant Others

14

Ophelia:
With and Without Fathers

In the second year of Ellen's illness, I found myself following the ambulance transporting her up a road that curved its way around the side of a mountain. At the top was a sprawling brick building where Ellen had been involuntarily committed for the next sixty days. It was late afternoon, and the sun reflected off the windows of the hospital in sparks of light that made me squint. The paved road gave way to gravel that crunched under my tires like breaking glass as we drew near the entrance.

The ambulance and my car pulled to a stop in unison, and I began the process of admitting Ellen. Unlike the first, or second, or third and fourth times she'd needed hospitalization, I was making the trip alone, since it required nearly a full day off work. At the time, my job was more expendable than my husband's.

"Hi, Mrs. Dellasega." A social worker greeted me with a big smile, then turned, still beaming, to Ellen. "Hello, Ellen." I supposed she was trying to be kind, but the continuing grin seemed out of place.

After all the forms were completed and Ellen was admitted, I made the two-hour drive home alone. My husband and I alternated visits after that, trying to make sure she saw one of us every week.

We're lucky—we have each other. Although he and I cope with Ellen's illness in entirely different ways (he works harder to make more money so we can afford care, while I arrange for and help deliver that care), there are two of us, which means twice as many vacation days to take off for her and double the adults to divide attention between the competing demands of our family.

The stories that follow made me realize how fortunate I have been to have a reliable husband who was always there for Ellen when she needed him. How much harder it must be to make this journey without the presence of another adult who may be the only one who truly understands and shares your pain!

Finding others to help is a critical survival strategy for mothers of struggling daughters. When fathers aren't available, grandparents, church members, and friends fill the void for some women. Incredible support has come from unexpected places, too: a teacher, a sibling, or a coach.

And of course there is the amazing solace that comes from other wise women whose journeys are similar to our own. I hope that my experience of discovering a vast but invisible network of moms like myself will free parents to reach out in their own communities and find the help they need.

On My Own

I gather that you are in the process of raising an adolescent and wondering how to get through this ordeal. I'm here to tell you that it is survivable and that eventually you may even celebrate the results of "hanging in" with your child(ren) through this challenging time!

Perhaps I've already provided the clue that indicates my children are (finally) grown. As a former single mom of two, I am experiencing immense gratification, knowing that my children are now well-adjusted, independent, happy, self-supporting members of society. Maybe just reading this will provide encouragement to moms in the midst of their children's adolescence, who are wondering whether it's all worthwhile. The rewards will come, I assure you, if you take time away from the task, do what you think is best, ask for guidance, support, and backup, when needed—and keep breathing!

My children's father and I were divorced when my daughter was nine, her brother six. It was in the months leading up to this devastating experience that I first got an inkling of how difficult surviving the adolescent years might be. We'd taken our daughter, B., to a therapist, at my insistence, after she tearfully proclaimed that she'd "just like to disappear." To me, this signaled a dreadful warning, not to be ignored; to her father, "she just needs more discipline."

The indication of future challenges came in the therapist's statement, "You and your daughter will have trouble separating when she's older because you're so much alike." At the time, I saw this as a relatively useless observation; I was far more focused on helping my daughter (and son, of course) survive the impending divorce. Little did I know that this prediction was significant. B. and I would eventually spend several years with our horns locked in an often vicious struggle for her independence, and my sanity!

I recall one prevalent internal experience during my children's teenage years: an intense "aloneness" when they were challenging me and my right to be "in charge." While at times I was certain my children would absolutely destroy one another in the throes of their sibling rivalry, when it came to supporting one another in their struggles with me, they were as thick as thieves! It was extremely painful, knowing that I needed to be strong enough to stick to my disciplinary guns, without anyone there to support me or back me up.

Fortunately, I was wise enough to connect with other single parents and find ways of verbalizing my angst, so I got support away from home. But those moments of standing firm with my decisions, by myself, while my children stuck together like glue, were sometimes enough to reduce me to blubbering. How I longed for a partner, beside me, occasionally stepping in and taking over the grind, telling my kids such things as, "Don't you dare speak to your mother like that!"

I have vivid memories of instances in dealing with my offspring that required calling in reinforcements, i.e., the police. This was not because my children had broken any laws, it was because I was alone and needed help! I believe this actually happened only once, when my fourteen-year-old ran out the door after a blowup with me; she was barefoot, it was dark and December, and we lived in Massachusetts! Having no idea where she had gone, I called for help—and I got it. In retrospect, my insight regarding this action was that I would do whatever seemed necessary, in the moment, to handle a difficult situation. I'm convinced this style of dealing with such challenges provides children with the security of knowing no matter what they do, Mom won't give up on them.

It occurs to me that much of today's laxity of guidelines and excessive permissiveness results from parents' feelings of guilt about being away from their children so much of the time. I, too, was extremely busy with college courses and employment, but this may be where single parenting was of benefit to my kids. When I was with them, they often got my undivided attention, since there was no husband or partner vying for my time. This, of course, is a two-sided coin; they also lacked a father's daily guidance, wisdom, discipline, and loving attention and were not privy to the invaluable lessons inherent in seeing two parents sharing their love and commitment to one another and their family.

In looking back, I wish I had remained more patient with my parental responsibilities during my daughter's high school years, perhaps being at home a bit more. My son had moved to a distant state to live with his father, so my daughter and I had three years to ourselves. Even today, B. remembers with noticeable resentment that I didn't seem to be around for her very much. My memory contrasts with hers; when I was home, she was the one who was seldom around. I'm afraid one or both of us have distorted the real scenario. Suffice it to say that any amount of attention from me probably wouldn't have made up for the absence of her brother and father, but I've always been the "safest" one to blame.

Blaming Mom is an important topic. I believe one must learn to withstand it—unscathed, if possible. Our interactions with our children can be the source of much of their anger and disappointment, a natural result of a parent's need to stifle one's offspring, at times. Holding fast to our standards and allowing our children to hate us, on occasion, is mature and responsible, and it provides the opportunity to stay firm in our loving, despite the wrath of our progeny. What better way for a child to learn that a human can dislike or censor another's behavior, while maintaining affection for that person? Could this be the true test of a loving parent: to love a kid—and herself—enough to be, temporarily, despised by that child?

Leslie Hilburn Fabian, Massachusetts

Daddy Died, Leaving a Wife and Daughter

In retrospect, I was often uncomfortable in the normal school atmosphere with peer parents. My daughter always attended private Catholic schools and I was acutely aware that I was a single mom; my husband died when she was only two. We were different, but it was not by choice. I wondered now if I was not a bit defensive about it and whether I unknowingly passed on my own feelings of parenting/family inadequacy to my daughter.

There were many school functions, plays and programs where two allotted seats went to the parents, and in the beginning I went and sat next to "the empty seat," where her father should have been. "The empty seat" that would have and should have been shared by the only other person who would fully understand the pride I had known with our daughter.

After a few years of this, I stopped going to these functions altogether and found other ways to celebrate with my daughter. This was my attempt to move away from "the empty seat." Again, years later, I wonder if perhaps these actions may not have led to some antisocial or some self-esteem issues. Of course, I could not see the harm in it at that time.

I believe that my daughter never really understood the loss of her dad or death until her senior year in high school. That year, one of her close classmates unexpectedly died. This brought to the surface so many feelings my daughter had yet to deal with: grief, rage, and anger. These were traits and characteristics that previously never described her.

She had one foot already headed out the door. Colleges had accepted her, she was working part-time, and her boyfriend took up a lot of her time. Somehow my influence was diminished.

We did not have the normal mother-daughter struggles that are really a natural progression to independence. I believe she would say I loved her and worked hard to keep it all together and going. I also believe she tried to keep the waters calm, even to her own detriment. The biggest problem was the type of boyfriends she would attract: men who were consistently less intelligent and motivated than she was

We had counseling and we had some family support. As a surviving parent and mother of a child, I would later learn just how easy I was to manipulate. I have read that all children test and manipulate to one degree or another. However, a surviving spouse with a child is an easy target for manipulation. You will feel sorry for your child, you will try and make up for this tremendous loss, but in the end that is the *worst* thing you can do.

Talk to your child, cry with your child, grieve with your child and remember crying never hurt anyone. As with any rainstorm, the sun will shine all the brighter when the rain is gone.

Bernadette A. Moyer, Maryland

My Journey with Amanda

At age forty-five, I was on my own after twenty-three years of marriage, a student at the University of Calgary, majoring in English literature with two children at home. My eldest daughter was doing well in her first year of university. My nine-year-old son was succeeding in school but was too quiet and I was worried about his lack of friends. On top of all this, my middle daughter, Amanda, had been permanently expelled from our city's high school for fighting, and I was now driving her fifteen miles up the highway to a school in another small town.

"Are you Amanda's mother?" A friendly face peered in my open car window when I came to pick her up shortly after she started there.

"Yes," I answered with some uncertainty, "Yes, I am."

"I'm Nancy Miller, one of Amanda's teachers. May I tell you what a lovely daughter you have?"

Completely taken back, I stammered "Why thank you."

Was she talking about my daughter—Amanda?

"She really is just delightful to teach, so funny . . . a pleasure in the classroom."

How much should I reveal? This teacher in my daughter's new school obviously did not know my daughter well. I murmured something about being happy to hear such comments, and, as she walked away with another teacher, I allowed myself to hope that this time, things would be better: Amanda would make friends with positive people, attend classes regularly, and stay out of trouble. The fall prairie sun was shining as Amanda and I drove home, chattering happily about the school's upcoming basketball tryouts. The teacher's words were still dancing about in my heart.

A short time later, I sat in Ms. Miller's office beside my daughter waiting for the vice principal to come and address us both, feeling like I was on trial along with my daughter. In all my life, I had never been called to a principal's office for any reason, but I was there now because I had failed as a parent. Amanda's crime: a substitute teacher had been humiliated and distressed to the point where she had fled to the office weeping and vowing never to teach the class again! My daughter had been the leader of the group of students who had caused and encouraged the situation. She faced expulsion from school for two weeks.

Amanda's face was surly.

She looked at me and through gritted teeth muttered, "Don't you dare cry!"

That did it. As Ms. Miller walked through her office door, tears splashed down the front of my blue silk blouse. I remember only one statement the vice principal made during that meeting, which resulted in Amanda being readmitted to the school. It was a turning point for me, if not for my child.

"Amanda," Ms. Miller said, "it's time for your mother to stop caring so much and time for you to start caring more!"

Several months passed reasonably smoothly. Amanda joined the drama club and made the school's basketball team. I was eager to show my support by driving her to the Saturday games in several of the small towns in the area. She would never really open up on our long drives together, but I plodded on. She spent long periods of time writing reams of poetry in her journals and painting pictures of flowers and of wild-eyed women with red lips and huge eyes. At home her confidant was her three-legged cat, Thomas.

Then came the incident that put us on the warpath again. One Friday night she and a girlfriend who was sleeping over stole my car in the early hours of morning, went on a joyride with several classmates, and ended up in a ditch. Eventually, the car had been pulled out by a rope attached to the flimsy bumper, which pulled it loose. Several days after this incident, unaware of the bumper's condition, I made the usual trek down the highway and onto the gravel road to Amanda's school to pick her up when I heard a strange noise. As I slowed down and glanced in my rearview mirror I was horrified to see the plastic bumper on my new après-divorce car fly off. Immediately, I pulled the car over, warily got out, and pulled the mangled piece of plastic from the mud. This had to do with Amanda. Driving on, clenching my teeth, I felt crazed.

Would my insurance cover the cost of a new bumper? No. I had to borrow the money to replace it.

Amanda and I stopped speaking. We were on our second counselor, as the first one said she felt unqualified to handle Amanda. I was encouraged to read books on parents who love too much, and Amanda started anger management therapy. The new therapist felt that I should lock my daughter out of the house if her curfew was not kept, but I could not agree to this. I recognized the need to establish firm boundaries, but my main concern was protecting Amanda from herself. I remembered several news stories where teens had been locked out of their homes and the results had been fatal.

It was many weeks before Amanda was allowed out of the house on weekends. One night she called me from a friend's house asking permission to stay overnight. After reminding her of our agreement that I pick her up at ten o'clock, she asked me if I would speak to her friend's father.

An adolescent male voice came over the phone, "This is Mr. Jones speaking. Can Amanda stay all night?"

"And how old are you?" I queried. "Nice try, Amanda," I told her, "but I'll be there in fifteen minutes. Be ready!"

It wasn't long before Amanda was expelled from school for the second time, again for fighting with another girl. I was expected to appear in order to have Amanda reinstated in class, but I remembered Ms. Miller's words from the last interview and decided for the first time to make Amanda responsible for her actions. She would stand alone. Surprisingly, Amanda calmly accepted my nonparticipation and must have done a splendid job of convincing the authorities, because that Monday morning she returned to class.

During these years the local police were frequent callers. One night a group of about seven kids formed a posse to revenge an alleged attack by Amanda. They began pummeling my living room windows with stones and kicking at my front door so hard my son and I were fearful they would break into the house. Shaking, I ran to my room and dialed "911." I later learned four of my neighbors had also called the police, who arrived quickly, but not before one of the girls kicked in the glass on my front door.

About this time my university "B" average began to decline. I just couldn't take any more and didn't know where to turn. I remember sitting beside Amanda in the new therapist's office. Behind a mirrored window sat a psychiatrist and several students of social work. Completely stressed out, I put my hands over my face and began to sob.

"I'm afraid I'm not going to be able to graduate. I'm afraid I'll become a bag lady."

"What do you think of that, Amanda?" asked Linda, our Ph.D. therapist. "Your mother feels like she can't continue her studies."

"My mother will survive. I think she'll be okay."

I looked at her in astonishment. Clearly this girl had no real grasp on all she was putting me through.

"You don't understand! I feel like I'm trying to swim across a lake with a brick tied to my waist!" I cried.

Amanda never did finish the school year. She ran away for a week to a small town with two of her girlfriends, returned, and spent the rest of the semester at home. That fall she went 1,500 miles away to my mother's home. My mother was certain that with the right discipline and firm boundaries she could help Amanda complete high school. This gave me a reprieve and allowed me to graduate, but Amanda obtained only a few more credits for eleventh grade before my mother was forced to ask her to leave.

My daughter arrived back at the airport looking completely un-apologetic, accompanied by a friend. Sherry, unlike previous friends,

was blond, vivacious and funny, and I really liked her. The girls had decided to work as cashiers for the summer at the Calgary Stampede and
Exhibition and would be sharing Amanda's room at home. The summer
went smoothly, with me driving the girls into town and picking them
up again in the late evening. With Sherry acting as a buffer, Amanda and
I did not discuss the previous months at her grandmother's. I was content to let peace reign and hope for the best.

At the end of the Stampede, the girls announced that they had decided to continue working with the exhibition and would follow it to
Toronto. I was not worried, knowing that the employees at the exhibition were like a family. I felt that the girls would be safe enough, and
my leap of faith was justified. By the summer's end Amanda not only
had a healthy bank balance but confidence in her work ethic and an
ability to live on her own.

Once back at home, she was offered a job working as a babysitter.
Martha, a woman Amanda had worked with at the Stampede, had a husband who was frequently out of town and needed a live-in caretaker for
her two daughters. Amanda was very good with the girls. She initiated
bedtime prayers and stories, as well as grace before meals. She seemed
to be remembering and implementing the very traditions she had experienced as a little girl. This surprised me, because I had almost forgotten about the things Amanda and our family shared, once upon a time.
It touched me that she had not. I found her surprisingly patient with
the children and once, when she thought I wasn't, she reminded me:
"Mom, they're just little!"

Eventually, she began to complain about being housebound with two
preschoolers. She cooked as well as cleaned and complained she wasn't
appreciated. I would nod and inwardly smile. When word arrived that
two of her friends were pregnant (unfortunately, one was Sherry), she
recoiled in horror, although she remained supportive until they each
gave birth. She kept in touch with her older sister, who was now working in a small-town high school teaching French, and vowed to complete her high-school diploma someday. I suggested she take an evening
class, but my words fell on deaf ears.

After a year, Amanda left her babysitting job and moved out into a
basement apartment in an old house. She began waitressing at a neigh-

borhood Greek restaurant and soon was made manager of the upstairs bar. She walked to and from work on aching legs, but her resolve was quietly building.

Today, at twenty-three, Amanda has grown into a caring and loving person, with a wonderful sense of humor. She lives in a downtown high-rise with her sister and works in a restaurant. The energy she used to put into anger now furthers her ambitions, and during the day she faithfully attends classes to fulfill requirements for her high school diploma. She maintains a B-plus average, and has a goal to enter nursing school. She has written many letters of apology and suffers because the relationship with her grandmother appears to be permanently scarred. Whenever she recalls the past she is quick to apologize to me for all the trouble she caused. My reply is that I have forgiven her and she must now forgive herself.

And on we march!

Karen Lowes, Canada

What role do fathers play when they are present? I was surprised by how often fathers *weren't* mentioned—in some stories, it's impossible to tell if the mother is currently married or not. That may be because they, like me, saw themselves as the person who most often actively intervened to deal with family problems. They were the ones who sensed when something was wrong, sought solutions, and tried to be involved in helpful ways.

Still, I have met and corresponded with many fathers who are extremely concerned about their daughters and intent on helping them in any way possible. In most cases that translated into being the "breadwinner" so a mother's effort was freed to focus on their struggling daughters. While no mother has told me she found it difficult to talk to her daughter about problems, fathers have said that discussing emotional issues was nearly impossible for them. Often, even talking or writing to me about the situations their girls were wrestling with was extremely distressing for dads.

The moms I have talked with describe the difference between themselves and their spouses this way: Mothers worry silently and continuously and, given the right circumstances, will talk about what's on their minds. Fathers, on the other hand, worry intensively, try to fix things immediately, and, if unsuccessful, go off to distract themselves with work or leisure activity. It was no big surprise to me when a recent report confirmed that men and women handle stress differently, with males gearing up for the traditional "fight-or-flight" response, and females "nesting" to protect their children and turning to friends for comfort.

The following story is a perfect illustration of the way mothers respond to situations in comparison to fathers. While Dale's husband was very involved in the trial they encountered, she was the one to recognize the emotional implications of what happened and to write poignantly about her feelings.

Skipping School

When I was in the seventh grade, I considered writing a book about what it felt like to be a seventh-grader. I wish I had. If I'd had that book the day our crisis occurred, maybe I would have had some insight into what my daughter was thinking. Instead, it came without warning, and our family was thrust into a nightmare that changed us forever.

8:15 A.M.: David, Karen's father, drops her off at school and heads for work. Karen waits until he leaves and then walks two miles to Peter's house.

10 A.M.: We receive the first sign of something amiss when the school secretary makes a routine telephone call to inquire about Karen's absence. Since David's office is two miles from the school and mine thirty minutes away, he is the designated parent in case of emergencies, so the secretary calls him.

Absent? How could Karen be absent? He had dropped her off at the door, watched her walk up the wide cement steps, reach out and take hold of the shiny brass door handle—and then he'd driven away. What could have happened in the next few seconds?

David thought a moment. "Have you spoken to Karen's friends?"

The secretary verifies they had. She pauses a moment and then offers the only clue. "There is an eighth-grade boy," she says. "His name is Peter and he is also absent."

David lets the implications of this information sink in.

"Peter's sister is flying home from college today," the secretary continues, "and he was supposed to go with his parents to pick her up. Yesterday he mentioned to some of the boys that he planned to tell his parents he was sick so he could stay home and watch cartoons. Karen has shown some interest in this young man. Perhaps—we don't know—it's a possibility she might be at his house."

When David calls me with the news, I am stunned. Up to this point, Karen has been a superior student with a level head. Skipping school to spend the day with a boy is out of character.

I put a lot of time, thought, and care into parenting our daughters and pride myself with the fact that I know them well. Now a wedge of doubt pokes its way into my psyche. Certainly there would have been a sign of some sort? What kind of a mother would have missed it? Who was I trying to fool—thinking I was a good parent?

Although we were confused about Karen's actions, we were still thinking clearly. What we needed to do seemed simple enough—find out exactly where Peter lived, call the house, see if Karen was there, pick her up, and deliver her back to school.

10:30 A.M.: No answer at Peter's house, even though we would later learn that Peter and Karen had really been sitting on the couch watching *Scooby Doo*. The school thought he was at the airport, so he didn't dare answer the phone.

10:45 A.M.: No answer at Peter's house.

11:00 A.M.: No answer at Peter's house.

12:05 P.M.: David parks in front of Peter's house and rings the doorbell twice. No one answers.

David called me at work after each of these occurrences to discuss our options. We hashed and rehashed the possibilities. By this time we had advanced to mild irritation with our teenager—it wasn't dark, so the strangling fear hadn't yet set in. We concurred that Karen would certainly appear at school dismissal—unaware the secretary had notified us of her absence.

3:30 P.M.: Karen does not appear at school dismissal. I encourage David to wait, certain she will show up. Meanwhile, Karen was sitting on the steps of her friend Jackie's apartment building three blocks away, confident that she had pulled it off. In the morning, she had told her sister, Laurel, about her plan for the day, concluding with, "After school, tell Dad I had to borrow something from Jackie. Have him pick me up there." She waited smugly for him to come.

4:00 P.M.: Karen is still not at the school. Without a dress rehearsal, Laurel, twelve, unorganized and forgetful, has missed her cue. She offers no information to David.

Jackie tells Karen what happened that day at school: "Everyone's talking about you. They think you and Peter did something. One of the teachers said, 'This is another Bill Clinton–Gennifer Flowers situation.'" Karen is stunned.

4:30 P.M.: David calls me for about the fiftieth time that day. We decide he should come home and we'll manage the situation from there. A chill creeps through me. If Karen did not spend the day at Peter's house, where was she? Surely Peter's parents wouldn't take her to New York without consulting us. Were Peter's and Karen's absences unrelated? Had we wasted valuable time on an erroneous assumption?

David pulled out of the school parking lot, feeling much like a father who finally makes the decision to turn his boat towards shore after his daughter disappeared beneath the waves.

Laurel nonchalantly asked, "Aren't you going to pick up Karen?"

"What are you talking about?" he asked. "How can I pick up Karen when I don't even know where she is?"

4:45 P.M.: Karen is surprised her father hasn't picked her up yet. She walks to the school, hides behind a tree, but doesn't see his car anywhere. She returns to Jackie's house, confused.

Once home, Laurel slips the cordless phone into her bedroom and whispers to her friend Stephanie, "My father says he won't pick up Karen."

Stephanie calls Alison. "Karen's father is so mad at her, he refused to pick her up at Jackie's."

Alison calls Jackie. "Karen's father is so mad at her, he doesn't ever want to see her again."

5:30 P.M.: Jackie gives Karen the news and the girls close in around her—the poor thing whose teacher thinks she did an immoral thing, the poor thing whose father never wants to see her again. They will take care of her. She can live in somebody's attic. They'll bring her food. The boys rally around Peter. One whisks him off on a bicycle to hide out at a friend's.

Despite the school's assurance that Karen's friends knew nothing, I decide to call them, starting with Jackie. "Jackie," I say, quelling a racing heart. "Have you seen Karen?"

"No," she answers. "I heard she's missing."

I call Julie. I call Roberta. I call Melissa. No one knows a thing but promises if she hears, she will call and let me know. Julie and Roberta and Melissa call Jackie and Jackie fills in Karen.

6:00 P.M.: We call the police.

"What is the nature of your emergency?" the officer asks. "Your call is being recorded."

I fight to keep my voice calm. "My daughter is missing," I say. I hear the words from down a long tunnel. My hands are ice. A vision flashes before me—Karen, mutilated, in a dumpster. "My husband dropped her off this morning—"

The police file a report, drive by Peter's home, knock on Peter's door. Only echoes respond.

8:30 P.M.: It is dusk now, and Karen has not been seen by anyone in more than twelve hours. I stand in front of the stove. We are hungry, so I cook something. The three of us take our places, leaving one empty seat. The table is in front of a picture window; beyond it the night closes in around us like a suffocating black blanket. In the silence, I am struck with the thought that *somebody* has to know *something*. I turn to Laurel.

I looked her in the eye and ask firmly: "Do you know where Karen is?"

"No," she says, shrugging. "She was at Melissa's but she isn't there anymore."

David and I erupt, screaming: "Why didn't you tell us?" "How long have you known this?" "What—" "Why—" "When—"

Laurel eyes David coolly, believing the convoluted story that started with her own mixed-up one-liner that we didn't even know yet. "You said you were so mad at Karen you didn't want to see her again."

"What are you talking about?"

I heard my normally calm husband lose it as I dashed for the phone.

Melissa denies knowing anything. I press and press. I tell her I know she knows. There is silence and then she says: "She's at Jackie's."

I call Jackie but cannot break her down. Seventh-grade girls are invincible in protecting or attacking each other.

I remember my friend Betty who lives in the same apartment building. I call, ask her to put down the phone, knock on Jackie's door, and see if Karen is there. She returns in two minutes with the pronouncement, "She's there."

I call Jackie again, my voice allowing no argument. "Betty just saw Karen. Put her on."

9:00 P.M.: I have found my daughter, but I do not know the one who takes the receiver and, with icy voice, refuses to come home. I tiptoe into this unfamiliar arena, cautious, wary.

"May I come and see you?" I ask, grasping at the only possibility I see towards understanding and reconciliation.

She agrees, then forcefully asserts, "Don't bring Dad."

I drive the twenty-five pitch-dark miles with a racing mind. What had happened? Why did it happen? Will she be there when I arrive or will she have run again? How will I handle this? I want to give her a piece of my mind. I want her to know what she put us through. I want to snap her back into place, to regain control.

As I weigh options, it is not a child psychology book I turn to for answers, but a real estate seminar I recently attended. "Let them speak first," the moderator said, and I decide to try it.

Karen rises from the steps when I pull up in front of the apartment building. She looks like she's been through a war, hair askew, slacks and shirt wrinkled and dirty. Her face is tight, her eyes daring me to even try to make her do anything she doesn't want to do. This is not the girl I sent to school that morning.

She gets in the car and we drive off. A few blocks away, I pull to the side of the road and cut the engine.

I turn to Karen and ask softly, "Can you tell me what happened?"

Crying and angry, she tells me the details, beginning with Peter's decision to cut school to watch cartoons and how she thought it would be funny to surprise him at the door. She tells me how she spent an innocent day with Peter, but then found out her Dad said he was so angry he never wanted to see her again. She describes her teacher's comment about a "Bill Clinton–Gennifer Flowers" situation and knows that all the students in the class are talking and saying she did things she didn't do.

In that moment, I am glad I let her speak first. My answer is not angry, but compassionate. She has already suffered the consequences of her own actions—there is no need for me to add additional pain to her wounds. I assure her that Dad never said what she thinks he said and ask if there's anything I can do for her now. She is not convinced about her father and will not come home. She asks me to talk to her teacher, so I do.

9:45 P.M.: I drop Karen back at Jackie's, where she will spend the night since it's Friday. I drive to her teacher's house, knock, and we talk. He is shocked when I attribute the Bill Clinton line to him, telling me it was a student comment, not his.

By the next afternoon, Karen reluctantly agreed to come home, and we spent a low-key weekend, trying to regroup.

The following Monday, I arrange with the principal to meet the seventh-grade girls—the same girls who had closed around Karen in protection, the same girls who had told me they knew nothing, the same girls who now participated in the false rumor that Karen had been promiscuous. The principal ushered them into her office without explanation, and each of them gasped when they saw me.

I began speaking and Melissa interrupted. "May I say something?" she asked.

"No," I said, staring her down. "You had the opportunity to speak on Friday and you didn't. Today is my day to talk." My tone was firm, not betraying the uncertainty I felt inside. "For nearly twelve hours, we didn't know if our daughter was dead or alive," I said. "When I called each of you for help, you didn't respond. I thought she was mutilated in a dumpster somewhere." Their heads were down and shoulders drooped. "Words were twisted and repeated in error so that Karen had nowhere to turn. She thought she couldn't come home. I'd like to think girls can always talk to their parents, but perhaps sometimes they can't. I'm going to ask Karen, and I'm asking you girls now—think of another adult that you can call collect anytime if you are in trouble and feel you can't call your parents. Choose someone you respect, an adult who can put a little perspective on things. I'd be happy to be that person for any of you—"

Within a week, summer vacation began, a time of healing. Somehow we patched our family together and limped on. It was over, but it wasn't over. We were changed. A marked awareness of vulnerability had seeped into my soul, and with chilling realization: I could not protect my daughter from everything in this world. She now possessed the power to bring tremendous harm to herself if she chose.

I began to doubt my ability to be a good parent. Karen had entered a gray land and I questioned whether I would be able to see through the mist to adequately interpret her intentions and say the right words so she would hear and heed. She was at a time of life when I could not afford to be naïve but, by the same token, to unjustly accuse might elicit the very behavior I was seeking to avoid. No ground seemed safe—it all oozed uncertainly beneath me.

Living in the shadow of Karen's marred reputation was probably the most difficult residual effect of the whole episode. Rumors about her promiscuity would not die. Four years later, an adult who had heard a twisted version of the story passed it on to a young man Karen was dating.

"Is this the kind of girl you want to be involved with?" she asked.

Karen and I now have a good relationship. I like this part of parenting—she is a competent college graduate, living on her own, responsibly and thoughtfully choosing a path for her life. We talk, laugh, and share experiences.

I wouldn't go back to the teen years for anything. There's still too much hurt there.

Dale Slongwhite, Massachusetts

15

Little Girl Grown:
Daughters Look Back

I hadn't anticipated receiving letters from daughters who had gone through crises in their teens and survived, but I did—so many that I decided to include a selection of them to show how they perceived the difficult years mothers were also writing about. These were the stories that offered the most hope to me, since they provided the wisdom of a glance back on adolescence. Based on their messages, I will never stop believing Ellen can recover and lead a wonderful life that satisfies her and reassures me that she is healthy and happy.

In three cases (noted at the end of these stories), the daughters of mothers who wrote stories included in the previous chapters offer their own perspective here. Reading about struggles from both the mother's and the daughter's perspective was a special gift, because it provided proof of the solidarity of maternal relationships, during and after troubled times.

Family Story

As a career officer, my father would take my family wherever the navy needed him, which meant we moved frequently. I knew my mother didn't like it. She was born and raised in a very large, stable family, living in the same town until she married. My grandparents still live in the same house to this day and just celebrated their sixtieth wedding anniversary last month.

Unfortunately, what my father despised in his own father was the exact same thing he became himself: a drinker. If he wasn't working thirteen-hour days, he was at the Officer's Club drinking. When he wasn't home, I longed to be with him. When he was home, he was a tyrant. Most of my teen years I assumed he hated me. He was always yelling and saying mean hurtful things to my mother, or me.

My younger brother, Christopher, was very quiet and seemed to miss the brunt of my father's wrath. I would spend most of my time either outside playing with friends or hiding in my room, dreading the possibility of my father coming home before I fell asleep.

My parents finally divorced. We had moved again, and being fourteen and having to deal with being the new kid on the block was tough. My father lived an hour away from us, and my mother was not assertive enough to handle my personality on top of the family dysfunction. I would basically intimidate her with profanity when I didn't want her around me.

It worked. I felt that since my parents really didn't have their stuff together, I could take advantage of the situation. I drank, smoked pot, and ran away. When my mother would threaten to call my dad, I laughed. He was so guilt ridden and busy sobering up that he would never dare tell me not to drink or do drugs. Besides, my father and mother weren't speaking to each other, so it was perfect, I thought.

I bounced between my mother and my father for several years, which didn't help matters. My father let me do whatever I wanted, and my mother nagged and pressured me. It was one extreme to the next. I never felt "centered." I was in constant flux, never feeling loved like I wanted. My family either gave me too much or too little of everything.

I was in constant trouble. Stealing, fighting, lying, you name it. If it was missing or broken, most likely I was involved. I cracked my cousin in the face on his birthday, and another time shook him so violently that he began to cry. My father swatted me on the butt. Apparently it didn't deter me, because as soon as my father turned around, I headed for my cousin again. For years he would start to cry whenever he saw me. I guess if I wasn't happy, I didn't want anyone else to be.

After my mother found out that at sixteen I was dating a twenty-four-year-old man and drinking more frequently, she decided enough was enough. She told me she was bringing me to the dentist, but it wasn't the dentist's office I saw once we arrived at this large facility with high fences surrounding the buildings. You had to be buzzed in by security to enter. It was called Summerville, a place where parents with problem teens went for help.

Once enrolled, you lived there, went to school there, and had chores and group meetings. Unfortunately, Summerville wasn't what I needed either. Remember that I always received too much or too little in my life and Summerville was a bit too much for me. There were kids in the facility who had multiple personalities, mental illness, or severe retardation. My roommate was a suicidal teen who would slash her wrists. There were kids in gangs, and drug addicts. I was just a kid who was lost.

What else was my mother to do? She was at her wit's end. I lived there for almost a year. I moved up in rank as I started to follow directions, and became more responsible. We had a daily chart on our progression, or regression. I saw all of these other kids having problems that most likely couldn't be corrected or would take years of therapy to resolve. I focused on myself and felt as though I had a new lease on life.

After I reached a certain level I was given weekend passes to stay with my mother. I didn't have very many friends, so I spent those days mostly with my mother and brother. We were getting along amazingly well.

One time, after church on Sunday, I was packing my clothes and getting ready to leave. My mother said she had to run an errand and would be back in an hour. When she arrived home, I asked her to hurry up because I had to get back to the school. She told me that I wasn't going back and that all of my belongings from Summerville were in her car. I asked why. She said she had seen such an improvement in me she felt I was ready to come home. When she mentioned this to my psychiatrist, he agreed. The Summerville staff disagreed, warning my mother I would become suicidal. That is when she realized they wanted the insurance money more than my recovery.

After I returned home, it was difficult to get back into the family routine because I had been told what to do and when for so long. I kept to myself and was a loner, finding it hard to make friends who didn't drink or smoke pot. Most of my old friends would tease me at school, calling me a snob. My grades were much improved, and my relationship with my mother had ups and downs, which continues to this day. I don't talk back with profanity, because that is not positive and produces nothing but hurt feelings.

My relationship with my father is the best ever. He has been sober for nineteen years, and we are closer now than we ever were.

I believe that my mother made a mistake putting me at Summerville and felt bad, but it shaped me up. I learned that regardless of how low and depressed you feel, things can get worse. Count your blessings. Have a strong and trusting relationship with your parents. It is hard work, but the benefits are fabulous.

Jennifer Kerry Day, Minnesota

Cutting

I can remember feeling depressed and anxious as early as the sixth grade. In the seventh grade, I cut my arms and wrists for the first time and carried a razor blade with me—always entertaining the thought of ending my life. It took me until my sophomore year of college, nine years later, to ask for help.

Healthy or unhealthy, during those years in between, I began to use exercise—sometimes in great excess—to "self-medicate" and stabilize my mood swings. The exercise also allowed me to create a fit young woman on the outside and mask my feelings of inner confusion. However, what brought me into the health services at my university was that due to overuse, I had injured my legs and could barely walk. My depression was so intense that I knew I would lose my scholarship if I did not try to put an end to what had consumed me for all of my adolescence.

Trying to find my voice at that given moment in my life was incredibly challenging but I put my faith in the mental health field to help put me back on my feet. I had no idea I was originally misdiagnosed, but the rapid mood swings, endless tears, and self-inflicted cuts on my arms suggested otherwise. When my first psychiatrist was unable to return my "concerned" phone calls regarding my rapidly changing mental state, my mother came to help me within hours of being informed of my problems. For the next several weeks she stayed with me, helping me prepare for school, cooking me warm, comforting food, and sitting and cuddling with me on the sofa.

Looking back on it, it was as though I was a little child again who was very sick with the flu or pneumonia and depending so greatly upon my mother's nurture. During all the unfortunate things that happened during that period in my life, my mother's love and presence literally kept me alive. She would not tolerate another misdiagnosis, nor would she allow any more of her daughter's pride and integrity to be stripped away. To this day, I continue to see my mother as my lifeline.

Though I wished my mother could stay with me forever, I knew she had a family waiting for her. Needless to say, she did not leave until a safety net was in place for me. For the past two years, I have been seeing a wonderful female psychologist who has helped empower me as a young woman trying not only to make sense of living with a bipolar disorder but also to rebuild the nine years I shut myself out of feeling and truly existing. Also, I am fortunate enough to be seeing a psychiatrist who cares about me beyond just being another paying client. This psychiatrist has helped me to find a medication with minimal side effects that made it possible for me to recently graduate from college after maintaining my scholarship and a respectable GPA.

Between my mother's undying faith in me and these two doctors, I have been able to return to athletics again, but this time as a person who is healthy mentally and physically. There has not been a day I have not thought about my mother coming out to help me and how hard it must have been for her to see her daughter incapable of making it through a day without extreme inner turmoil. I am also thankful every day when I realize how far I have come, and as a result, I continue to grow both in mind and spirit daily.

My mother has always had a way of making things better and not only did her assistance help two years ago, but it has brought our relationship to a more mature understanding of each other. I see her now as both a wonderful, caring mother and a strong, beautiful woman.

Allie, Midwest

(Allie is the daughter of Sophia Rodgers, author of "Excerpt from 'Losing Time,'" Chapter 7.)

Time Away

I don't remember how it started, really, but its progression was almost startling. I say "it" for lack of a better name. "It" really was a long series of events, all leading to the eventual removal of myself from my life, my situation, and the world, as I knew it. Everything I had ever known was left behind, so I could experience what would become a therapy session that would rock my world.

I started smoking marijuana at the age of fifteen, leading to the habitual use of a variety of drugs for a two-and-a-half-year period, during which time I alienated my close friends and my family. I felt no remorse for what I was doing at the time. On the contrary, I believed I was the one being mistreated. My mother's attempts at giving me assistance were futile. I withdrew further every time. She tried many routes: being a friend, keeping me home, and getting professional help for my obvious drug addiction, but I was stubborn and headstrong.

She is the only person I've ever fought so hard against. I resented her, was irritated by her, and did everything I could to make myself believe I was the victim, which included making Mom the "bad guy."

Soon she had no choice but to let me go. She watched me walk away. Watched as I almost completely left her life—figuratively and for the most part literally. I would come home on occasion when I was really hungry, or when I needed a place to sleep. The majority of my time was spent in the home of the boy who would eventually become the father of my unborn child.

I thought Mom had just let me go, but in all actuality she was making arrangements. She, my brother, dogs, and I were headed to Mexico for an indefinite period of time. I went along. I guess I could have fought that too, but I knew it was time. I needed to get out.

About two weeks after we left I missed my period. I had a sneaking suspicion I was pregnant, but said nothing. It wasn't until I started getting nauseous, and my breasts were visibly swollen, that I told my mom. She was more supportive than most mothers would have been. Alone in that foreign land, she became my life support. We started rekindling a relationship that we both faintly remembered. It was like rediscovering some sweet flavor you had almost forgotten.

On the day the Mexican culture honors the souls of children who have passed over, I miscarried. I will never forget the day, but unfortunately its poetry is too sweet to ever be conveyed through words. But my mother was there. She had stuck with me through it all.

The loss of the baby marked a new beginning for me. I began working up to six days a week, entered into a romantic relationship with a boy from Guadalajara, and felt a new sense of freedom. I was back in control of my life.

When we returned to the United States, six months after arriving in Mexico, I continued this changed behavior. I am now eighteen years old, have a full-time job as an assistant preschool teacher, and am living on my own. I feel healthier and more alive than I ever have. I know that where I am today is because of our trip to Mexico.

I will never be able to convey to my mom the gratitude she deserves, but will continue to love her, and to make her proud as long as I am on this earth. Thank you, Mommy. I want you to know that I think you did an excellent job raising us, and I love you more than anyone in the world.

Erika Hess, Idaho

(Erika is the daughter of Kim Hess, author of "All She Needs Is You," Chapter 13.)

Celebration

Yesterday, I turned twenty-eight. I spent it at the zoo with my daughter, son, and mother (dinner would be later with my husband). I couldn't have had a better birthday. Our house is under construction with a new addition. I have embarked on a career with my own company, working from home with my two young children beside me. I have the best life right now. I would go back and change nothing!

Eight years ago I would have stated that differently. My mother raised me. She and my father divorced when I was a year old. She remarried when I was two. I adored my stepfather and called him Daddy. Even my mother took a backseat to him. So it should come as no surprise when at the age of ten, my mother announced her intention to divorce him and I my intention to divorce her. This event kicked off what would become a decade-plus of tears, pain, separation, hardships, joy, communication, and through it all, love.

With glasses and braces and a brain, I moved to a new town at the beginning of junior high school. This did not bode well for me. I struggled to make and maintain friendships. My mother pushed communication in a big way. I was a teenager who didn't want to. Conflict was heavy in the air in our house.

My mother's new boyfriend moved in with us. I was terrible to him. I threw his clothes away, hid his mail, and ignored him when he spoke to me. The only time I talked to my mother was to ask to visit my stepfather. She sent me to a psychiatrist, who had been my parents' marriage therapist. Needless to say, it didn't work out.

When I entered high school, I entered the world of alcohol and partying and deception. I readily deceived my mother on an almost hourly basis. Freshman year wasn't too bad; I still had the braces and glasses. The following summer, the braces came off, contacts went in, and the high life began. I went from looking twelve to looking twenty-two. My dance card was full!

I went out and got drunk every weekend. I never drank any other time, unless it was a holiday and there was a party, and never got into drugs. I tried pot but it made me silly and I am not silly by nature.

To maintain control, my mother would ground me. I would go to my father's then and go out, always finding ways around my punishment. As a single parent, it was difficult for my mother to notice this. I took a lot of chances and almost never got caught.

My mother left for Vermont with her newest boyfriend (second since the divorce, six years earlier) to stay at his cabin with no phone. I was to stay at my girlfriend's house. It changed to my two best friends staying at my house and we forwarded her phone line to my house.

We went out and got a guy to buy us a large bottle of liquor. My friend sat in the backseat and I drank most of it. The last I remember from that night was about 7:30 P.M. We were cruising the avenue, a long road in our city, something that was done by everyone on the weekend.

I woke up to bright lights, a mask over my mouth, an IV in each arm, and electrodes monitoring my heart. A nurse, looking stiff and matronly, came over to the bed and noticed I had opened my eyes. I asked where I was.

"The emergency room. You nearly died."

She scared me. She told me that at .1 amount of alcohol I would be too drunk to drive. She told me that at .3 I would be close to being in a coma. I was at .28 when they brought me to the hospital. To add to this, my body temperature was at 92. It was November and I had taken my coat off after I threw up on it.

I vowed not to drink again. The hangover lasted for three days, but the aftermath of my mother's reaction lasted much longer. I lost her trust and the thin connection we had made since her divorce.

I didn't drink again—that year. The following summer I only had one beer at parties and not always. Then came senior year.

My mother went away. I had parties most of the first month of senior year—well controlled but large nonetheless. I also got into nightclubs at this point with my older friends. Drinking was easier there.

From the age of seventeen through twenty-one, I partied, dating many men and never settling down. I wasn't sexual until after senior year, and then I was safe and cautious. My relationship with my mother was in the far background. Being with my friends and having fun was so much more important.

When I was twenty, I got kicked out of my house. Tension had been building and my mother had lost control over me, so I moved in with my father. This was unreal for her. That birthday was horrible. I grew close to my father and continued having a good time. I moved back to my mother's temporarily and then out on my own.

We worked on a new relationship at this point. After a year on my own, I got a roommate. In one month, she did many of the same things

I did to my mother: not cleaning up after herself, being inconsiderate of others, coming in at all hours (loudly), taking my clothes, etc.

I called my mother up crying, "I am so sorry for everything I did. I love you."

I wound up moving back home for about a year, and we became friends who could communicate and live together amicably. During this time, the worst "bump" in our road came. I was twenty-two when a stalker came into my life; I had dated him for two months and then he stalked me for eight. I was out of my mind and so was my mother. I had to quit my job, and we had our phone number changed. We had beer bottles smashed on our driveway every night. I was followed everywhere.

It was during this time that an ex-boyfriend decided to reenter my life, another one I should have kept the door shut on. He had two children by two different women, one prior to our relationship, the other after. I didn't want to get involved with anyone, but he had changed from the way he was when we had dated and we became friends. One night a few months later, we had sex. That night I knew I had no feelings for him, so I avoided his calls and he stopped calling.

Two months later, I found out I was pregnant. I had no job, lived at home, and had just returned to college. I still had a stalker and now was pregnant. Needless to say, emotions were high.

My mother was calm but I could see her heart had broken. She pushed me to think hard about having an abortion but didn't force me. When I decided to do it, she went along, stayed, and cried with me. Although I was angry with her at first, I realized that I was the one who made the choice. She thought for a long time that I felt she had forced me, but she also knew that I never did anything I didn't want to.

Since then, our relationship has grown steadily stronger. When I got married, she and my father gave me away. She lives only two miles from my house. I spend Mother's Day with my children, but the day she gave birth to me is our day. We celebrate every one together!

Meghan Rita, Connecticut

Step by Step

Bulimia. To this day, that word gives me the chills. It represents a very desperate and lonely time in my life, a period when I was so scared and overwhelmed I had to turn to bulimia for comfort.

I will never forget the first time that I was bulimic. I was in my junior year at U.C. Berkeley, and it just happened. I was feeling lonely and had baked some bran muffins for comfort—planning to eat just one—but eating all eight of them. I couldn't stop. An insane feeling came over me and I frantically stuffed all of the muffins down my throat, as I had many times before. But this time was different—I threw up afterwards.

There was no food left in my system. Whatever it was that had made me feel so overwhelmed and sad and lonely in the first place was purged out of my system. I was hooked. I remained severely bulimic for the next eight years.

What caused the bulimia? I wish I could answer that. It was not any one thing. I came from a very loving home. My parents were divorced and I moved around a great deal as a child, but I was always loved. My mother was incredibly supportive of me and I was very secure with her love. However, throughout my childhood, I remember feeling "less-than" and lonely. I felt inadequate. I was afraid of myself—my intense emotions and endless needs.

In my mind, my mother was perfect. I idolized her. I used to wear her clothes—and judged my body by hers. She is extremely slender and I desperately wanted to look like her. I judged my insides by her outsides—if I could *look* like her, then I would *feel* better. I also compared myself to billboard models and actresses, condemning myself for not being disciplined enough to look like them. I somehow decided that I was a worthless person because I did not look like a model.

I started to turn to food for comfort when I was about seventeen years old. At that time, my mother was living in Mexico and I was in northern California. I was too young to be on my own, but very determined. I found myself reaching out to food whenever I felt alone or overwhelmed or simply, whenever I *felt*. Feelings were all too much for me. I would avoid my true feelings at any cost because I was terrified by them.

Right before the bulimia started, my mother went through a nervous breakdown. She moved to LA and I spent a summer living with her. It was horrific for me to see my mother that way. I was terrified of her instability and vulnerability. I started to eat more and more to escape my own feelings. The bingeing of food eventually led to purging.

For whatever reason, I just could not eat in front of my mother. The idea of eating in front of her repulsed me. I guess I thought she could see through me. If I ate in front of her, my eating disorder would be exposed. She would see the madness that happened when I ate.

When I first became bulimic, I lost about thirty pounds. The more weight I lost, the more confident I felt around people—especially men. I started to crave the attention of men—I needed their constant devotion in order to feel good about myself.

I remained bulimic throughout my twenties—no one knew except my mother. I went to graduate school, had many boyfriends and serious relationships, and got a great job that took me traveling throughout the world, but I could not stop the bulimia. I learned to *manage* it, to *live* with it—or so I thought.

At twenty-eight, I found cocaine. Cocaine put an immediate end to bulimia. It stopped my appetite and removed the obsession to eat. It felt like a lifesaver. The obsession with food was removed overnight. I surrendered to cocaine in gratitude and relief.

Over the next three years, I overdosed twice and was rushed to the hospital. I went to four drug rehabs, lost my great job in NY, lost my apartment, my boyfriend, every penny I had in the world, my self-respect, and my laughter. But, I was thin, and, I was not bulimic. At that time, I actually thought this was progress.

At thirty-one years old, I went home to my mother's house. I was beaten, scared, sick, thin, addicted, and suicidal. My mother was amazing—she had the perfect mix of being understanding and loving while also having tough love. She suggested that I go to therapy, but did not push the idea on me. My mother simply gave me the number of a therapist and left it at that. I ended up calling the therapist for help on my own time—because I *wanted* help.

With the help of the Twelve Step Program and therapy, I learned slowly to surrender to this disease of addiction and to recover on a daily basis. My bulimia, drug addiction, and alcoholism were the same. They were simply parallel manifestations of the same problem: my inability to cope with my feelings and my low self-esteem coupled with unrealistic expectations of myself.

The Twelve Step Program has saved my life. I am no longer bulimic today—haven't been for two years now. I am clean and sober.

My life has changed dramatically. I attend AA meetings regularly and I have a therapist who is also in recovery from an eating disorder. I wake up each day and pray to stay clean and sober and free from addiction and obsession.

My mother has always remained supportive of me. She has understood and witnessed all sides of my addictions and has loved me regardless. I wish that I had not caused her so much pain and heartache—it hurts me to know how much she has suffered due to my addictions. For a long time, I wanted to blame my mother for my disorders. I needed to point the finger at someone. However, my eating disorder and my drug addiction have been my own path. They did not have anything to do with her. I needed to experience it all—for me—in order to become who I am today.

I now have a wonderful home—with a fridge full of healthy (and some not-so-healthy) food. I enjoy eating. I run or do yoga almost every day—for both my body and my mind. Like most women, I think about my weight. I would love to lose five pounds, but I am not willing to cause myself any damage in order to do so.

Recovery from an eating disorder is possible. However, I do not think that I could have done it alone. My friends and my family tried to help me, but I needed help from others who had also suffered from addiction. I needed to listen to those people who had already recovered from eating disorders and drug addiction. They were the only ones who really understood.

My mother and I are very close today. She is my best friend. In many ways, I needed to claim my addictions and my recovery for myself in order to grow into my own womanhood. I no longer compare myself to my mother, but rather enjoy our similarities and our differences. We have gone through a great deal together and have grown much closer.

Michele Earl, California

(Michele is the daughter of Maureen Earl, who wrote "Letter to My Family," in Chapter 2, and "Letter to a Friend," in Chapter 12.)

Mother Lost

My mother died at the age of forty-nine from a rare and crippling disease called scleroderma. I was twenty-six years old at the time, mother to a two-year-old daughter and eight months pregnant with my son. I miss my mother terribly and try to keep her memory alive through the stories I now tell my children about their grandmother. I have named my third child Lena in honor of her memory.

I wish I could say I was the ideal, perfect daughter, but I cannot. Although I was extremely intelligent, as a teenager, I was also rebellious and disobedient. Mama could talk to me until she turned blue in the face, but I wouldn't listen. I did things my way. Her characterization of me was I had to "bump my own head." My family's characterization of me was I was rude, fast, smart-mouthed, cocky, and had a bad attitude. My grandmother's favorite words were that I was the "black sheep of the family who would end up pregnant without a husband." The one thing that hurt the most was when my own mother looked me in the eyes, called me "bitch" and told me to get out after I'd stayed out all night with some friends of mine.

During my high-school years, my troublesome behaviors included sneaking away from the house. Whenever Mama was away, I found ample opportunity to do the same. It was hard for her to enjoy a social life because she always had to worry about what I was doing. I also had quite a mouth and had no restraint when it came to speaking my mind. There was no one in the family that could outtalk me. I threw horrible temper tantrums and said awful things to make anyone in my path feel as bad as I was feeling.

I was the middle of three girls and needless to say, I did not get along with my siblings very well, especially my oldest sister. We fought constantly, not only verbally but also physically, as we often came to brutal blows. After each fight, it never failed that all blame was placed on me. The customary saying was, "Well, you know how she is" (referring to me). It was always assumed that I was responsible for starting the trouble.

The main thing that bothered my mother about my behaviors was my association with the opposite sex. I was smart, petite and extremely pretty. (I got my good looks from her.) Boys my age, as well as older men, were attracted to me like magnets. I was preyed upon everywhere I went. I did nothing to attract this kind of attention; as a matter of fact, I tried to conceal anything about me that suggested sex and did not act in any way like I thought I was pretty. I don't know what it was; I must have had some kind of look that suggested hungriness and neediness.

To make a long story short, I was promiscuous. My first love affair was with one of my teachers, also a married man. At the end of my freshman year, after we'd formed what I considered to be a very tight friendship, he violated me. We continued on throughout my high school career, a relationship that I found to be both comforting and tormenting at the same time.

My teen years were troubling for my entire family and me. We constantly argued and fought. There was rarely a moment of peace or pleasure. I was angry and resentful and the atmosphere was thick whenever I was around. My mama, already suffering from a terminal illness, suffered even more trying to deal with my rebellion. She even said to me once that I was incorrigible and threatened to send me to a girl's home. At times, I wish she would have. Although I had my share of problems, I thank God I never turned to drugs and alcohol or even cigarettes. I was pretty much a loner and isolated myself from my family as much as possible. I never smiled or laughed. I buried myself in my books and used sex like a junkie uses drugs as my means of escape and pleasure.

Why was I this way? Because no one ever listened and no one was ever there for me. I felt like I didn't matter. I was angry with everyone in my life because although they said they loved me and wanted the best for me, no one ever cared enough to show that love in a constructive way. From sixth grade through twelfth grade, I played volleyball, basketball, and ran track, and not one member of my family cared to even show up at a game, meet, or awards banquet. I stopped bringing a report card home in fifth grade, and no one ever asked what kind of grades I was making. I stayed focused enough in that area to make honor roll all my life.

My mama was ill and I suspect she was also abused as a child. She was never violent towards us, except for verbally, but was also the sweetest thing in our life. I have to accept that she did the best she could and all that she knew how to do. She often seemed very proud of us. I know that she was concerned with her health, but I needed her there to just love me, to just be there sometimes.

I was rebellious because no one in my family believed in me. Like for instance, the relationship with my teacher. I wanted so much to tell that he raped me that first time, but I was scared to death of what they would say about me. I remember going home, getting in a tub of hot water and scrubbing and soaking for hours, trying to get his touch off of me. Eventually, I learned to crave it because that was the most love, tenderness, and kindness I'd ever been shown in my life. All I wanted was for someone to listen to me, not judge me, not hit me, and to truly love me. Because I didn't get this at home, I made some very bad choices.

I do miss my mama and regret all the problems I put her through. I'm glad that she lived long enough for me to become a mother. Those last two years together were phenomenal. I was able to apologize for my actions and to thank her for believing in me the most. I know now that she was struggling with issues of health and her own past, but at least she never stopped talking to me and encouraging me. She didn't judge me as the bad seed like most people but did know the real me.

I found her journal after she died and read it, expecting to find horrible things about me, but I didn't. She actually understood me and knew what I was going through. She knew I was starving for love and acceptance and in the best way she knew how with her circumstances, she was trying to give it to me. I guess it was just a little too late when I went to her.

I struggle with issues from the past, too, but now that I'm a mother, I remember to always try to be there for my children. My children and I share a very open relationship. We talk about everything. I try to find the good in them instead of tearing them down with negative, hurtful words. My husband and I try to make them believe that they are everything and can do anything they put their minds to. We both try hard to not make the same mistakes our parents made with us. I do thank my mother most of all for her humanity. Through her I learned to respect life and love people. I will always remember her telling me, "No one is better than you, but you're no better than anyone else, either." Today, those words define who I am.

Lynne L., Nebraska

PART SIX

Into the Future

16

Where We Are Now

January 2001.

Shortly after Ellen left Utah and returned to the boarding school for "at-risk" children where she'd been admitted the previous fall, I received a call at work.

"Your daughter has a bad case of B-R-A-T," the voice on the other end of the phone concluded. "We want her out of here now."

Once again, crisis struck. When I phoned my husband to tell him the news, he voiced the same fear that was making my gut clench.

"If she comes home, she'll destroy our family."

A series of temporary arrangements were strung together until another catastrophe occurred and I decided it was time to get her.

"I'm bringing her home," I informed Paul, my maternal instincts overriding his commonsense argument that her presence would fling our house back into a state of chaos. He was probably right, but she was my daughter and she needed me, so I left to get her before we could argue about it.

"I'll take her away somewhere," I promised Paul and Joe when I returned a few hours later, remembering how that strategy had worked for Kim Hess author of "All She Needs Is You" in Chapter 13. As it turned out, we were only able to spend two days in a hotel in Lancaster, but during that time I began to believe Ellen had changed. Although her eating disorder was still clearly out of control, there was a softness to her I hadn't seen in years.

In the days that followed our trip, I noticed her singing: sometimes an irritating rap song with no more than four words, and other days, lilting fragments from Alanis Morissette. We began to take nightly walks, gazing up at the stars as she talked honestly about her life and held my hand. She and Joe watched videos together, and when she drove, he sat in the front seat with her.

About two weeks after Ellen returned, I was feeling both uplifted by the change in her attitude and overwhelmed by the continuing severity of her bulimia (each morning we would rise and see dishes and food containers spread from the family room to the kitchen). How long could her body withstand the daily purging? Everywhere I looked in my life, there seemed to be problems that had me in tears at 8 A.M. Although I tried to hide them, Ellen went off to work, returning that night with a slightly bedraggled plant in her hand.

"Here. This is for you. It's sort of like me, some parts are withering but other parts are still growing," she said, then gave me a hug. "Don't you know the only reason I want to be a mother someday is because of you?"

I was speechless, but in a positive way.

In my research, any good study raises as many questions as it answers. When I first thought about writing a book two years ago, I believed that by the time I reached the last chapter, our journey through troubled times would be over. Although that hasn't happened, Ellen is a different girl than the one I've described in these pages. Her struggles are still obvious, but her mood has changed dramatically, and, in some ways, my daughter is coming back to me.

There are other things I've learned. An incredible number of young women all across the country are in crisis, challenged by problems not of their doing that are nonetheless life threatening. These are girls who come from homes where there has been enough money, food, clothing, shelter, and love, and whose parents have followed "the rules" for good child rearing. Despite this, the pain these young Ophelias experience is deep and persistent, and the road to recovery often long and difficult. But I have no answer as to why this happens.

What helps mothers so they can support their daughters during this demanding and potentially dangerous time? We do—the sisterhood of women that stretches from one end of this country to the other. Within this safety net, we are free from judgment, loneliness, and despair, sustained by the wisdom and support of others who truly understand our anguish. I encourage every mother who is out there suffering in silence to reach out to someone in her community who may need her help. Both of you will benefit.

And what of the future? Will Ellen continue to recover, or will our dark journey through the world of anorexia and bulimia continue? Perhaps her words hold the best answer:

2/18/2001

In two more weeks I will be seventeen. The last three years of my life have been hell. It's been like a dream, a really bad dream that I couldn't wake up from. When I look back, I wish I could take the time all back and redo it. I feel like I have lost out on so much, like I've completely wasted a huge chunk of my life.

I struggle mostly with bulimia and anger management. Food is like a drug, and like any other drug it is out of control for me. I also struggle with depression. The bulimia and depression are like triggers for each other, I struggle with eating, and this depresses me, and when I am depressed it just triggers my eating disorder more.

I know that more than anything I have hurt my mom, but through all the hurt we have still managed to have a close relationship. I love my mom more than anything now because I can finally see how much she loves me. She has stuck by me through all this. Our relationship has definitely been challenged in many ways—we have had a lot of problems thrown at it. I think only the relationship between a mother and a daughter could survive what we have gone through.

There have been many times where my mom has been mad at me, and I have been mad at her, and I have thought our relationship was destroyed. But each conflict we have gotten through has only improved our relationship. I am very lucky to have the good relationship that I have now with my mom; we very easily could have learned to hate each other these past three years. I'm very thankful we didn't.

Everything my mom has done in my whole life was done with the intention of helping me, I know that. The last three years in particular she has endlessly tried to help me. And even if she didn't cure me, it is enough for me to know that she tried to help. The best thing she has done for me is stick by me and never stop loving me. I think that is all she really could do. I know that if she had a magic wand to wave over me and cure me, she would. But I know now that all she could do was love me and love me some more and that is the best thing she could have done for me.

As my birthday approaches, I have mixed feelings about the future. Sometimes I feel really hopeful that I eventually will be free of my eating disorder, and other times I feel completely hopeless. Everyone says that they know I will recover, and sometimes I believe them. I would really like to believe that I will recover, but sometimes I just don't feel strong enough. I guess the only thing I know for sure about the future is that I will have a lot of challenges thrown at me, and I'm going to have to stay strong to get through it all.

Ellen Dellasega, Hershey, Pennsylvania

APPENDIX:
WHERE TO FIND HELP

I wish this was a longer or more definitive list, but as I mentioned in the introduction, I didn't find much out there when I went looking for help. However, these sources are ones I can say I have used and found beneficial.

Books

Carol Maxym, Ph.D., and Leslie York, M.A. (February 2000). *Teens in Turmoil: A Path to Change for Parents, Adolescents, and Their Families.* ISBN: 0140286039. The authors present advice for recognizing problem situations and handling them either on your own or with help from others. Leslie York is the parent of a "teen in turmoil." Dr. Maxym is also an educational consultant with a web site of her own: http://www.drcmaxym.com.

Deborah Spungen. (August 1996). *And I Don't Want to Live This Life.* ISBN: 0449911411. Deborah Spungen's honest biography of her daughter Nancy (murdered by singer Sid Vicious of the Sex Pistols) was gritty and a bit hard to take, but it was reassuring to read about her emotional responses and her many attempts to help her child.

Ruth Bell Graham and Gigi Graham Tchividjian. (July 1999). *Prodigals and Those Who Love Them.* ISBN: 080105897X. This book was reassuring to me if only because Ruth Bell Graham is the wife of a world-famous evangelist—if her teens (sons) could struggle, surely any-one's can. The analogy to the Prodigal Son and that story's ultimately positive outcome also helped me reframe my situation.

Organizations

The Ophelia Project (TOP) of Erie, Pennsylvania, is a nonprofit, nonde-nominational, grassroots volunteer organization dedicated to saving the selves of girls by protecting and reconnecting families. With branches across the country, the Ophelia Project has a number of beneficial pro-grams for adolescent girls, boys, and their moms.

The Ophelia Project
P.O. Box 8736
Erie, PA 16505-0736
http://www.opheliaproject.org

Focus Adolescent Services

Focus Adolescent Services Resources is an Internet clearinghouse of re-sources to help families with troubled teens. This state-specific site is chock-full of resources and has a toll-free hotline (1-877-FOCUS-AS). Although there is some advertising for emotional-growth boarding schools, counseling centers, and other programs, most of the articles on this site are appropriate for just about every aspect of parenting a teen you can think of.

http://www.focusas.com

Focus on the Family

This Christian organization has a number of helpful resources, includ-ing books and tapes from their popular radio series. I found the audio-tapes by Ruth Graham Bell and David Jeremiah, both parents of strug-gling teens, helpful.

http://www.family.org

Tough Love

TOUGHLOVE International is a nonprofit, self-help organization that provides ongoing education and active support to families, empowering parents and young people to accept responsibility for their actions. Their support network strives to make communities safe places to live.

http://www.toughlove.org

Web Sites

Help for Struggling Teens is a resource for parents and professionals trying to help at-risk teenagers. If you're at the point of considering outside help (a wilderness program or boarding school), this site, created by educational consultant Lon Woodbury, can be a resource.

http://www.strugglingteens.com

The web site Bridge to Understanding was established by another educational consultant group (Thomas Croke and Associates). I actually spoke with Mr. Croke and found him quite supportive, although we did not use his services. The on-line articles and Parents Forum were helpful to me when I searched for a wilderness program for Ellen—within twenty-four hours I had feedback from other parents who had sent their children to the same places I was considering.

http://www.bridgetounderstanding.com/

The Center for Youth and Parent Understanding is a nonprofit Christian organization committed to building strong families by serving to bridge the gap between parents and teenagers. This group offers a lot of on-line articles, some with heavy Christian orientation, others of general interest (i.e., a newsletter on development).

http://www.cpyu.org/mission.html

http:/teenagerstoday.com is a website from iparenting.com that covers the teen years. Experts provide answers to pressing questions posted by parents, and a community bulletin board allows parents to interact with each other. A list of resources and tools for parents is also available.

http:/www.parentingteens.com offers information, insight, and support for parents of teens. A free newletter is available, along with a "teen expert" who helps answer questions. Other features include a forum, chatroom, bookstore, and a parenting support group.

My Web Site!

The web site Surviving Ophelia is a resource you can use to connect online with other moms. Please feel free to use the Post a Problem feature to add any resources you've found particularly helpful during your parenting career, or share a story of your own.

http://www.cheryldellasega.com

Newsletters

Parenting Today's Teens
http://www.parentingteens.com

Parenting of Adolescents with Denise Witmer
http://www.parentingteens.about.com/parenting/parentingteens/

An on-line newsletter from California offers support and information for parents of teenagers and kids. In any given issue you will find articles on subjects such as college, body piercing, and driving. Up soon will be a discussion forum for parents. This site's a favorite of mine!
http://www.parent-teen.com

INDEX